CORPORATE SUSTAINABILITY & RESPONSIBILITY

An Introductory Text on CSR Theory & Practice – Past, Present & Future

Wayne Visser

KALEIDOSCOPE
Futures ▷▷▷▶▶

Paperback edition first published in 2013
by Kaleidoscope Futures Ltd.
68 Britten Close, London NW11 7HW

Cover photography and design by Wayne Visser and Kaleidoscope Futures Ltd. Cover photograph of glass mosaic on La Trobe University Campus, Melbourne, Australia.

ISBN 978-1-908875-11-2

CONTENTS

Acknowledgements   1

Figures & Discussion Questions   2

Chapter 1: Definitions and Drivers of CSR   **5**

1.1 Definitions   5

1.2 The DNA Model of CSR   7

1.3 Local CSR Drivers   9

1.4 Global CSR Drivers   11

1.5 The Business Case for CSR   12

1.6 The Problem of Uneconomic CSR   15

1.7 The Failure of CSR?   16

Chapter 2: The Evolution of CSR   **19**

2.1 Ancient History   19

2.2 Industrial Welfare   20

2.3 Questioning Business   21

2.4 Spaceship Earth   23

2.5 CSR Theory   24

2.6 Legislating CSR   25

2.7 Stakeholder Theory   27

2.8 Triple Bottom Line   28

2.9 Supply Chain Integrity   30

2.10 Corporate Governance   31

2.11 Ethical Investment   32

2.12 Bottom of the Pyramid (BOP)   33

2.13 Codes and Standards   36

2.14 The Way Forward   37

Chapter 3: CSR Around the World   **39**

3.1 Global and Local CSR   39

3.2 CSR Around the World   40

3.3 CSR in Developing Countries   42

3.4 The Literature on CSR in Developing Countries   43

3.5 Global Research on CSR   44

3.6 Research on CSR in Asia   45

3.7 Research on CSR in Africa   46

3.8 CSR Research in Latin America   47

3.9 Myths about CSR in Developing Countries   49

3.10 An Alternative CSR Pyramid   50

3.11 Anglo American's CSR Pyramid   53

3.12 Going Native and Becoming Indigenous   54

3.13 Corporate Shared Value   56

3.14 Social Entrepreneurs on a Mission   58

3.15 Glocal CSR in Practice   59

Chapter 4: Implementing CSR   **62**

4.1 Values: It's in his Kiss   62

4.2 Vision: A Jumbo Quest   67

4.3 Work: An Elephants Playground?   72

4.4 Governance: Council of the Animals   77

4.5 Relationships: Walking Gently as Giants   81

4.6 Communication: The Rumble in the Jungle   85

4.7 Services: The Genius of Nature   89

Chapter 5: Leadership For CSR   **93**

5.1 Definitions and Theories of Leadership   93

5.2 Defining Sustainability Leadership   94

5.3 A Model of Sustainability Leadership   96

5.4 Traits of Sustainability Leaders   98

5.5 Styles of Sustainability Leaders   100

5.6 Skills of Sustainability Leaders   102

5.7 Knowledge of Sustainability Leaders   103

5.8 Characteristics of Sustainability Leaders   105

5.9 Actions of Sustainability Leaders   107

5.10 Sustainability Leadership at General Electric (GE)   108

5.11 Sustainability Leadership at GlaxoSmithKline (GSK)   110

5.12 Sustainability Leadership at Skanska, Unilever and IBM   111

5.13 The Paradox of CSR Leadership   112

5.14 Distributed Sustainability Leadership   115

Chapter 6: CSR and Change — 117

6.1 Creative Destruction — 119

6.2 Change Management — 120

6.3 Leadership for Change — 122

6.4 Wheels of Change — 124

6.5 Theory U — 125

6.6 Mapping the Innovation Territory — 127

6.7 We Are the Champions — 128

6.8 Types of CSR Change Agent — 130

6.9 Dynamics of CSR Change Agents — 131

6.10 Applying the CSR Change Agents Model — 133

Chapter 7: Cases In CSR — 133

7.1 A Little World (ALW) — 137

7.2 Anglo American — 139

7.3 Big Pharma — 140

7.4 Big Tobacco — 142

7.5 BP — 148

7.6 Cabbages & Condoms — 149

7.7 Cadbury — 154

7.8 CIDA Campus — 155

7.9 Coca-Cola — 157

7.10 Corporate Leaders Group on Climate Change — 161

7.11 Enron — 162

7.12 Freeplay — 164

7.13 GlaxoSmithKline (GSK) — 166

7.14 Google — 168

7.15 Grameen Bank — 169

7.16 Interface FLOR — 174

7.17 Lehman Brothers — 178

7.18 McDonald's — 180

7.19 Nike — 183

7.20 Patagonia — 188

7.21 Seventh Generation — 189

7.22 Shell   191
7.23 Tesco   192
7.24 Vodafone   194
7.25 Walmart   200

Chapter 8: The Future Of CSR   **200**
8.1 The Age of Greed   200
8.2 Executive Greed   201
8.3 Banking Greed   202
8.4 Financial Market Greed   204
8.5 Corporate Greed   205
8.6 Capitalist Greed   206
8.7 The Ages and Stages of CSR   208
8.8 The Age of Responsibility   210
8.9 Web 2.0: Seeds of a Revolution   212
8.10 The Birth of CSR 2.0   213
8.11 Principles of CSR 2.0   215
8.12 Shifting from CSR 1.0 to CSR 2.0   219
8.13 Drivers of the Future   220
8.14 Future Uncertainties   225
8.15 Future Scenarios   230
8.16 Future Options   233
8.17 Decisions   237
8.18 A Test for Future-Fitness   238
8.19 Predictions for the Next 10 Years   242

Concluding Thoughts   **246**
References   247
About the Author   261
Other books by Wayne Visser   262

ACKNOWLEDGEMENTS

This book is a compilation and adaptation of selected extracts from the author's articles, chapters and books published over the past 20 years. For reference, see *Other Books by Wayne Visser* at the end of the book.

Discussion Questions & Figures

Discussion Questions

1.1: CSR Definitions	9
1.2: CSR Drivers	12
1.3: CSR Business Case	16
1.4: The Failure of CSR	18
2.1: Industrial Welfare	21
2.2: Limits to Growth	24
2.3: Carroll's CSR Pyramid	26
2.4: Stakeholders and the Triple Bottom Line	29
2.5: Accountability and Corporate Governance	33
2.6: Bottom of the Pyramid (BOP) and Codes	37
3.1: CSR Around the World	42
3.2: CSR in Developing Countries	45
3.3: CSR in Developing Regions	48
3.4: CSR Pyramid for Developing Countries	54
3.5: CSR, BOP and CSV	57
3.6: Social entrepreneurship and Glocality	61
4.1: Values	67
4.2: Vision	71
4.3: Work	77
4.4: Governance	81
4.5: Relationships	85
4.6: Communication	89
4.7: Services	92
5.1: Leadership and Sustainability	96
5.2: Traits and Styles of Sustainability Leaders	101
5.3: Skills and Knowledge of Sustainability Leaders	107
5.4: Sustainability Leadership Cases	112
5.5: Paradoxes of Sustainability Leadership	116
6.1: Creative Destruction & Change Management	120
6.2: Leadership & Systems Change	123
6.3: Theory U and Social Innovation	126

6.4: CSR Champions & Change Agents ... 132

7.1: A Little World ... 137

7.2: Anglo American ... 138

7.3: Big Pharma ... 140

7.4: Big Tobacco ... 142

7.5: BP ... 148

7.6: Cabbages & Condoms ... 149

7.7: Cadbury ... 154

7.8: CIDA Campus ... 155

7.9: Coca Cola ... 157

7.10: Corporate Leaders Group on Climate Change (CLG) ... 161

7.11: Enron ... 162

7.12: Freeplay ... 164

7.13: GlaxoSmithKline (GSK) ... 165

7.14: Google ... 167

7.15: Grameen Bank ... 169

7.16: Interface FLOR ... 174

7.17: Lehman Brothers ... 178

7.18: McDonald's ... 179

7.19: Nike ... 182

7.20: Patagonia ... 187

7.21: Seventh Generation ... 189

7.22: Shell ... 191

7.23: Tesco ... 192

7.24: Vodafone ... 194

7.25: Walmart ... 199

8.1: The Age of Greed ... 208

8.2: The Ages and Stages of CSR ... 210

8.3: CSR 2.0 and the Age of Responsibility ... 214

8.4: Shifting from CSR 1.0 to CSR 2.0 ... 220

8.5: Future Scenarios ... 239

8.6: A Test for Future-Fitness ... 241

8.7: Ten-Year Predictions ... 245

Figures

3.1: CSR Pyramid for Developing Countries   51
5.1: The Cambridge Sustainability Leadership Model   97
8.1: The Kaleidoscope 5-S Future-Fitness Framework   240

CHAPTER 1: DEFINITIONS AND DRIVERS OF CSR

1.1 Definitions

The first thing to note is that CSR, in this book, is taken to stand for Corporate Sustainability and Responsibility, rather than the more commonly used Corporate Social Responsibility.

The second point is that CSR is a contested concept, which to a greater or lesser extent draws from and overlaps with related concepts like sustainable development, corporate citizenship, corporate (social) responsibility, environmental management, business ethics and stakeholder management.

I have been guided in my own synthesis definition of CSR by having the dual perspective of both an academic and a practitioner. In my work as a consultant in the field, especially as Director of Sustainability Services for KPMG, I observed that the focus in business is most often on what these terms have in common, while in my subsequent academic career, I learned that theoreticians like to emphasise the semantic differences. Both perspectives are important.

The third point is that CSR is in no way an objective, scientific or neutral concept, but rather a normative construct, which always contains a set of implicit or explicit values.

For the purposes of this book, I offer four definitions of CSR, which are all different ways of saying the same thing. I suggest you use whichever one resonates the most with your way of thinking.

Definition 1
CSR is the ability of business to respond with care to society's needs.

Definition 2
CSR is the way in which business consistently creates shared value in society through economic development, good governance, stakeholder responsiveness and environmental improvement.

Definition 3
CSR is an integrated, systemic approach by business that builds, rather than erodes or destroys, economic, social, human and natural capital.

Definition 4
CSR is a values-laden umbrella concept, which refers to the way in which the interface between business, society and the environment is managed.

Definition 5

Another alternative is from the ISO 26000 standard on Social Responsibility, which was launched in November 2010. Its definition is much more unwieldy, which is what happens when you try to get the countries of the world to agree on a concept. I present it here for completeness.

According to ISO 26000, social responsibility is the responsibility of an organisation for the impacts of its decisions and activities on society and the environment, through transparent and ethical behaviour that:

> Contributes to sustainable development;
> Takes into account the expectations of stakeholders;
> Is in compliance with applicable law and consistent with international norms of behaviour; and
> Is integrated throughout the organisation and practiced in its relationships.

Definition 6

A much more succinct, policy-based definition comes from the European Commission (EC), in its updated CSR Strategy (launched in October 2011).

According to the European Commission, CSR is the responsibility of enterprises for their impacts on society.

The EC adds that respect for applicable legislation, and for collective agreements between social partners, is a prerequisite for meeting that responsibility. To fully meet their corporate social responsibility, enterprises should have in place a process to integrate social, environmental, ethical, human rights and consumer concerns into their business operations and core strategy in close collaboration with their stakeholders, with the aim of:

> maximising the creation of shared value for their owners/shareholders and for their other stakeholders and society at large; and
> identifying, preventing and mitigating their possible adverse impacts.

The EC Strategy on CSR concedes that complexity of that process will depend on factors such as the size of the enterprise and the nature of its operations. For most small and medium-sized enterprises, especially microenterprises, the CSR process is likely to remain informal and intuitive. To maximise the creation of shared value, enterprises are encouraged to adopt a long-term, strategic approach to CSR, and to explore the opportunities for developing innovative products, services and business models that contribute to societal wellbeing and lead to higher quality and more productive jobs.

The EC elaborates that to identify, prevent and mitigate their possible adverse impacts, large enterprises, and enterprises at particular risk of having such impacts, are encouraged to carry out risk-based due diligence, including through their supply chains. Certain types of enterprise, such as cooperatives, mutuals, and family-owned businesses, have ownership and governance structures that can be especially conducive to responsible business conduct.

Other definitions (of which there are no shortage) are likely to be some version of the six provided above.

1.2 The DNA Model of CSR

I extend my own definition of CSR (Definition 2 above) into a DNA Model of CSR. In one sense, it is not so different from other models we have seen before. We can recognise echoes of Carroll's (1991) CSR Pyramid, Freeman's (1984) Stakeholder Theory, Wood's (1991) ideas around Corporate Social Performance, Elkington's (1994) Triple Bottom Line concept, Prahalad & Hart's (2002) Bottom of the Pyramid (BOP) model, Porter & Kramer's (2006) Strategic CSR proposal and the ESG approach of the Socially Responsible Investment movement, to mention but a few related concepts. And that is really the point – the DNA Model of CSR integrates what we have learned to date. It presents a holistic view of CSR.

The essence of the CSR DNA model are the four DNA Responsibility Bases, which are like the four nitrogenous bases of biological DNA (adenine, cytosine, guanine, and thymine), sometimes abbreviated to the four-letters GCTA (which was the inspiration for the 1997 science fiction film GATTACA). In the case of CSR, the DNA Responsibility Bases are Value creation, Good governance, Societal contribution and Environmental integrity, or VEGS if you like. Each DNA Base has a primary goal and each goal has key indicators. The goals and key indicators are what begin to show the qualitative and quantitative differences between other models of CSR and my CSR DNA model. Let's look at each element of the DNA of CSR in turn.

Value Creation

Value Creation refers to much more than financial profitability. The goal is economic development, which means not only contributing to the enrichment of shareholders and executives, but improving the economic context in which a company operates, including investing in infrastructure, creating jobs and providing skills development. There can be any number of key performance indicators (KPIs), but I want to highlight two that I believe are essential: beneficial products and inclusive business. Do the company's products and services really improve our quality of life, or do they cause harm or add to the low-quality junk of what Charles Handy (1998) calls the 'chindogu society'? And how are the economic benefits shared? Does wealth trickle up or down? Are employees, SMEs in the supply chain and poor communities genuinely empowered?

Good Governance

Good Governance is another area that is not new, but in my view has failed to be properly recognised and integrated into CSR theories and practices. The goal of institutional effectiveness is as important as more lofty social and environmental ideals. After all, if the institution fails, or is not transparent and fair, this undermines everything else that CSR is trying to accomplish. Trends in reporting, but also other forms of transparency like social media and brand- or product-linked public databases of CSR performance, will be increasingly important indicators of success, alongside embedding ethical conduct in the culture of companies. We can expect tools like GoodGuide, KPMG's Integrity Thermometer and Covalence's EthicalQuote ranking will become more prevalent.

Societal Contribution

Societal Contribution is an area that CSR is traditionally more used to addressing, with its goal of stakeholder orientation. This gives philanthropy its rightful place in CSR – as one tile in a larger mosaic – while also providing a spotlight for the importance of fair labour practices. It is simply unacceptable that there are more people in slavery today than there were before it was officially abolished in the 1800s, just as regular exposures of high-brand companies for the use of child-labour are despicable. This area of stakeholder engagement, community participation and supply chain integrity remains one of the most vexing and critical elements of CSR.

Environmental Integrity

Environmental Integrity sets the bar a lot higher than simply minimising damage. Rather, it aims at maintaining and improving ecosystem sustainability. The KPIs give some sense of the ambition required here – 100% renewable energy and zero waste. We cannot continue the same practices that have, according to WWF's Living Planet Index, caused us to lose a third of the biodiversity on the planet since they began monitoring 1970. Nor can we continue to gamble with the prospect of dangerous – and perhaps catastrophic and irreversible – climate change.

A final point to make is that, in taking CSR to mean Corporate Sustainability and Responsibility, I am also proposing a new interpretation for these terms. Like two intertwined strands of a rope, sustainability and responsibility can be thought of as different, yet complementary elements of CSR. Hence, sustainability can be conceived as the destination - the challenges, vision, strategy and goals, i.e. what we are aiming for – while responsibility is more about the journey – our solutions, responses, management and actions, i.e. how we get there.

Discussion 1.1: CSR Definitions

1. How has the definition of CSR evolved since Carroll's (1979) four-part conceptualisation?
2. Will the new ISO 26000 definition of social responsibility help or hinder the development of CSR as a profession?
3. What are the strengths and weaknesses of Visser's DNA Model of CSR be improved?

1.3 Local CSR Drivers

Now that we have some basic definitions and a holistic model of CSR, we need to understand why do companies do CSR. What makes it a worthwhile corporate practice? In other words, what are the Drivers of CSR? In fact, each region, country and community has a different combination of CSR drivers. Hence, the art of the so-called 'business case for CSR' is to determine which incentives and pressures are most applicable to a given local context. Of the ten typical CSR drivers I have identified, five are local (or internal) drivers, namely pressures from within the country or community. These are briefly discussed below.

Cultural Tradition

In many countries and regions, CSR draws strongly on deep-rooted indigenous cultural traditions of philanthropy, business ethics and community embeddedness. For example, in a survey of over 1,300 small and medium-sized enterprises in Latin America, Vives (2006) found that the region's religious beliefs are one of the major motivations for CSR. In Asia, a study by scholars Chapple & Moon (2005) reached a similar conclusion, namely that 'CSR does vary considerably among Asian countries but that this variation is not explained by [levels of] development but by factors in the respective national business systems'. And in Africa, I have found that the values-based traditional philosophy of African humanism (ubuntu) is what underpins much of the modern, inclusive approaches to CSR on the continent (Visser, 2006b).

Political Reform

CSR cannot be divorced from socio-political reform processes, which often drive business behaviour towards integrating social and ethical issues. For example, the political and associated social and economic changes in Latin America since the

1980s, including democratization, liberalization, and privatization, have shifted the role of business towards taking greater responsibility for social and environmental issues. In South Africa, the political changes towards democracy and redressing the injustices of the past have also been a significant driver for CSR, through the practice of improved corporate governance, collective business action for social upliftment, black economic empowerment and business ethics. Likewise, more recently, the goal of accession to EU membership has acted as an incentive for many Central and Eastern European countries to focus on CSR, since the latter is acknowledged to represent good practice in the EU.

Socio-economic Priorities

CSR is typically shaped by local socio-economic priorities. For instance, while poverty alleviation, health-care provision, infrastructure development and education may be high on many developing country agendas, this stands in stark contrast to many Western CSR priorities such as consumer protection, fair trade, green marketing, climate change concerns, or socially responsible investments. Stephen Schmidheiny questions the appropriateness of imported CSR approaches, citing examples from Latin America where pressing issues like poverty and tax avoidance are central to CSR, but often remain left off of international CSR agendas.

Governance Gaps

CSR is frequently seen as a way to plug the 'governance gaps' left by weak, corrupt, or under-resourced governments that fail to adequately provide various social services (housing, roads, electricity, health care, education, etc.). Crane & Matten (2005) see this as part of a wider trend in developing countries with weak institutions and poor governance, in which responsibility is often delegated to private actors, be they family, tribe, religion, or increasingly, business. A survey by WBCSD (2000) illustrates this: when asked how CSR should be defined, Ghanaians stressed 'building local capacity' and 'filling in when government falls short'.

Crisis Response

Crises often have the effect of catalyzing CSR responses, albeit mostly of the philanthropic kind. For example, the economic crisis in Argentina in 2001 marked a significant turning point in CSR, prompting debates about the role of business in poverty alleviation. Similarly, Hurricane Katrina in the USA and HIV/AIDS in South Africa had the effect of galvanizing CSR. The examples are endless, be they the industrial accidents of the 1970s and 1980s (Seveso, Bhopal, Exxon Valdez), the environmental and human rights fiascos of the 1990s (Shell, Nike, McDonald's) or the corporate governance and natural disasters of the 2000s (Enron, Katrina, Sichuan).

1.4 Global CSR Drivers

Other sets of drivers are more global (or external) and tend to have an international origin. Remember, it is the varied combination of drivers that determines glocality.

Market Access

The flipside of the socio-economic priorities driver is to see these unfulfilled human needs as an untapped market. This notion underlies the now burgeoning field of 'bottom of the pyramid' (BOP) strategies. CSR may also be seen as an enabler for companies in developing countries trying to access markets in the developed world. For example, a survey of CSR reporting among the top 250 companies in Latin America found that businesses with an international sales orientation were almost five times more likely to report than companies that sold products regionally or locally (Araya, 2006).

International Standardisation

Codes are frequently a CSR response, especially in sectors where social and environmental issues are deemed critical, such as textiles, agriculture or mining. Often, CSR is driven by standardisation imposed by multinationals striving to achieve global consistency among its subsidiaries and operations in developing countries. For example, a study by Chapple & Moon (2005) in Asia found that 'multinational companies are more likely to adopt CSR than those operating solely in their home country, but that the profile of their CSR tends to reflect the profile of the country of operation rather than the country of origin.'

Investment Incentives

The belief that multinational investment is inextricably linked with the social welfare of developing countries is not a new phenomenon. However, increasingly these investments are being screened for CSR performance. Hence, socially responsible investment (SRI) is becoming another driver for CSR in many countries. Often, this is as a result of global SRI funds and indexes, like the Dow Jones Sustainability Index and FTSE4Good, but the influence of regional and national SRI instruments is also on the rise, with Brazil and South Africa among the first to go glocal in this respect. In addition, there are sector-based indexes emerging, like the ICT Sustainability Index launched in 2008.

Stakeholder Activism

In the absence of strong governmental controls over the social, ethical and environmental performance of companies in some countries, activism by stakeholder groups has become another critical driver for CSR. In developing countries, four stakeholder groups emerge as the most powerful activists for CSR, namely development agencies, trade unions, international NGOs and business associations. These four groups provide a platform of support for local NGOs, which are not always well developed or adequately resourced to provide strong advocacy for CSR. The media is also emerging as a key stakeholder for promoting CSR

Supply Chain Integrity

Another significant driver for CSR, especially among small and medium-sized companies, is the requirements that are being imposed by multinationals on their supply chains. This trend began with various ethical trading initiatives, which led to the growth of fair trade auditing and labelling schemes for agricultural products. Later, poor labour conditions and human rights abuses resulted in the development of certifiable standards like SA 8000. Major change has also been achieved through sector-based initiatives such as the Forest Stewardship Council and more recently, through the 'Walmart effect', involving choice editing by large retailers to source only from sustainable and responsible suppliers.

Discussion 1.2: CSR Drivers

1. What are the strongest drivers of CSR in your country?
2. Do the drivers of CSR differ between developed (or high income) countries and developing (or emerging) countries and, if so, how?
3. What do you expect will be the strongest CSR drivers over the next 5 years?

1.5 The Business Case for CSR

The World Business Council for Sustainable Development (WBCSD), which is the strongest proponent of the business case for CSR, suggests that it is predicated on five 'returns': operational efficiency; risk reduction; recruitment and retention of talent; protecting the resource base of raw materials; and creation of new markets, products and services.

Similarly, I believe there are ten powerful arguments that help to build the business case for CSR.

CSR raises the bar of legislation

In virtually every country in the world, as well as at an international level, legislation regulating environmental and social impacts is becoming more stringent. Unsustainable and irresponsible companies will find themselves incurring significant fines, penalties and clean-up or compensation orders, as well as being targeted for litigation, while sustainable and responsible companies will escape these costly outcomes.

CSR quantifies external impacts

Governments, using a variety of economic instruments such as taxes, subsidies and permits, are gradually forcing companies to reap the full cost or benefit of what they sow in terms of environmental and social impacts. Unsustainable and irresponsible companies will be net payers due to their negative contribution, while model CSR companies will be net receivers for their positive contribution.

CSR extends stakeholder accountability

Stakeholder groups have become powerful, well-organised agents in society, increasingly backed by the weight of the law, international NGO networks, public support and media interest. Unsustainable and irresponsible companies will waste inordinate amounts of time, energy and money trying to manipulate or fight its stakeholders, while sustainable and responsible companies will engage constructively with these groups.

CSR shapes public reputation

Stakeholder support of companies will to a greater degree be influenced by their public reputation, with unsustainable companies suffering from consumer boycotts, civil lawsuits and disruptive NGO activism. The profitability and share prices of unsustainable and irresponsible companies will be directly affected by repeated damage to their reputation, while model CSR companies will attract loyal support.

CSR introduces new rules of trade

Compliance with internationally recognised social and environmental standards is becoming a prerequisite for engaging in responsible global trade. Despite the counterproductive efforts of the World Trade Organisation, CSR-friendly countries and companies will increasingly refuse to trade with predatory companies which do not bear one or more approved marks of CSR. For example, most large global retail chains now do audits on the working conditions of their overseas suppliers.

CSR spawns new markets

The switch to a more sustainable economy will create new market opportunities in such areas as clean technology, ethical consumer products, ecotourism, sociocultural tourism and professional advisory services. Traditional exploitative markets of unsustainable and irresponsible companies will decline, while strategically sustainable companies will invest in the growing markets surrounding CSR.

CSR affects costs and liabilities

Dealing with corporate environmental and social impacts or infringements is becoming more expensive, as a result of taxes, fines, penalties, legal costs, damage claims, clean-up costs and compensation payments. By avoiding these costs, and identifying savings opportunities through eco-efficiency, cleaner technology and improved stakeholder relations, model CSR companies will be more profitable than their unsustainable and irresponsible counterparts.

CSR affects access to finance

Since the financial services sector faces indirect risks from funding or investing in unsustainable companies or projects, banks and insurance companies will increasingly scrutinise their business partners and clients on CSR criteria. Sometimes, this is through socially responsible investment funds and stock market indexes such as the Dow Jones Sustainability Index or FTSE4Good. Access to finance by unsustainable and irresponsible companies will become more difficult and expensive, while analysts, investors and lenders will actively seek to support companies with CSR best practices.

CSR expands corporate governance

All around the world, corporate governance codes, which are considered the ground rules for good business practice, are incorporating CSR principles into their requirements for risk management, ethics and reporting on nonfinancial matters. Unsustainable and irresponsible companies will more frequently fail the corporate governance acid test applied by stock exchanges, analysts and investors, while model CSR companies will excel.

CSR motivates employees

In the knowledge and service economy, companies are increasingly dependent on recruitment and retention of highly skilled workers. Since employees prefer to work for organisations that give them a sense of purpose and pride, irresponsible and unsustainable companies will struggle in the battle for talent, while businesses with strong CSR practices will benefit from increased staff attraction, commitment, retention and productivity.

1.6 The Problem of Uneconomic CSR

Despite these arguments, we must also concede that the much touted 'business case for CSR' is not nearly as obvious, certain or practiced as many assume. We must look beyond the rhetoric and turn to academic research. For a comprehensive review of these academic arguments and studies, see Carroll & Shabana (2010). To summarise here, however, the studies show a lack of consensus. For example, Griffin & Mahon (1997) reviewed 25 years of studies and found that a majority showed a positive link between CSR and financial performance, while Margolis & Walsh (2001) reviewed 80 studies, of which 42 showed a positive relationship, 19 demonstrated no relationship and four found a negative one.

Orlitzky, Schmidt & Rynes (2003) reviewed 52 studies and in most (but not all) cases, the studies suggest a positive association between CSR and profitability. Two reports by SustainAbility – Buried Treasure and Developing Value – also suggest mixed results. Some relationships between CSR factors and business success factors are stronger than others, and in many cases, no relationship exists.

Laffer et al. (2004), on the other hand, in a review of Business Ethics magazine's 100 Best Corporate Citizens found 'no significant positive correlation between CSR and business profitability as determined by standard measures.' Vogel (2005), author of The Market for Virtue, concludes that 'there is no definitive answer to the question of a financial link. It depends on an individual company's circumstances. Academics searching for a definitive corporate responsibility-financial performance link are barking up the wrong tree.'

I tend to agree. There are far too many variables to isolate the impact of CSR on financial performance, except through very specific examples like eco-efficiency. What's more, are typical measures of CSR a reliable proxy for sustainability and responsibility? After all, if we had correlated Enron's CSR and financial performance prior to its demise, it would have pointed to a strong positive relationship, which makes a nonsense of the whole exercise.

I have a more fundamental problem with the misleading nature of CSR business case rhetoric however. The real question we should be asking is: Does the market consistently reward sustainable and responsible performance by companies? Even without checking the data, we know intuitively from what we see going on in the world that the answer is an unequivocal no.

With very few exceptions, the global markets today reward the externalisation of social, environmental and ethical costs over the short term. New York Times journalist and author Thomas Friedman (2008) calls this 'the privatization of benefits and the socialisation of costs', while activist writers like Naomi Klein

(2000) call it 'the race to the bottom', referring to tendency for companies to locate their production in places with the lowest labour or environmental standards, and hence the lowest costs.

To underscore the point, the Vice Fund (VICEX) in the U.S., which only invests in the so-called 'sin' industries like tobacco, alcohol, gambling and armaments consistently outperforms the market over the long term, including socially responsible funds like the Domini Social Equity Mutual Fund (DSEFX). However, we don't need to go to extremes to prove the uneconomic nature of responsibility. Why are fairtrade and organic products, or renewable energy, more expensive than more mainstream products? Why does Exxon remain one of the largest and most profitable companies in the world? The fact of the matter is that, beyond basic legal compliance, the markets are designed to serve the financial and economic interests of the powerful, not the idealistic dreams of CSR advocates or the angry demands of civil society activists.

As it turns out, business leaders agree. The survey of 766 CEOs by Accenture & UN Global Compact (2010) found that 34% cited lack of recognition from the financial markets as a barrier to achieving their CSR goals. Nestle's Executive Vice President of Operations and GLOBE, Jose Lopez (2010), is candid: 'At the same time that we are coming out with a lot of discussions regarding the importance of sustainability, the market continues. I had hoped that after the world lost 5 trillion dollars in market capitalisation out of this nonsense financial crisis that companies would start to be measured by something else other than market capitalisation. But the world doesn't seem to be going anywhere other than to measure companies by their market capitalisation.'

Discussion 1.3: CSR Business Case

1.   Which elements of the business case for CSR are most convincing? Why do you say so?
2.   How has the business case for CSR changed over the past 20 years?
3.   What changes in economic conditions, government policies, business actions and public attitudes would strengthen the business case for CSR?

1.7 The Failure of CSR?

In light of the preceding section on the business case, my usual starting point for any discussion on CSR is to argue that it has failed. In my book, The Age of Responsibility, I provide the data and arguments to back up this claim (Visser, 2011). But the logic is simple and compelling. A doctor judges his/her success by whether the patient is getting better (healthier) or worse (sicker). Similarly, we should judge the success of CSR by whether our communities and ecosystems are getting better or worse. And while at the micro level – in terms of specific CSR projects and practices – we can show many improvements, at the macro level almost every indicator of our social, environmental and ethical health is in decline.

I am not alone in my assessment. Indeed, Paul Hawken (1994) stated in The Ecology of Commerce that 'If every company on the planet were to adopt the best environmental practice of the "leading" companies, the world would still be moving toward sure degradation and collapse.' Unfortunately, this is still true nearly 20 years later. Co-founder and former CEO of Seventh Generation, Jeffrey Hollender agrees, saying: 'I believe that the vast majority of companies fail to be "good" corporate citizens, Seventh Generation included. Most sustainability and corporate responsibility programs are about being less bad rather than good. They are about selective and compartmentalized "programs" rather than holistic and systemic change' (Hollender & Breen, 2010).

In fact, there is no shortage of critics of CSR. For example, Christian Aid (2004) issued a report called 'Behind the Mask: The Real Face of CSR', in which they argue that 'CSR is a completely inadequate response to the sometimes devastating impact that multinational companies can have in an ever-more globalized world – and it is actually used to mask that impact.' A more recent example was an article by Karnani (2010) in the Wall Street Journal called 'The Case Against Corporate Social Responsibility', which claims that 'the idea that companies have a responsibility to act in the public interest and will profit from doing so is fundamentally flawed.'

This is not the place to deconstruct these polemics. Suffice to say that they raise some of the same concerns I have – especially about the limits of voluntary action and the 'misdirection' that CSR sometimes represents. But I also disagree with many of their propositions – such as the notion that CSR is always a deliberate strategy to mislead, or that government regulation is the only solution to social and environmental problems.

Be that as it may, there are a number of ways to respond to my assertion that CSR has failed. One is to disagree with the facts and to suggest that things are getting better, not worse, as do the likes of Bjørn Lomborg (2001) in his Skeptical Environmentalist. That is his (and your) prerogative. However, I find the evidence, which is widely available from credible sources like the United Nations, both compelling and convincing.

Second, you might argue that solving these complex social, environmental and ethical problems is not the mandate of CSR, nor within its capacity to achieve. My response is that while business certainly cannot tackle our global challenges alone, unless CSR is actually about solving the problems and reversing the negative trends, what is the point? CSR then becomes little more than an altruistic conscience-easer at best; a manipulative image-management tool at worst.

My approach is to say that while CSR as it has been practised in the past has failed, that doesn't mean that a different kind of CSR – one which addresses its limitations and reforms its nature – is destined to fail in the future. However, we will need a new approach, which I call transformative CSR (or systemic CSR or CSR 2.0), which I discuss in more detail in the final chapter on the future of CSR.

Discussion 1.4: The Failure of CSR

1. Do you agree with Visser's proposition that CSR has failed? How would you support your argument?
2. Which social, environmental and ethical problems (in your country, or the world) are getting worse and which show improvement?
3. Enron and Lehman Brothers both went bankrupt despite having CSR programs. Could better or different CSR practices have prevented their collapse?

CHAPTER 2: THE EVOLUTION OF CSR

This chapter explores how we got here – tracing a brief history of the corporate sustainability and responsibility movements.

2.1 Ancient History

Much like the origins of philanthropy, we can go back many thousands of years to discover the wellspring of responsible business practices. One of the clearest threads of ethical debate relating to business has been the practice of giving loans and, more specifically, charging excessive interest on loans, which became known as 'usury'.

The practice of usury can be traced back approximately four thousand years and during its subsequent history it has been repeatedly condemned, prohibited, scorned and restricted, mainly on moral, ethical, religious and legal grounds. Among its most visible and vocal critics have been the religious institutions of Hinduism, Buddhism, Judaism, Islam and Christianity, as well as ancient Western philosophers, politicians and various modern socio-economic reformers.

The earliest references to usury are in the Hindu Vedic (2,000-1,400 BC) and Sutra (700-100 BC) texts, as well as the Buddhist Jatakas (600-400 BC). Among the Ancient Western philosophers who condemned usury can be named Plato, Aristotle, the two Catos, Cicero, Seneca and Plutarch. The criticism of usury in Islam was well established during the Prophet Mohammed's life and reinforced by various of his teachings in the Holy Quran, dating back to around 600 AD. The original word used for usury in this text was riba which literally means 'excess or addition'. In Judaism, the Hebrew word for interest is neshekh, literally meaning 'a bite'.

In Christianity, the anti-usury movement reached its zenith in 1311 when Pope Clement V made the ban on usury absolute. This stance gradually weakened over the centuries, especially with the rise of pro-capitalist Protestantism, but even Luther and Calvin expressed reservations. Calvin, for instance, set out seven crucial instances in which interest remained sinful. Furthermore, the architects of capitalism and modern economic theory, Adam Smith and John Maynard Keynes, both felt that interest should be strictly controlled, to prevent its negative effects.

And what where these negative effects? There are six principle arguments against the practice of usury, namely that: it represents unearned income; it is a form of double-billing; it exploits the needy; it is a mechanism for the inequitable redistribution of wealth; it is an agent of economic instability; and it results in discounting the future. These critiques are explored in more detail in a paper I co-authored with Alastair McIntosh and published in Accounting, Business & Financial History (Visser & McIntosh, 1998). For the purposes of this chapter, I simply use them to illustrate that there has been a raging debate about the ethics of business for millennia.

2.2 Industrial Welfare

The responsible business movement has more recent, direct and concrete roots through the emergence of the Industrial Welfare Movement in Victorian times, of which Cadbury was a part. As Carroll (2009) describes in The Oxford Handbook of Corporate Social Responsibility, one of the pioneers was John H Patterson, founder of National Cash Register in the 1884. Much like Cadbury, he ensured the provision of hospital clinics, bathhouses, lunchrooms, recreational facilities and even profit sharing for his employees. He became especially know for constructing the first 'daylight factory' buildings in 1893, with floor-to-ceiling glass windows that let in light and could be opened to let in fresh air.

Around that time, the limits of industrial welfare were being challenged and tested in the courts. In a landmark case of 1883, West Cork Railroad tried to compensate employees for job losses when the company was closing down. However, the court forbade any payments, ruling that it could only spend money for the purposes of carrying on the business. Around the same time, the piano manufacturer Steinway was also taken to court, because it had bought a tract of land to be used for a church, library and school for employees. In this case, however, the court condoned the expenditure, since it could be regarded as a strategy for improving employee relations.

Hence, right back in the 1880s, the fault line between business interests and stakeholder interests was drawn and the need to make a 'business case' for responsibility was firmly established. Bear in mind that this was still the era during which a Charter of Incorporation was only bestowed on those businesses that were socially useful – for example, water utilities or railroads. As legal academic and author of The Corporation, Joel Bakan (2004), put it to me: 'The original notion of the corporation was that the sovereign would grant the status of corporation to a group of business people in order to acquit themselves of some responsibility to create something that was in the public good. ... The notion that this was simply about creating wealth for the owners of the company was alien' (Bakan, 2008). How different the world might have been if this principle remained in force.

However, by the end of the Civil War, charters were available under any business pretext and were nearly impossible to revoke.

Another American pioneer in the Industrial Welfare Movement was Pullman Palace Car Company, which created a model industrial community in 1893 in the south of Chicago (much like Cadbury's Bourneville Village), including higher standards of housing, lighting, playgrounds, a church, an arcade, a theatre, a hotel and (somewhat more dubiously) a casino. The crucial lesson from these 19th century trailblazers was that they clearly understood that treating employees well was not only a noble thing to do, but was also good for business.

Despite these early signs of enlightenment, the industrial welfare movement was stopped in its tracks in the early 20th century by the combined forces of Frederick Taylor's doctrine of scientific management – based on his time-and-motion productivity studies – and the commercial success of Henry Ford's production line model. Glimmers of hope re-emerged with Elton Mayo's Hawthorne Works experiments of the 1920s, showing that a better working environment (lighting, heating, etc.) resulted in improved productivity. In fact, many concepts like group dynamics, teamwork and organisational social systems all stem from Mayo's pioneering efforts. Even here, however, as with the court cases 50 years earlier, the insidious business case principle was being reinforced: better treatment of employees was only justified if it improved profitability.

Discussion 2.1: Industrial Welfare

1. Usury is given as an example of business ethics concerns going back thousands of years. Can you think of any other ancient business ethics concerns?
2. What motivated the early industrial welfare pioneers to go beyond the law and ahead of common practice at the time?
3. Has the emergence of bureaucratic management practices improved or compromised corporate responsibility?

2.3 Questioning Business

By the late 1930s, we see the seeds of an intellectual movement being sown, with the first books exploring social responsibility emerging, including Chester Barnard's (1938) The Functions of the Executive, J.M. Clark's (1939) Social Control of Business and Theodore Krep's (1940) Measurement of the Social Performance of Business. These were not simply academic ramblings, but rather reflected the growing sentiments in the populace at large.

Asked in a 1946 Fortune Magazine survey, 'Do you think that businessmen should recognise responsibility for the consequences of their actions in a sphere wider than that covered by their profit-and-loss statements', 93.5% of the public said 'yes'. And asked, 'What proportion of the businessmen you know would you rate as having a social consciousness of this sort?' most responded either 'about half' or 'about three quarters' (Fortune, March 1946, 197-8, cited in Bowen, 1953: 44).

Just a few years later, we see the first cracks in the great edifice of industrial growth starting to appear, with Aldo Leopold (1949), self-appointed spokesperson for the decades-old conservation movement, saying in his Sand County Almanac that 'our bigger-and-better society is like a hypochondriac, so obsessed with its own economic health as to have lost the capacity to remain healthy'. American economist Howard Bowen (1953) reflected on this seminal movement in his book, Social Responsibilities of Business, using the term social responsibility for the first time in a book title, earning him the accolade in some people's eyes as 'the father of corporate social responsibility'.

However, it wasn't until the 1960s that business received its first serious critique for a failure of social responsibility, in the form of Rachel Carson's (1962) Silent Spring. In this scientific treatise, Carson lambasts the chemical industry for the accumulation of toxins like DDT in the environment, and their deadly bio-accumulative consequences up through the food chain. Indeed, many today regard Silent Spring as the birth sign of the modern environmental movement. Her poetic words still haunt and echo down the ages:

'It was a spring without voices. On the mornings that had once throbbed with the dawn chorus of robins, catbirds, doves, jays, wrens and scores of other bird voices, there was now no sound; only silence lay over the fields and woods and marsh. Even the streams were now lifeless. No witchcraft, no enemy action had silenced the rebirth of new life in this stricken world. The people had done it themselves.'

Big business received its second shock attack, from legal activist Ralph Nader (today better known as a serial minority candidate for the U.S. Presidency). In Nader's (1965) book, Unsafe at Any Speed: The Designed-In Dangers of the American Automobile, he went to war with the auto industry in general and General Motors in particular. 'A major contemporary problem', he said, 'is how to control the power of economic interests which ignore the harmful effects of their applied science and technology.'

2.4 Spaceship Earth

Around the same time, Kenneth Boulding (1966), Barbara Ward (1966) and Buckminster Fuller (1969) gave the public a metaphor to visualise society's growing predicament: Spaceship Earth – the planet as a closed system (apart from solar input). 'One of the reasons we are struggling inadequately today,' said Fuller, 'is that we reckon our costs on too short-sighted a basis and are later overwhelmed with the unexpected costs brought about by our short-sightedness.'

It was precisely those 'unexpected costs' that the Club of Rome decided to make explicit when they commissioned their Limits to Growth study (Meadows et al., 1972). The findings were based on the world's first global computer simulation of five major trends: accelerating industrialization, rapid population growth, widespread malnutrition, depletion of non-renewable resources and a deteriorating environment. Their overall conclusion, based on a range of scenarios, was that 'the behaviour mode of the system is clearly that of overshoot and collapse.'

Today, over 35 years later, co-author of the report, Jorgen Randers, sees no deviation from the path. In an interview, Randers (2008) told me: 'The real message of the Limits to Growth is that on a finite earth with rapid physical expansion, one must be very careful in not postponing action when problems start to emerge. You need to act very quickly ... And of course now, with climate change, we are seeing exactly the phenomenon that we were describing. So most likely this will be the overshoot and collapse, or an example of this, that we spoke about.'

Another intellectual that added his voice of warning was E.F. Schumacher (1973), author of Small is Beautiful. 'Economic growth,' he said, has become 'the abiding interest, if not the obsession, of all modern societies.' As a result, we have 'ever bigger machines, entailing ever bigger concentrations of economic power and exerting ever greater violence against the environment.' These 'big is beautiful' trends do not represent progress. On the contrary, he said 'they are a denial of wisdom. Wisdom demands a new orientation of science and technology towards the organic, the gentle, the non-violent, the elegant and beautiful.'

So by the end of the 1970s, it was clear that 'Spaceship Earth' was on a collision course. Moreover, it was clear that it was our industrial model of growth that was propelling humanity towards self-destruction. Right around that time, British scientist James Lovelock (1979) gave us a theory of how Earth might react, given the threat. I am referring, of course, to the Gaia Hypothesis – the idea that the earth acts like a living, self-regulating organism. In an interview with me, Lovelock (2008) reflected on our current state of affairs:

'Living things, when threatened or stressed, at first resist – and the [Earth] system's been doing that for quite a while now ... But somewhere around about 1900 we began to go beyond the limit. So now the system is doing the other thing that living things do and fleeing to a safe place that it knows. And the safe place which it's been at many times before is the hot regime where the global temperature is 5 or 6 degrees planet-wide hotter than now.'

Discussion 2.2: Limits to Growth

1. Warnings about the 'limits to growth' go back nearly 50 years. Why has it been so difficult to heed these warnings?
2. Did the early activists who were questioning the industrial growth model have credibility, and if so, why?
3. Can you think of any examples of new projects, products, businesses or cities that are being designed using 'spaceship earth' principles?

2.5 CSR Theory

Business was not deaf to these criticisms and warnings, nor completely unresponsive. In the West, labour conditions were steadily improving, the discipline of Human Resources was emerging and in 1977, Revered Leon Sullivan launched what might be regarded as the first CSR code – the Sullivan Principles, which set out the minimum acceptable labour practices for companies to remain in the discriminatory apartheid South Africa. Several companies had also begun tackling the issues of waste. For example, 3M's Pollution Prevention Pays programme began in 1975, avoiding more than 2.6 billion pounds of pollutants and saving more than $1 billion over the next 30 years. Germany was also a forerunner, launching its Blue Angel eco-label in 1978. What was still missing, however, was widespread agreement of what exactly business's obligations to society were.

This void was filled by American academic Archie Carroll (1979) who provided the first popular definition of corporate social responsibility (CSR), namely that it is the economic, legal, ethical and discretionary or philanthropic expectations that society has of business. Based on subsequent empirical work, the definition was later presented as a pyramid of weighted importance, with economic responsibility at the base (i.e. most important), followed by legal and ethical dimensions and final philanthropy at the apex (i.e. least emphasised). Despite considerable evolution in theory and practice since the 'CSR Pyramid' was first published, it has – together with Carroll's four-part definition – endured remarkably well (Carroll, 1991).

One of the reasons for the CSR Pyramid's longevity – besides its intuitive logic and business-friendly conceptualisation – is that it can be applied in practice. For example, Unilever did two studies to investigate its economic impacts, in Indonesia (Clay, 2002) and South Africa (Kapstein, 2008). What they found was that in Indonesia, while they employed over 7,000 directly, they also created over 293,000 jobs indirectly through the supply chain. In South Africa, the ratio of direct to indirect jobs was 1: 22. That in itself is a remarkable economic contribution, but it represents only one of numerous 'economic multipliers' identified by the International Business Leaders Forum (Nelson, 2003).

According the IBLF, in addition to creating jobs, companies generate investment, produce safe products and services, pay taxes, invest in human capital, establish local business linkages, spread international business standards, support technology transfer, and build physical and institutional infrastructure. Recognising this greater set of economic impacts and contributions, beyond simply generating returns for shareholders, many companies are now including Economic Value Added statements in their annual reports.

The legal dimension of Carroll's CSR Pyramid is more controversial, since many regard social responsibility as a purely voluntary activity. Pragmatically speaking however, many governments are weak, failing or corrupt and without the capacity to effectively police or enforce implementation of their legislation. Hence, voluntary legal compliance becomes genuine social responsibility. Legal responsibility also raises issues like tax avoidance, negative political lobbying and bribery and corruption, all of which should be acknowledged and addressed by responsible companies.

2.6 Legislating CSR

Of course, legal issues vary by region and by country. I can still remember a safety, health and environmental governance audit on a chemical company that I did when I was Director of Sustainability Services at KPMG. We visited facilities in five countries – South Africa, Germany, Netherlands, Italy and the USA – and one of the things we asked was for their records of legal non-compliance, including fines and penalties. This was a relatively trivial matter in all countries but one, the United States. First, they had not just a few but thousands of non-compliances, which probably said more about the country's onerous legal requirements than the company's negligence. For instance, when we asked to see their air pollution permit documentation, they pointed to an entire bookshelf of lever arch files. Second, they didn't know what liability these non-compliances represented, because they were in constant negotiation with the government (applying the

Federal Sentencing Guidelines principles) over the exact settlement amount of these.

On the question of legal responsibilities, I am often asked when I give talks whether CSR should be legislated. My answer is always the same: That depends what you mean. If you mean, should the government require companies to spend a certain percentage of their profits on CSR-related activities, as is being proposed in India and Nigeria, the answer is no. After all, that's just another kind of tax. What we need is for governments to have effective regulation of the issues that CSR is trying to tackle – pollution, labour conditions, environmental degradation, human rights and corruption.

One such issue where there is extensive legal reform happening is transparency. According to 2010 research across 30 countries by KPMG, GRI & UNEP (2010), there are already 142 country standards or laws with some sustainability reporting requirement or guidance, of which 65% are mandatory.

The issue of ethical responsibility could be the subject of an entire book itself – and indeed it already is (Crane & Matten, 2010). With ancient roots in philosophy, business ethics has exploded as area of study and practice, especially since it became strongly linked to the corporate governance movement of the 1990s. The financial scandals of Enron and WorldCom in 2001 (and many others since, like Parmalat and Lehman Brothers) have only served to concentrate the spotlight on business ethics, especially in America. We have seen the recruitment of armies of Ethics Officers, the drafting of endless Codes of Conduct and the widespread introduction of management tools like whistle-blowing. Many seem to forget the fact that many similar ethics policies and procedures already existed in the companies that so spectacularly imploded. This should serve as a warning about the limitations of the cult of management when it comes to responsibility.

The final element of Carroll's CSR Pyramid, philanthropic responsibilities, is already a familiar subject in CSR circles. I will just say that it is to his credit that Carroll represents philanthropy as the least significant part of CSR, as it serves as a useful reminder to many of those, especially in developing countries, who still equate CSR with philanthropy. Not that Carroll's Pyramid is inscrutable. In fact, I have written and published several critiques of the model (see, for example, Visser, 2006b).

Discussion 2.3: Carroll's CSR Pyramid
1. Do you agree with Carroll's inclusion of economic and legal dimensions as part of the definition CSR?
2. What are the strengths and weaknesses of Carroll's CSR Pyramid model?

3. Some argue that CSR be mandatory. What are the pros and cons of this argument?

2.7 Stakeholder Theory

In the 1980s, another American academic, Ed Freeman (1984), introduced a conceptual framework which has become central to all discussions of responsibility, namely Stakeholder Theory. According to the theory 'business can be understood as a set of relationships among groups which have a stake in the activities of that business, i.e. stakeholders. Stakeholders are those individuals or groups that can affect or can be affected by the achievement of the firm's core purpose' (Freeman in Visser et al., 2010). Implicitly, the stakeholder concept was (and remains) a challenge to the increasing domination of shareholder interests as the primary measure of effective management.

Stakeholder theory had an immensely hubristic effect, not only generating lively academic debate, but also achieving widespread application in business, as stakeholder management. Much of the early work was done around creating 'stakeholder maps', which plotted a company's relationship to all its 'interested and affected parties'. However it quickly became evident that such a broad scoping exercise inevitably results in everybody being included a stakeholder, which is not very useful. Hence, the practice of distinguishing between primary and secondary stakeholders emerged, or producing stakeholder webs in which not all stakeholders are equidistant from the centre. One of the most useful academic contributions to this evolving practice was Mitchell, Agle and Wood's (1997) proposition that stakeholders be ranked in three dimensions: power, legitimacy and urgency.

Of course, relations with stakeholders are not always consensual. I remember asking one CEO in America to tell me about his stakeholder relationships. He asked what I meant, so I said, 'You know, NGOs, civil society organisations and the like'. 'They are not stakeholders,' he growled, 'they are the enemy!' Hard to believe, but I'm not kidding. One useful matrix that I use classifies stakeholders on two axes: supportive or non-supportive, and active or inactive. Hence, supportive, active stakeholders are 'advocates', non-supportive, inactive stakeholders are 'apathetic', supportive, non-active are 'dormant' and non-supportive, active are 'adversarial'. By implication, engagement approaches should vary depending on the type of stakeholder.

Ten years after its introduction by Freeman, the concept of stakeholder engagement was enshrined for the first time as a fundamental element of good management when it was included in the King Code on Corporate Governance in South Africa in 1994. Today, stakeholder theory continues to be refined and expanded, with countries like Malaysia even considering changing their corporate law to give more prominence to stakeholders. Indeed, I often think that until we get this right – until stakeholders are given their legal, rightful and equal place at the negotiating table of business – all efforts at responsible business amount to little more than window dressing.

2.8 Triple Bottom Line

While this largely socially-dominated agenda was evolving, the environmental movement in the wake of Rachel Carson's (1962) Silent Spring continued to develop in parallel. 1970 saw the formation of Greenpeace, the celebration of the first Earth Day and became the base year of the WWF Living Planet Index. Soon after, in 1972, the United Nations convened a seminal conference on the Human Environment in Stockholm. Then a series of industrial disasters shook the world – a chemical explosion near Seveso in Italy in 1976, the Union Carbide gas leak in Bhopal in India in 1982, the Chernobyl nuclear accident in the Ukraine in 1986 and the Sandoz chemical spill into the Rhine River in Basel, Switzerland, in the same year – all with devastating human and ecological impacts.

Partly as a result of these disasters, as well as the increasingly worrying data on the state of the world being published by organisations like the Worldwatch Institute and the World Resources Institute, the UN formed the World Commission on Environment and Development (WCED), chaired by former Norwegian Prime Minister, Gro Harlem Brundtland. In 1987, the Commission released its report, Our Common Future, which included the now famous definition of 'sustainable development' – 'development that meets the needs of the current generation without compromising the ability of future generations to meet their needs' (WCED, 1987). The landmark 'Earth Summit' in Rio De Janeiro followed in 1992, attracting 172 governments, 108 heads of state and around 47,000 people.

At last, business had a concept that they could wrap their emergent responsibility practices around. In preparation for the Earth Summit, they produced a set of 50 case studies, published in a book called Changing Course (Schmidheiny & WBCSD, 1992). They also set up the Business Council for Sustainable Development (BCSD) and, through the International Chamber of Commerce, launched the Business Charter for Sustainable Development. This opened the floodgates for a new era of codes, standards and guidelines.

One of the first to emerge was EMAS – the Eco-Management and Auditing Scheme – in 1993, and then a few years later, in 1996, the ISO 14001 standard on Environmental Management. ISO 14001 followed in the footsteps of the immensely successful ISO 9001 quality standard. According to the ISO (2010) survey, at least 250,972 ISO 14001 certificates were issued in 155 countries by the end of 2010, up 12% from the previous year. 50% of certifications are now in the Far East and 41% in Europe, although Central and South America saw growth of 64% in 2010.

Much of the emphasis in the 1990s was still on eco-efficiency (coined and promoted by the World Business Council for Sustainable Development) and cleaner production (promoted by UNEP), since this produced the win-win outcome of environmental improvements and financial returns, thereby making a 'business case' for sustainable development.

At the time, John Elkington recalls feeling 'uneasy' with the eco-efficiency agenda, both because it narrowly focused on financial aspects, rather than wider economic impacts, and also because it ignored the social dimension of human rights, labour issues, community impacts and the like. To correct this, he introduced the idea of the 'triple bottom line' of sustainability: integrated, balanced economic, social and environmental performance. Reflecting on its success, Elkington (2008) told me, 'It was, for corporate leaders, like popping a pill where you suddenly saw the world slightly differently.'

Elkington (1997) pulled together his ideas on sustainability in Cannibals With Forks. The title came from a quote by the Polish poet, Stanislaw Lec, who said, 'Would it be progress if cannibals learned to eat with forks?' For Elkington, the cannibals were companies – displaying aggressive, acquisitive behaviour in the marketplace – and the fork was the three prongs of the triple bottom line. The concept was widely adopted and later institutionalised through the Dow Jones Sustainability Index and the Global Reporting Initiative's Sustainability Reporting Guidelines, launched in 1999 and 2000 respectively.

Discussion 2.4: Stakeholders and the Triple Bottom Line

1. As an organisation, how would you choose between the often conflicting interests and demands of stakeholders?
2. Some argue that the environment and future generations are stakeholder groups without a voice (and hence, more easy to ignore). Would you agree?
3. What are the strengths and weaknesses of Elkington's triple bottom line concept? Is anything missing from the model?

2.9 Supply Chain Integrity

Elkington was right to shine a spotlight on business's attention deficit on social issues. This was spectacularly illustrated when, in November 1997, Nike was exposed for using sweatshops in Asia. This bombshell came just five months after Nike had, together with its peers, launched the World Federation of Sporting Goods Industry Code of Conduct. The scandal erupted when a report on labour conditions in one of their contract supplier factories in Vietnam, prepared by Nike's own auditors, Ernst & Young, was leaked to an activist NGO (TRAC/Corporate Watch) by a disgruntled employee. The firestorm of bad publicity that rained down on Nike resulted in, among other things, Nike being sued for violating California's Business and Professionals Code.

Partly in response, in 1998, Social Accountability International (SAI) launched SA 8000, a standard especially focused on labour conditions in the supply chain. SAI is now one of the world's leading social compliance training organisations, having provided training to over 20,000 people, including factory and farm managers, workers, brand compliance officers, auditors, labour inspectors, trade union representatives and other worker rights advocates. Today, SA 8000 certification covers over 2,000 facilities in 64 countries, across 66 industries, and over 1.1 million employees.

Perhaps it is not surprising that Nike's supply chain is now one of the most scrutinised in the world. The three main product lines of Nike's brand – footwear, apparel and equipment – are made by approximately 600 contract factories that employ more than 800,000 workers in 46 countries around the world. In 2005, Nike was the first company in its industry to disclose its factory list. They now claim to visit each factory, on average, 1.77 times per year, while the exact number of visits per individual factory depends on a factory's rating, its strategic importance and its performance history. In 2009, they also conducted 33 deeper studies, called Management Audit Verifications (MAV), and 267 environment, health and safety reviews.

Another standard that emerged as a result of these social engagement trends in the 1990s was Accountability's AA 1000 Framework, launched in 1999 as 'an accountability guideline on social and ethical accounting, auditing and reporting, including stakeholder engagement'. Under this umbrella, a number of related standards were spawned, including an Assurance Standard (AA 1000AS), Stakeholder Engagement Standard (AA 1000SES), Purpose and Principles (AA1000PP) and Framework for Integration (AA 1000FI).

Former CEO of Accountability, Simon Zadek (2008), told me that the standards were a response to the tension between intensive and extensive accountability 'with the modern corporation being the quintessential example of extreme forms of intensive accountability, to very narrowly defined sets of stakeholders ... What's happened in the last decade and a half in the corporate responsibility space, conceptually, is that the pressure on companies has been to play out an increasingly extensive accountability model', i.e. being forced to take into account a wider set of stakeholder interests.

2.10 Corporate Governance

In many ways, the 1990s were a decade of increasing convergence in responsibility, with not only the social and environmental agendas on the rise, but also the corporate governance movement taking hold. The UK took the lead, establishing a Committee on the Financial Aspects of Corporate Governance in 1991 under the chairmanship of Sir Adrian Cadbury, then Director of the Bank of England and retired Chairman of Cadbury Schweppes. The Committee's report in 1992 – the so-called Cadbury Report, including its code of best practice – set the standard for other similar initiatives around the world.

One of the first to follow was South Africa's King Committee on Corporate Governance in 1993, which issued its King Report and Code in 1994 under the chairmanship of former High Court judge and director of several companies, Mervyn King. In many ways, King went further than Cadbury, going beyond the purely financial aspects of corporate governance and incorporating the concept of wider stakeholder accountability. Without a doubt, the different emphases were shaped by the operating context. At the time, London was still one of the great financial capitals of the world and South Africa was having its first democratic elections.

This divergence, which began as a fissure, became a canyon when subsequent updates were issued. The Cadbury Report was followed by the Greenbury Report in 1995, Combined Code in 1998 (updated in 2003 and 2006), the Turnbull Report in 1999, the Higgs Review in 2003, the Smith Report 2003 and the Walker Review in 2009, all of which continued to focus mostly on financial and organisational aspects of corporate governance (structure of the board, audit committees, remuneration committees, etc.). Hence, issues like sustainability and responsibility have to be inferred through generic clauses on risk and reputation, or passing references to environment, health and safety.

By contrast, updates to the King Report in 2002 and 2009 increasingly placed sustainability and responsibility at the heart of corporate governance. King II, for instance, included a substantial section on business ethics and an entire chapter on 'integrated sustainability reporting'. King III goes even further placing. As Mervyn King puts it, 'the philosophy of King III revolves around leadership, sustainability and corporate citizenship'. In an interview I conducted with King (2010), he emphasised that directors are accountable to the company first, not shareholders, and a broader set of stakeholders provide a better perspective on what is good for the company in the long term.

These alternative views of corporate governance are all the more insightful considering the accounting scandals that came to characterise the first decade of the 21st century, from the collapse of Enron and WorldCom in the U.S. in 2001, to Parmalat in Europe in 2003 and of course devastating fallout from the 2008 financial meltdown, including Lehman Brothers and numerous others. America's post-Enron response was the Sarbanes-Oxley Act, over which Mervyn King remains deeply sceptical.

2.11 Ethical Investment

A related trend to corporate governance in the Age of Management was the rise of socially responsible investment (SR). Steve Lydenberg (2005), author of Corporations and the Public Interest, explains that the history of SRI can be divided into two general periods, the first running from 1970 to the mid-1990s, and the second from the mid-1990s to the present (Lydenberg in Visser et al., 2010).

In the first period, SRI was largely a North American phenomenon. Starting in the early 1970s, a limited number of SRI unit trusts (mutual funds) and money managers began serving retail investors and small institutions. Large institutional investors then became involved in SRI through the anti-apartheid South Africa divestment movement, which began in the 1970s and culminated in the early 1990s. Ultimately scores of U.S. state and local pension funds, among others, screened billions of dollars in assets according to companies' labour records and levels of involvement in South Africa.

Throughout this period and continuing to today, U.S. religious organisations played a leading role in shareholder activism through the annual filing of hundreds of shareholder resolutions on social and environmental issues. Simultaneously, a number of community development banks, credit unions, and revolving loan funds were founded and attracted support from SRI investors.

During the second period, SRI developed into a worldwide phenomenon, starting in the United Kingdom, where it took root in the 1980s, and extending rapidly to Europe, and then to Asia, Africa, and Latin America. Starting in the late 1990s, Australia and Japan also developed active markets for SRI unit trusts (mutual funds) and the stock exchanges of South Africa, Israel, and Brazil launched 'SRI indexes' to encourage CSR among companies listed in those countries. Since 2000, a number of the public and private pension funds in Norway, Sweden, Denmark, the Netherlands and France have also imposed a variety of social and environmental standards in the management of a part, or all, of their assets.

Reflecting the global nature of this expansion, the United Nations became increasingly active in promoting SRI through the UN Environmental Programme's Financial Initiative and the launch in 2006 of the Principles for Responsible Investment. In Europe, SRI assets under management increased from €2.7 trillion to €5 trillion between 2007 and 2009 (Eurosif, 2010), while SRI now represents an estimated $3.07 trillion out of $25.2 trillion in the U.S. investment marketplace, according to the Social Investment Forum website. A report by Robeco and Booz & Company (2009) predicts that these will reach $26.5 trillion by 2015 – over 15% of the global total.

Discussion 2.5: Accountability and Corporate Governance

1. What is the difference between responsibility and accountability?
2. What are the respective merits and demerits of the British, South African and American approaches to corporate governance?
3. Some argue that SRI is simply reinforcing a short-term shareholder-driven capitalist model that is at the heart of our global unsustainability. What do you think?

2.12 Bottom of the Pyramid (BOP)

One of the most popular new visions of CSR is C.K. Prahalad and Stuart Hart's concept of doing business at the 'bottom of the pyramid' (BOP), the roughly 4 billion people living on less than PPP$1,500 a year. The concept was popularised in several academic papers (notably, Prahalad & Hart, 1992) and subsequently by Prahalad's (2004) book The Fortune at the Bottom of the Pyramid. Prahalad argues that the poor, defined as people living on less than $2 per day, at purchasing power parity (PPP) rates, represent a market size of PPP$13 trillion. Allen Hammond (2007), vice president of World Resource Institute (WRI), believes it may be as much as $15 trillion a year. Estimates in The Next 4 Billion, drawing on income data from 110 countries and standardized expenditure data from 36 countries across the globe, are lower at $5 trillion, but still by no means trivial.

Much of this colossal market will remain untapped, however, unless business learns to do business differently. In order to access the BOP, argue Prahalad and Hart, several myths need to be busted. For example, contrary to popular belief, BOP markets are brand-conscious and connected and BOP consumers accept new technology. However, in order to do business with these markets, companies have to create the capacity to consume, by making products affordable, accessible and available. The provision by Hindustan Lever of single-serve sachets of shampoo in India is now a classic – and much debated – case in point.

Building trust is also a prerequisite. I remember asking Muhammad Yunus (2008b) why the Grameen Bank had succeeded where so many other commercial banks had failed in doing business with the poor. His answer was that he began the bank in an area that he had lived and worked in for many years. He had built up social capital and earned their trust. As a result, he was able to grow a $2.5 billion banking enterprise with over 7 million active clients, affecting 35 million family members. Most remarkably, Grameen's loan repayment rate is over 98%, with borrowers of the Bank own 90% of its shares. By 2007, the microcredit model had scaled to over 50 countries, with 3,316 microcredit institutions reaching over 133 million clients. Of these, 93 million (up from 7.6 million in 1997) were among the poorest when they took their first loan. And of these poorest clients, 85%, or 79 million, were women.

The BOP model has been hotly debated and criticised. Speaking to me in an interview, Hart (2008) conceded two main problems: One is that 'companies will take existing, unsustainable polluting or toxic products or product systems or manufacturing processes, strip some cost out of them and take it out into these under-served markets, and then just do a lot more environmental damage.' The second, captured by Aneel Karnani (2007) in 'The misfortune at the bottom of the pyramid', is that companies are entering rural villages and urban slums and shanty towns and just 'selling stuff to poor people that they really don't need, extractive products that are just going to take what little cash they have in their pockets, extract wealth, not create it, and at the end of the day do more harm than good from the standpoint of poverty alleviation.' To this, Yunus (2008b) added, 'Our primary responsibility is to lift [the poor at the bottom of the pyramid], rather than see it as an opportunity to make money. So we should not look at them as consumers of our product. We should see them as potential producers; potential creative people who can take charge of their own life and transform it.'

Taking these concerns into account, Hart, with Erik Simanis and others at Cornell University, has been leading an initiative to create a BOP Protocol, or BOP 2.0 model. Hart (2008b) describes it as 'a new business process for actually engaging in those communities, building trust and then co-creating businesses.' There is an attitude difference that embodies humility. 'It's a co-creation methodology, rather than a talk-down imposition where the presumption is rich people are smarter, poor people are dumb and are victims. You have to change your mindset and think: we could be partners and colleagues and we could actually work together to develop a business that combine the best of both. We could bring incredible next generation, clean technology, but there's a lot of local knowledge, that if we combine those together, imagine what sort of interesting business we could create that could make a better way to live.' And as an example of scalability in this approach, he cites a BOP Protocol initiative in the U.S. with Ascension Health, which is the third largest hospital corporation in the United States, focussed on the 50 million people in the U.S. with no health insurance.

Another example of BOP scalability is the Tata Nano, the $2,500 car launched in 2008 in India. The mission began back in 2003, when Ratan Tata, chairman of Tata Motors and the $50 billion Tata conglomerate, set a challenge to build a 'people's car'. Tata gave an engineering team, led by 32-year-old star engineer Girish Wagh, three requirements for the new vehicle: It should be low-cost, adhere to regulatory requirements, and achieve performance targets such as fuel efficiency and acceleration capacity. By design, it is small and eco-efficient and while many wring their hands over the environmental impacts of a billion Indians driving a car, and the safety record of the Nano, no one has an ethical right to deny the same access to individual mobility that virtually the whole population of the developed world enjoys.

Other big companies have also got involved. For example, Philips is actively targeting rural India with two products: the smokeless chulha, or stove, and lighting products in the Philips Sustainable Model in Lighting Everywhere (SMILE) range. 'At Philips, we have a strategy in place to address the needs of consumers at the bottom of the pyramid,' said Philips India CEO Murali Sivaraman. 'We look at this section of society as a viable market and have developed products catering to their needs.'

Similarly, Envirofit, a spinout from the University of Colorado, claims that its $20 stoves cut smoke and toxic emissions by 80%, and halve the amount of fuel that is needed. It aims to sell 10 million in the developing world over the next five years. According to Simon Bishop, head of policy at the Shell Foundation, which seed funded the Envirofit venture, 'Everything we do is about applying business thinking to poverty and environmental issues. There is never going to be enough aid to go around so what you need to do is to focus our limited resources on self-financing mechanisms that can make a big impact.'

2.13 Codes and Standards

Looking back, we can see that the 1990s were the decade of CSR codes – not only EMAS, ISO 14001 and SA 8000, but also the Forest Steward Council (FSC) and Marine Stewardship Council (MSC) Certification Schemes, Green Globe Standard (tourism sector), Corruption Perceptions Index, Fairtrade Standard, Ethical Trading Initiative, Dow Jones Sustainability Index and OHSAS 18001 (health & safety), to mention just a few. But all that was just a warm up act when we look look at the last 10 years, when we have seen codes proliferate in virtually every area of sustainability and responsibility and all major industry sectors. So much so that in the A to Z of Corporate Social Responsibility, we included over 100 such codes, guidelines and standards – and that was just a selection of what it out there (Visser et al., 2010). To illustrate the point, here is a sample of what has been thrust onto corporate agendas since the year 2000:

The Carbon Disclosure Project; Global Alliance for Vaccines and Immunisation; GRI Sustainability Reporting Guidelines; Kimberley Process (to stop trade in conflict diamonds); Mining and Minerals for Sustainable Development (MMSD) Project; UN Global Compact; UN Millennium Development Goals; Voluntary Principles on Human Rights; FTSE4Good Index; Global Business Coalition on HIV/AIDS; Global Fund to Fight AIDS, Tuberculosis and Malaria; Business Principles for Countering Bribery; Publish What Pay Campaign; Johannesburg Declaration on Sustainable Development; London Principles (finance sector); AA 1000 Assurance Standard; Equator Principles (finance sector); Extractive Industries Transparency Initiative (EITI); Roundtable on Sustainable Palm Oil; Global Corruption Barometer; UN Convention Against Corruption; UNEP Finance Initiative; UN Norms on Business and Human Rights; World Bank Extractive Industries Review; AA 1000 Standard for Stakeholder Engagement; EU Greenhouse Gas Emissions Trading Scheme; Millennium Ecosystem Assessment; ISO 14064 Standard on Greenhouse Gas Accounting and Verification; Stern Review on the Economics of Climate Change; Bribe Payers' Index; UN Principles for Responsible Investment; ClimateWise Principles (insurance sector); UNEP Declaration on Climate Change; UN Principles for Responsible Management Education (PRME);

Bali, Poznan and Copenhagen Communiqués (climate change) ... and many, many more.

No wonder companies are suffering from code fatigue and audit exhaustion. It is the supreme paradox of the Age of Management – companies are pressured to standardise their efforts on sustainability and responsibility, while stakeholders and critics (myself included) remain unconvinced that this approach identifies or addresses the root causes of the problems we face. Many of the institutional failures over the past 20 years have, I would argue, been systemic failures of culture, rather than bureaucratic failures of management; they have more to do with a prevailing set of values than a particular set of procedures.

Discussion 2.6: Bottom of the Pyramid (BOP) and Codes

1. Some argue that BOP strategies are a new type of economic colonialism or exploitation of the poor. What do you think?
2. What are the strengths and weaknesses of the BOP model?
3. What are the main benefits and limitations of voluntary CSR codes and standards?

2.14 The Way Forward

So where does this leave us? As I explain later in this book, and in detail in *The Age of Responsibility* (Visser, 2011), this historical development of CSR represents the passage of business through four Ages and Stages of CSR: Defensive CSR in an Age of Greed, Charitable CSR in an Age of Philanthropy, Promotional CSR in an Age of Marketing and Strategic CSR in an Age of Management. Collectively, these have brought us to a point of crisis in CSR. Specifically, CSR is failing to turn around our most serious global problems – the very issues it purports to be concerned with – and may even be distracting us from the real issue, which is business's role causal role in the social and environmental crises we face. The way I see it, that leaves us with three options for taking CSR forward, which I like to think of as the Parrot, Ostrich and Phoenix scenarios.

The Way of Parrot is to tell it like it is: recognise the limitations of CSR and admit to its primary role as a business tactic for reputation management.

The Way of the Ostrich is the status quo: pretend that CSR is working and that more of the same will be enough.

The Way of the Phoenix is the transformative agenda: reconceptualise CSR as a radical or revolutionary concept that challenges the intransigent business and economic model and offers genuine solutions to our global challenges.

The Way of the Phoenix is what I call Transformative CSR, or CSR 2.0, and is what we are just starting to see rising from the ashes of the previous ages, as we enter a new Age of Responsibility.

CHAPTER 3: CSR AROUND THE WORLD

3.1 Global and Local CSR

The term 'glocal' – a portmanteau of global and local – is said to come from the Japanese word dochakuka, which simply means global localisation. Originally referring to a way of adapting farming techniques to local conditions, dochakuka evolved into a marketing strategy when Japanese businessmen adopted it in the 1980s. It is said that the English word 'glocal' was first coined by Akio Morita, founder of Sony Corporation. In fact, in 2008, Sony Music Corporation even trademarked the phrase 'go glocal'. It was subsequently introduced and popularised in the West in the 1990s by Manfred Lange, Roland Robertson, Keith Hampton, Barry Wellman and Zygmunt Bauman.

The underlying concept of 'think global, act local' claims somewhat more varied origins. In a broad, abstract sense, it is captured in the ancient Hermetic idea of 'as above, so below' – the macrocosm is reflected in the microcosm and vice versa. Or as Goethe put it: 'If (we) would seek comfort in the whole, (we) must learn to discover the whole in the smallest part'. More concretely and recently, the Scots town planner and social activist Patrick Geddes applied the concept in his 1915 book, Cities in Evolution, saying: 'Local character is thus no mere accidental old-world quaintness, as its mimics think and say. It is attained only in course of adequate grasp and treatment of the whole environment, and in active sympathy with the essential and characteristic life of the place concerned.'

Sometimes, glocality maintains its geographical origins. For example, Neighborhood Knowledge California (NKCA) is a project of the Advanced Policy Institute (API) at the University of California, Los Angeles, which serves as state wide, interactive website that assembles and maps a variety of databases that can be used in neighborhood research. Its aim is to promote greater equity in housing and banking policy. In addition, it functions as a geographic repository for users to map their own communities by uploading their own datasets.

When and by who the phrase 'think global, act local' was first applied to environmental issues is a matter of some dispute. It may have been introduced by David Brower, founder of Friends of the Earth, in 1969, or by Rene Dubos as an advisor to the 1972 UN Conference on the Human Environment. Also, in 1979, Canadian futurist Frank Feather chaired a conference called 'Thinking Globally, Acting Locally'. Whatever its origins, the notion of glocality has entered into the popular consciousness. It was perhaps given its most visible and practical expression when the Rio Earth Summit issued Local Agenda 21 in 1992, which was a programme of action for applying the global principles of sustainable development in local contexts. Today, there is also a Glocalist magazine in Austria that offers a daily online newspaper, weekly digital magazine and monthly print magazine.

In a CSR context, the idea of 'think global, act local' recognises that most CSR issues manifest as dilemmas, rather than easy choices. In a complex, interconnected CSR 2.0 world, companies (and their critics) will have to become far more sophisticated in understanding local contexts and finding the appropriate local solutions they demand, without forsaking universal principles. It is also a caution against applying global models and standards, without allowing for the flexibility of local adaptation and expression. This chapter explores some of the diverse ways that CSR is manifesting in different regions and countries of the world.

3.2 CSR Around the World

The importance of glocality for CSR really struck home to me when, in 2008 – together with my co-author, Dirk Matten – I launched my book The A to Z of Corporate Social Responsibility (Visser et al., 2010) in several regions and countries around the world, from Guatemala and South Africa to China and the UK. What became blindingly obvious was that while CSR had some global principles that most countries agreed on, the local manifestations were distinctive in each local case.

This led me to undertake a two-year research project that culminated in The World Guide to CSR (Visser & Tolhurst, 2010), profiling CSR in five regions and 58 countries. In her review of the book, Israeli CSR expert Elaine Cohen captures some of the essence of the idea of glocality: 'The country profiles [offer] a local flavour and sometimes even a little local language – tzedakah, the Hebrew word for charity; sanpo yoshi – 'three-way good' in Japan; choregia, the ancient form of sponsorship in Greece; and ubuntu in Southern Africa, which relates to community culture, to name but a few examples.'

International comparative CSR research bears out my personal experiences and the content of *The* World Guide to CSR. One of the best studies was done in 2006 by my Cambridge colleague, Jeremy Baskin, which looked at the reported CSR behaviour of 127 leading companies from 21 emerging markets across Asia, Africa, Latin America, and Central and Eastern Europe. It also compared the findings with over 1,700 leading companies in high-income OECD countries. The first finding was that CSR varies by region and level of economic development: it is highest in

Europe, followed by Japan and North America, all of which are ahead of emerging markets. However, this conclusion masks a greater diversity of performance. For example, on community, philanthropy and human resource aspects, emerging markets have better CSR disclosure than North America and Japan, while on environmental issues, Japan is roughly on par with Europe and ahead of emerging markets and North America. The study also showed that, among the BRICS countries, CSR is strongest in South Africa, followed by Brazil, India, Russia and China.

Two GlobeScan surveys (2005 and 2007) also illustrate the glocality of CSR. In the first, the public was asked: What is the most important thing a company can do to be seen as socially responsible? The results showed that in the U.S., Canada and Brazil, community involvement was perceived as most important, while in Australia, UK and much of Europe it was protecting the environment, and in Mexico and China, quality and safety of their products was the priority. In the second survey, the public was asked: How responsible should companies be held for their impact on society? The findings were that more than 80% of Brazilians hold business responsible for its performance across 10 dimensions of CSR, as compared with only 59% of British, 57% of Americans, 53% of Indians and 46% of Chinese.

Perceptions of companies' CSR performance also varies by region. In Globescan's (2011) Survey of Sustainability Leaders, Walmart is ranked 1 in North America, 8 in Europe and 5 in Emerging Markets, while Unilever is ranked 1 in Europe, 4 in North America and 3 in Emerging Markets, and Natura is ranked 1 in Emerging Markets but doesn't even feature in the North American and European top ranks.

Another study, by EIRIS (2007), found that the percentage of high impact companies with advanced environmental policies was 90% in Japan and Europe, as compared with 75% in Australia and New Zealand, 67% in the USA and 15% in Asia (excluding Japan). Furthermore, it was determined that 75% of European companies operating in high-risk countries had developed a basic human rights policy, as compared with only 40% of U.S. companies.

All of these studies, and many more besides, provide evidence for glocality. CSR varies by country and by region – in terms of its level of maturity, the issues it prioritises and the approaches that it adopts. This variation is especially evident between developed and developing countries, which has been a particular fascination for me in my work in CSR.

Discussion 3.1: CSR Around the World

1. How can a multinational company practice glocality, when labour and other standards are so different around the world?
2. How would you describe CSR in your country, and how does this vary from other countries you know about?
3. Which country do you think is leading the world on CSR? Why do you think so?

3.3 CSR in Developing Countries

The challenge for CSR in developing countries is framed by a vision that was distilled in 2000 into the Millennium Development Goals—'a world with less poverty, hunger and disease, greater survival prospects for mothers and their infants, better educated children, equal opportunities for women, and a healthier environment.' Unfortunately, these global aspirations remain far from being met in many developing countries today. The question addressed by this chapter, therefore, is: What is the role of business in tackling the critical issues of human development and environmental sustainability in developing countries?

To begin with, it is worth clarifying my use of the terms developing countries and CSR. There is an extensive historical and generally highly critical debate in the development literature about the classification of countries as 'developed' and 'less developed' or 'developing'. Without reviving that debate here, suffice to say that I use 'developing countries' because it is still a popular term used to collectively describe nations that have relatively lower per capita incomes and are less industrialized.

This is consistent with the United Nations Developments Program's (UNDP) categorization in its summary statistics on human development and is best represented by the World Bank's classification of lower- and middle-income countries. It should be noted, however, that the UNDP's classification of high, medium and low development countries produces a slightly different picture than the World Bank's list of which countries are developed and developing.

As I've noted in the opening chapter, CSR is also a contested concept. However, for the purposes of this chapter, I use CSR in developing countries to represent the formal and informal ways in which business makes a contribution to improving the governance, social, ethical, labour and environmental conditions of the developing countries in which they operate, while remaining sensitive to prevailing religious, historical and cultural contexts.

The rationale for focusing on CSR in developing countries as distinct from CSR in the developed world is fourfold:

1. Developing countries represent the most rapidly expanding economies, and hence the most lucrative growth markets for business;
2. Developing countries are where the social and environmental crises are usually most acutely felt in the world;
3. Developing countries are where globalization, economic growth, investment, and business activity are likely to have the most dramatic social and environmental impacts (both positive and negative); and
4. Developing countries present a distinctive set of CSR agenda challenges, which are collectively quite different to those faced in the developed world.

3.4 The Literature on CSR in Developing Countries

The CSR literature can be grouped into four dominant CSR themes: social, environmental, ethics, and stakeholders. What is immediately evident in applying this categorization to the literature on CSR in developing countries is that, in contrast the Lockett et al.'s (2006) findings that most CSR articles in top management journals focus on ethical and environmental themes, most scholarly work on CSR in developing countries focuses on the social theme.

In part, this reflects the fact that corporate *social* responsibility is the preferred term in the literature to describe the role of business in developing countries, as opposed to, say, business ethics, corporate citizenship, corporate sustainability, or stakeholder management. More than this, however, social issues are generally given more political, economic, and media emphasis in developing countries than environmental, ethical, or stakeholder issues. And there is also still a strong emphasis on the philanthropic tradition in developing countries, which is often focused on community development.

Lockett et al. (2006) also classify CSR papers by epistemological approach and find a roughly even split between theoretical and empirical research, which is also the case in the literature on CSR in developing countries, although the latter has a slight weighting towards empirical work. What is interesting is that, whereas Lockett et al. (2006) find that 89% of theoretical CSR papers are non-normative, in the CSR in developing countries literature, the balance is far more evenly split. This is largely due to the relatively large number of papers on the role of business in development, which tend to adopt a normative, critical perspective.

In terms of empirical research, there are also differences. According to Lockett et al. (2006), the CSR literature is dominated by quantitative methods (80%). In contrast, CSR papers on developing countries are more likely to be qualitative. Lockett et al. (2006) suggest that their findings probably reflect the positivist editorial tendencies of many of the top management journals, rather than the inherent epistemological preference of CSR scholars. And indeed, the CSR and development journals in which most developing country papers are published seem to have more interpretive or epistemologically flexible editorial policies.

I have found that most research on CSR in developing countries to date has either generalized about all developing countries, or focused at a national (rather than a regional) level (Visser, 2008a). Despite the focus on countries in the literature, only about a fifth of all developing countries have had any CSR journal articles published on them. Of these, the most commonly analyzed and written about countries are China, India, Malaysia, Pakistan, South Africa, and Thailand. Analysis at a regional level (notably Africa, Asia, and Latin America) is becoming more common, but papers at the sector, corporate, or individual level remain relatively scarce.

3.5 Global Research on CSR

Although the literature often frames the debate about CSR in a global context, there is very little empirical research on the nature and extent of CSR in developing countries. Baskin's (2006) research, which compares CSR in 21 emerging markets with high-income OECD countries, is a notable exception. He finds that emerging market companies have a respectable representation in the Dow Jones Sustainability Index and show rising levels of take-up of the Global Reporting Initiative and ISO 14001.

More specifically, over two-thirds of the emerging market companies in the sample either produced a sustainability report or had a specific section on their website or in their annual report covering CSR. Interestingly, emerging market companies are also more inclined to report extensively on corporate social investment activities than OECD companies.

Other areas of reported CSR performance examined by Baskin (2006) show that emerging markets lag the OECD significantly on reporting on business ethics and equal opportunities (with the exception of South Africa), are roughly on a par for environmental reporting, and show comparable reporting variance on women on company boards (e.g. high in Norway and South Africa, low in Japan and Latin America), training and occupational health and safety (e.g. high in South Africa and Western Europe, low in North America and Asia).

Despite the limitations of using reporting as an indicator of CSR performance and the danger of representing regions by just a few countries (e.g. only two of the 53 countries in Africa were included in the sample), the Baskin (2006) study does provide some insight into the level of CSR activity in developing countries, concluding that 'there is not a vast difference in the approach to reported corporate responsibility between leading companies in high income OECD countries and their emerging-market peers. Nonetheless, corporate responsibility in emerging markets, while more extensive than commonly believed, is less embedded in corporate strategies, less pervasive and less politically rooted than in most high-income OECD countries' (46).

An older, yet more comprehensive piece of international research is the Millennium Poll on Corporate Social Responsibility (Environics, 2000), which surveyed 25,000 citizens in 23 countries and on 6 continents. It found that citizens in 13 of 23 countries thought their country should focus more on social and environmental goals than on economic goals until 2010. Two in three citizens wanted companies to go beyond their historical role of making a profit, paying taxes, employing people and obeying all laws; they wanted companies to contribute to broader societal goals. Actively contributing to charities and community projects didn't nearly satisfy people's expectations of CSR – there were 10 areas rated higher. Around half were paying attention to the social behaviour of companies and over 20% of consumers reported either rewarding or punishing companies based on their perceived social performance, and almost as many again considered doing so.

Discussion 3.2: CSR in Developing Countries

1. To what extent is the distinction between developed and developing countries still useful for analysis and understanding?
2. If you accept the distinction, what are the main differences between CSR in developed and developing countries? If you don't explain why.
3. What might be the methodological problems with research like the Millennium Poll on CSR? What are the implications for our understanding of CSR?

3.6 Research on CSR in Asia

Asia is the region most often covered in the literature on CSR in developing countries. In this section, I give a flavour of some of the early academic research on CSR in Asia, which has a significant focus on China (e.g. Zhuang & Wheale, 2004), India (e.g. Balasubramanian et al., 2005), Indonesia (e.g. Blowfield, 2004), Malaysia (e.g. Zulkifli & Amran, 2006), Pakistan (e.g. Lund-Thomsen, 2004) and Thailand (e.g. Kaufman et al., 2004). Other countries that have had less attention include Bangladesh (Nielsen, 2005), the Pacific Forum Islands (Prasad, 2004), Sri Lanka (Luken & Stares, 2005), and Vietnam (Prieto-Carron, 2006).

The Journal of Corporate Citizenship special issue on CSR in Asia (Issue 13, Spring 2004) provides a good overview of the status of the debate. Editors Birch & Moon (2004) note that CSR performance varies greatly between countries in Asia, with a wide range of CSR issues being tackled (e.g. education, environment, employee welfare) and modes of action (e.g. foundations, volunteering and partnerships).

A number of quantitative studies confirm this picture of CSR variance. In a survey of CSR reporting in Asia, Chapple & Moon 2005) found that nearly three quarters of large companies in India present themselves as having CSR policies and practices versus only a quarter in Indonesia. Falling somewhere between these two extremes are Thailand 42%), Malaysia 32%) and the Philippines 30%). They also infer from the research that the evolution of CSR in Asia tends to occur in three waves, with community involvement being the most established form of CSR, following by successive second and third waves of socially responsible production processes and employee relations.

In a comparative survey of CSR in 15 countries across Europe, North America, and Asia, Welford 2005) speculates that the low response rates from countries like Hong Kong, Malaysia, Mexico, and Thailand may in itself be an indicator of CSR being less prevalent in developing countries. This seems to be borne out by the research findings, in which these countries fairly consistently underperform when compared with developed countries across 20 aspects of CSR measured by the survey. More specifically, Malaysia is generally the weakest in terms of CSR performance, with Thailand being relatively strong on external aspects such as child labour and ethics) and Hong Kong being generally better on internal aspects such as non-discrimination and equal opportunities).

3.7 Research on CSR in Africa

In this section, I explore some of the early academic research on CSR in Africa, which is heavily dominated by South Africa (Visser, 2006a), while other pockets of research exist for Côte D'Ivoire (e.g. Schrage & Ewing, 2005), Kenya (e.g. Dolan & Opondo, 2005), Nigeria (e.g. Amaeshi et al., 2006), Tanzania (e.g. Egels, 2005), and Mali and Zambia (e.g. Hamann et al., 2005). Very few papers are focused on industry sectors, with traditionally high impact sectors like agriculture (e.g. Blowfield, 2003), mining (e.g. Kapelus, 2002), and petrochemicals (e.g. Acutt et al., 2004) featuring most prominently.

Two good sources of literature on the region are Corporate Citizenship in Africa (Visser et al., 2006) and the Journal of Corporate Citizenship special issue on CSR in

Africa (Issue 18, Summer 2005). The latter concludes that 'academic institutions and researchers focusing specifically on corporate citizenship in Africa remain few and under-developed' (Visser et al., 2005: 19).

This is confirmed by a review of the CSR literature on Africa between 1995 and 2005 (Visser, 2006a), which found that that only 12 of Africa's 53 countries had any research published in core CSR journals at the time, with 57% of all articles focused on South Africa and 16% on Nigeria. The latter partly reflects the high media profile generated around corporate citizenship issues and the petrochemical sector, especially focused on Shell and their impacts on the Ogoni people (Ite, 2004).

My review also found that, in contrast to the socially oriented focus of the literature on CSR in developing countries more generally, business ethics dominates as a research topic in the region, accounting for 42% of all articles on CSR in Africa over the past decade. Partly, this reflects the collective weight of the ethics-focused journals in the study. But it is also because CSR debates in Africa have historically been framed in terms of the ethics of colonialism and apartheid and the prevalence of corruption and fraud on the continent.

This pattern is unsurprisingly also reflected in CSR research on South Africa. For example, in a previous review I found that, of the pre-1994 literature, most dealt with the ethical investment issues relating to apartheid; and since the transition to democracy in 1994, many papers now focus on the individual ethics of South African managers (Visser, 2005). I expect that other themes, such as stakeholder engagement, social responsibility, and health (including HIV/AIDS) will move up the agenda as CSR increasingly addresses these issues in an African context. In practice, however, it is likely that the economic and philanthropic aspects of CSR (rather than the legal and ethical responsibilities) will continue to dominate CSR conceptualization and practice in Africa (Visser, 2006b).

3.8 CSR Research in Latin America

In this section, I point to some of the early academic research on CSR in Latin America, which is the least covered of the developing country regions (Haslam, 2007), with the focus mainly on Argentina (e.g. Newell & Muro, 2006), Brazil (e.g. Vivarta & Canela, 2006) and Mexico (e.g. Weyzig, 2006), although Nicaragua (Prieto-Carron, 2006) and Venezuela (Peindado-Vara, 2006) also feature.

One helpful collection of papers is the Journal of Corporate Citizenship special issue on CSR in Latin America (Issue 21, Spring 2006). De Oliveira (2006) notes that the CSR agenda in Latin America has been heavily shaped by socio-economic and political conditions, which have tended to aggravate many environmental and social problems such as deforestation, unemployment, inequality, and crime. Schmidheiny (2006) frames this in a constructive way, claiming that many Latin Americans see CSR as the hope for positive change in the face of persistent poverty, environmental degradation, corruption and economic stagnation.

The trend towards increasing CSR in the region has been generally upward. For example, Correa et al. (2004), cited in Schmidheiny (2006), reported that by 2004, there were more 1,000 Latin American companies associated with EMPRESA (the American CSR network), 300 were members of the World Business Council for Sustainable Development, 1,400 had obtained ISO 14001 certification, and 118 had signed up to the UN Global Compact. Furthermore, the CSR debate is alive and well, with the CSR track in Brazilian Academy of Management (ENANPAD) in 2005 attracting the largest number of articles (De Oliveira, 2006).

Araya's (2006) survey of CSR reporting among the top 250 companies in Latin America also gives some indication of practices in the region. At the time, 34% of the top companies published sustainability information in a separate report, the annual report, or both, mostly from the energy and natural resources sectors. The annual report was the more common format (27%, versus 16% using separate reports), with Brazilian companies being the most likely to report (43% disclose sustainability information in annual reports and 22% in sustainability reports), as compared with Mexico (33% and 25%) and Chile (22% and 16%). Even companies with European and American origins are less likely to be reporters than Brazilian companies.

The picture for small and medium-sized enterprises (SMEs) is slightly different. In a survey of over 1,300 SMEs in Latin America, Vives (2006) found that SMEs in Chile and Argentina have the highest level of CSR activity, while those in Brazil and El Salvador have the lowest. Most CSR by SMEs is focused on internal activities (especially employee welfare), whereas external (philanthropic) and environmental activities are less common.

Discussion 3.3: CSR in Developing Regions

1. How do you perceive the differences between CSR in Asia, Africa and Latin America?
2. Do you think there is a trend of convergence or divergence of CSR practices in the regions?
3. How does CSR in the region you're from (or living or studying in) compare with other regions?

3.9 Myths about CSR in Developing Countries

I first tackled this question of whether the conceptions and models of CSR developed in the West are appropriate for developing countries by setting out what I believe to be seven popular myths about CSR in developing countries (Visser, 2003).

Most of these myths exist as a result of the feeding frenzy that inevitably occurs every time the media has hunted down and sunk its teeth into one or other juicy story of corporate exploitation. The myths are also sustained, however, by whole legions of largely well-intentioned people who have vested interests in promoting their particular brand of the truth about CSR. Let's look at these myths briefly.

Myth 1 – Economic growth is not compatible with CSR

What the Index for Sustainable Economic Welfare (ISEW) and UN Human Development Index (HDI) show is that GDP growth and quality of life move up in parallel until social and environmental costs begin to outweigh economic benefits. Most developing countries have yet to reach this divergence threshold. For them, economic growth and the expansion of business activities is still one of the most effective ways to achieve improved social development, while environmental impacts are increasingly being tackled through leapfrog clean technologies.

Myth 2 – Multinationals are the biggest CSR sinners

On the ground in most countries, multinationals are generally powerful forces for good, through their investment in local economies, creation of jobs, upgrading of infrastructure, provision of basic services and involvement in community development and environmental conservation. The cumulative social and environmental impacts of smaller companies, which operate below the radar of the media and out of reach of the arm of the law, are typically far larger than that of the high profile multinationals.

Myth 3 – Multinationals are the biggest CSR saviours

Not only do large companies have limited influence over government policy, but most multinationals, despite large capital investments, provide only a minuscule proportion of the total employment in developing countries. The real potential saviours are small, medium and micro enterprises (SMMEs), including social enterprises, which are labour intensive and better placed to effect local economic development. If the social and environmental impacts of these SMMEs can be improved, the knock on benefits will be proportionally much greater than anything that multinationals could achieve on their own.

Myth 4 – Developing countries are anti-multinational

Developing countries are often caught in a no-man's land of under-development in a competitive, monetized, global economy, and the sooner they can modernise and integrate, the better for them. Most often, developing country communities welcome multinationals and their CSR initiatives. This is not the same as saying that the developing world should repeat the past mistakes of the developed countries, such as highly polluting industrialisation, nor that multinationals should not be required to be responsible and held accountable.

Myth 5 – Developed countries always lead on CSR

There are countless examples of how developing countries are proving themselves highly adept at delivering the so-called triple bottom line of sustainability, namely balanced and integrated social, economic and environmental benefits. It is actually not surprising, since in developing countries, these three spheres are seldom separable – economic development almost inevitably results in social upliftment and environmental improvement, and vice versa.

Myth 6 – Codes can ensure CSR in developing countries

The past few years have seen a mushrooming of corporate responsibility codes, standards and guidelines, which developing countries are keen to adopt, if only to satisfy their Western partners. This standardisation trend is both inevitable and necessary in a globalising world which is desperately searching for an alternative to command-and-control style business regulation in order to satisfy the governance and accountability void which still exists. But it would be a big mistake – for companies, civil society, or regulators – to assume that this codification is a reliable predictor of social and environmental impacts at grassroots level.

Myth 7 – CSR is the same the world over

One of the biggest fallacies is that, in a globalised world, CSR can somehow conform to a unitary model. Of course, we need universal principles, like the UN Global Compact, and perhaps even process frameworks, like ISO 14001. But standardised performance metrics, like those of the Global Reporting Initiative and the numerous sustainability funds and indexes, start to tread on shaky ground. The tendency is for developed country priorities to receive emphasis and for northern NGO agendas to dominate.

3.10 An Alternative CSR Pyramid

Having unmasked these myths, I decided to look at Archie Carroll's CSR Pyramid of economic, legal, ethical and philanthropic responsibilities (described in the Chapter

2) and see how well it fitted the African context (Visser, 2006b). My conclusion was that 'the relative priorities of CSR in Africa are likely to be different from the classic, American ordering' and that 'Carroll's CSR Pyramid may not be the best model for understanding CSR in general, and CSR in Africa in particular.' I then broadened this to propose an alternative CSR Pyramid for developing countries, which I will describe briefly below (Visser, 2008a).

Of course, I was not the first to question Carroll's model. Leading CSR academics, Crane & Matten (2010) observed that 'all levels of CSR [described in Carroll's pyramid] play a role in Europe, but they have different significance, and furthermore are interlinked in a somewhat different manner'. In the same way, my contention is that the order of the CSR layers in developing countries – if these are taken as an indicator of the relative emphasis assigned to various responsibilities – differs from Carroll's classic pyramid. Hence, in developing countries, economic responsibilities still get the most emphasis. However, philanthropy is given second highest priority, followed by legal and then ethical responsibilities.

Figure 3.1: CSR Pyramid for Developing Countries

Copyright Wayne Visser 2012

Economic responsibility is the most obvious and important focus of CSR. It is well known that many developing countries suffer from a shortage of foreign direct investment, as well as from high unemployment and widespread poverty. Therefore the economic contribution of companies in developing countries is highly prized, by governments and communities alike. Hence, in developing countries, CSR tends to stress the importance of 'economic multipliers', including the capacity to generate investment and income, produce safe products and services, create jobs, invest in human capital, establish local business linkages, spread international business standards, support technology transfer and build physical and institutional infrastructure.

Philanthropic responsibility is next most important for several reasons. First, there are often strong indigenous and religious traditions of philanthropy. Second, the socio-economic needs of developing countries are so great that philanthropy is an expected norm – it is considered the right thing to do by business. Third, companies realise that they cannot succeed in societies that fail, and philanthropy is seen as the most direct way to improve the prospects of the communities in which their businesses operate. Fourth, over the past 50 years, many developing countries have become reliant on foreign aid or donor assistance. Hence, there is often an ingrained culture of philanthropy. And finally, developing countries are often still at an early stage of maturity in CSR, sometimes even equating CSR and philanthropy, rather than embracing the more embedded approaches.

Legal responsibility generally has a lower priority than in developed countries because the legal system does not function as well. This does not necessarily mean that companies flaunt the law, but there is far less pressure for good conduct. This is because, in many developing countries, the legal infrastructure is poorly developed, and often lacks independence, resources and administrative efficiency. Corruption and the government capacity for enforcement in particular remain serious limitations and reduce the effectiveness of legislation as a driver for CSR.

Ethical responsibility has an influence on the CSR agenda in developing countries, but it remains limited. Despite progress on issues of corporate governance in some countries, these are still the exception rather than the rule. For instance, in Transparency International's annual Corruption Perception Index and Global Corruption Barometer, developing countries usually make up the bulk of the most poorly ranked countries. Furthermore, survey respondents from these countries generally agree that corruption still affects business to a large extent. The World Bank's Investment Climate Survey paints a similar picture.

It is important to say that this CSR pyramid is an illustration of how CSR typically manifests in developing countries, rather than an aspirational view of what CSR in developing countries should look like. For example, I am not proposing that legal and ethical responsibilities should get such a low priority, but rather that they do in practice. By contrast, if we were to envisage an ideal CSR Pyramid for developing countries, I would argue that improved ethical responsibilities, incorporating good governance, should be assigned the highest CSR priority. In my view, governance reform holds the key to improvements in all the other dimensions, including economic development, rule of law and voluntary action. Hence, embracing more transparent, ethical governance practices should form the foundation of CSR practice in developing countries, which in turn will provide the enabling environment for more widespread responsible business.

3.11 Anglo American's CSR Pyramid

Let's use the global mining company Anglo American as an example to illustrate this alternative CSR pyramid. On economic responsibilities, they state that 'our economic contribution extends far beyond the profits we generate.' They divide this contribution into two categories: 1) value added in the course of production and the wider effects of these activities (e.g. through payments to suppliers and multiplier effects) and through investments in staff development, technology transfer and investment; and 2) the value to society of their products, which are used in the manufacture of goods that underpin the modern way of life and for which there are few ready substitutes. Hence, their Value Added Statement includes disclosures for employment, distribution of economic benefits to employees and suppliers, tax and related payments to government, capital expenditure, black economic empowerment and returns to shareholders. Seen this way, Anglo American's economic contribution in Africa exceeds the GDP of many individual African countries.

Demonstrating glocality, Anglo American is now subject to the South African Mining Charter, which is a legally binding commitment by the industry to increase the access of previously disadvantaged individuals to the mineral resources of the country and their associated economic benefits. They do this through prioritised development and promotion of previously disadvantaged employees, entering into financial partnerships with empowerment companies and procurement from black-owned firms. In addition, Anglo American established the Anglo Khula Mining Fund to promote the entry of black economic empowerment participants into junior mining companies.

In terms of philanthropic responsibilities, Anglo American declared in one of its CSR reports that 'in developing countries there is still a significant role for philanthropic programmes.' Their primary vehicle for charitable engagement in Africa is the Anglo American Chairman's Fund, which was established in 1975 and aims 'to enable people to take greater control over their daily lives'. One of the major focuses of this fund in Africa – demonstrating glocal prioritisation – is HIV/AIDS.

On legal responsibilities, not surprisingly, Anglo American claim legal compliance as one of their fundamental business principles, saying 'we respect the laws of host countries' and 'we will comply with all laws and regulations applicable to our businesses and to our relationships with our stakeholders.' Nevertheless, each year they disclose legal actions against the company for breaches of safety legislation and environmental incidents, both resulting in fines. The point is not so much the company's commitment to legal compliance, but rather that it is given relatively less importance as a driver in the pursuit of CSR, as compared with economic and philanthropic pressures.

Finally, regarding ethical responsibilities, Anglo American notes its support for the Extractive Industries Transparency Initiative (EITI) 'as a means of increasing stakeholder confidence, reducing opportunities for embezzlement and stimulating debate around how revenues are allocated most effectively in resource-dependent economies.' In their statement of business principles Anglo American also insist that 'we are implacably opposed to corruption. We will not offer, pay or accept bribes or condone anti-competitive practices in our dealings in the marketplace and will not tolerate any such activity by our employees.' In 2003, they launched a whistle-blowing facility in order to allow employees to anonymously report any violations of Anglo American's business principles or any legal or ethical concerns.

Discussion 3.4: CSR Pyramid for Developing Countries
1. Does Visser's proposed CSR pyramid match your perception, knowledge or experience of CSR in developing countries?
2. Visser calls for CSR to be led by a governance revolution in developing countries. What is your view?
3. What are the strengths and weaknesses of Visser's CSR pyramid?

3.12 Going Native and Becoming Indigenous

In practice, making CSR in countries around the world requires a special skill, which Stuart Hart (2005), in his book Capitalism at the Crossroads, calls 'native capability'. When I interviewed him, Hart (2008) explained it like this: 'Where multinationals have engaged with Base of the Pyramid (BOP) communities, in rural areas or slums and shanty towns, it's almost always been through an NGO partner; they outsourced it to that partner. Very seldom would you see employees or staff from multinationals actually being in those places. That's beginning to change. People from the company actually have to be in those spaces and develop relationships on the ground. You can't just outsource the work to NGOs and expect any capability to develop.

'So it's really a new capability,' says Hart, 'the idea of native capability or becoming indigenous, and it requires effort to develop it. But if you do it and do it well, it can yield new business opportunities based on trust and social capital that makes you virtually impossible to dislodge. So from the standpoint of sustainable competitive advantage, becoming embedded in the community, developing that sort of social capital and trust and relationship, is the highest form of sustainable competitive advantage.'

One of the companies that Hart is working with – through the BOP 2.0 Protocol initiative – is SC Johnson, particularly in Kenya. I remember hearing a story, told by one of the people working on this project, which provides a perfect example of what glocality and native capability is all about. He explained that SC Johnson saw great opportunities for selling their household cleaning products to poor communities in rural Kenya. However, after some consultation with the community, they quickly discovered that tackling hygiene and cleanliness issues of the communal toilets was their real top priority. SC Johnson was delighted, as they have a great range of toilet cleaning detergents and related products.

However, when they brought samples for testing, the community was extremely disappointed. 'They don't work!' said the community. 'But they must work', said SC Johnson, 'we have tested them extensively in America and customers are very happy with the results'. 'Well, they might work for the private toilets of America,' said the community, 'but they don't work for the communal toilets of Kenya'. Slightly nonplussed, SC Johnson went 'indigenous' and sent a team to investigate on the ground. And indeed, 'on the ground' was the key, because the walls and floors of the communal toilets were all made from dried mud. And – unsurprisingly – SC Johnson's cleaning products weren't designed to work on mud surfaces. So they went back to the drawing board and designed something that would work. They had learned the lesson of developing native capabilities.

One of the ways for of assessing glocality in terms of the UN Millennium Development Goals (MDGs) is a tool developed by Business in Development (NCDO) and Sustainalytics called the online MDG Scan. Companies can create a free account on the website and insert key performance data relating to the company's presence in developing countries. The MDG Scan then converts this data into numbers of beneficiaries in developing countries whose lives have been positively affected by the company's activities. The Scan measures this positive contribution to the MDGs through a company's economic value added, employment creation, products and services and community investments. It's by no means comprehensive, but for many companies, it will be a good start.

Ted London (2009) also reported in Harvard Business Review on a framework he has developed, which is aimed at helping BOP ventures assess the impact their initiatives are having locally, in the short term and over time. It measures how a venture affects the wellbeing of its critical constituencies in three important dimensions: their economic situation, their capabilities and their relationships. Another initiative is the Impact Reporting and Investment Standards (IRIS) developed by the Acumen Fund, The Rockefeller Foundation and B Lab, in conjunction with PwC and Deloitte, in an attempt to better assess social and environmental impacts.

3.13 Corporate Shared Value

Porter & Kramer (2011) build on BOP and related concepts to propose 'shared value creation' as the next big thing for business. 'The capitalist system is under siege,' they declare. 'In recent years business increasingly has been viewed as a major cause of social, environmental, and economic problems. Companies are widely perceived to be prospering at the expense of the broader community. Even worse, the more business has begun to embrace corporate responsibility, the more it has been blamed for society's failures.'

The problem, according to Porter and Kramer, is that companies remain trapped in an outdated approach to value creation. They continue to view value creation narrowly, optimizing short-term financial performance in a bubble while missing the most important customer needs and ignoring the broader influences that determine their longer-term success.

As far as solutions go, Porter and Kramer see CSR as something of a red herring, despite the authors having written a previous paper extolling CSR as a route to competitiveness (Porter & Kramer, 2006). Now they see CSR as a 'mind-set in which societal issues are at the periphery, not the core' and 'a reaction to external pressure—[which has] emerged largely to improve firms' reputations.'

By contrast, they argue that the principle of shared value involves creating economic value in a way that also creates value for society by addressing its needs and challenges. 'Businesses must reconnect company success with social progress. Shared value is not social responsibility, philanthropy, or even sustainability, but a new way to achieve economic success. It is not on the margin of what companies do but at the center.'

This redefinition of corporate purpose from profit maximization to shared value creation – which the authors claim is starting to be embraced by the likes of GE, Google, IBM, Intel, Johnson & Johnson, Nestlé, Unilever, and Wal-Mart – requires 'a far deeper appreciation of societal needs, a greater understanding of the true bases of company productivity, and the ability to collaborate across profit/nonprofit boundaries.'

And how can companies create shared value? There are three distinct ways, according to the authors: by reconceiving products and markets, redefining productivity in the value chain, and building supportive industry clusters at the company's locations. 'Each of these is part of the virtuous circle of shared value; improving value in one area gives rise to opportunities in the others.'

Porter and Kramer are keen to emphasise that corporate shared value is not about sharing the value already created by firms—a redistribution approach. Instead, it is about expanding the total pool of economic and social value. They illustrate this with the example of cocoa farmers in the Côte d'Ivoire, where fair trade can increase farmers' incomes by 10% to 20%, while shared value investments can raise their incomes by more than 300%.

Fair trade, they explain, aims to increase the proportion of revenue that goes to poor farmers by paying them higher prices for the same crops. 'Though this may be a noble sentiment, fair trade is mostly about redistribution rather than expanding the overall amount of value created. A shared value perspective, instead, focuses on improving growing techniques and strengthening the local cluster of supporting suppliers and other institutions in order to increase farmers' efficiency, yields, product quality, and sustainability. This leads to a bigger pie of revenue and profits that benefits both farmers and the companies that buy from them.'

If we succeed, Porter and Kramer believe this shared value approach will drive the next wave of innovation and productivity growth, reshape capitalism and its relationship to society, and legitimize business again.

Discussion 3.5: CSR, BOP and CSV

1. What common criticisms do the bottom of the pyramid (BOP) and corporate shared value (CSV) approaches have of CSR?
2. Is CSV different from the BOP idea of indigenous co-creation, and if so, how?
3. What are the main limitations of Porter and Kramer's shared value creation model?

3.14 Social Entrepreneurs on a Mission

Many of the models discussed – such as BOP and CSV – require a special breed individual to implement their vision; people who have become popularly known as social entrepreneurs and form part of the social enterprise movement. There are examples throughout history of companies that have worked for social benefits – think for example of the credit unions started in the 1850s in Germany by Franz Hermann Schulze-Delitzsch – but the movement really only gained formal recognition in the 1980s. This was the decade in which Bill Drayton founded Ashoka in Washington, D.C., Muhammad Yunus registered Grameen Bank as an independent bank, and former Archbishop of Panama Marcos McGrath and Swiss businessman Stephen Schmidheiny set up FUNDES in Panama, all with a mission to support social entrepreneurs.

Since 1981, Ashoka has elected over 2,000 leading social entrepreneurs as Fellows, providing them with living stipends, professional support, and access to a global network of peers in more than 60 countries. Ashoka defines social entrepreneurs as those 'who have innovative solutions to social problems and the potential to change patterns across society. They demonstrate unrivalled commitment to bold new ideas and prove that compassion, creativity, and collaboration are tremendous forces for change.' Put more simply, 'the life purpose of the true social entrepreneur', says Bill Drayton (2010), 'is to change the world.'

And many have done just that. Ashoka evaluates the impact of its Fellows five years after their election and start up. In 2010, the Corporate Executive Board Company reported the results of a survey of Ashoka's impact, which they conducted in 12 languages across the globe. They found that 52% of the Ashoka Fellows had changed national policy within five years and 76% had changed the pattern in their field nationally (on average 3.2 times) within the same five years. 'These results are especially striking', reflects Drayton (2010), 'since five years is early in the lifecycle of the social entrepreneur.'

The social enterprise movement was given a boost in the 1990s with the establishment of the Schwab Foundation for Social Entrepreneurship (started by the World Economic Forum's founder, Klaus Schwab), which supports 'pragmatic visionaries who achieve large scale, systemic and sustainable social change through new invention, a different approach or a more rigorous application of known technologies or strategies.' Jeff Skoll, first president of eBay, also set up a fund – the Skoll Foundation – to support social entrepreneurs. 'I like to support causes where a lot of good comes from a little bit of good,' says Skoll. 'In other words, where the positive social returns vastly exceed the amount of time and money invested.'

One of the projects supported by the Skoll Foundation was a series of studies by SustainAbility on social entrepreneurship. The first report, Growing Opportunity, concluded that three different mindsets have characterized business thinking in relation to social and environmental issues (SustainAbility & Skoll Foundation, 2007). 'If 1.0 was about compliance and 2.0 about citizenship, 3.0 is about creative destruction and creative reconstruction.' They identified five main components to this Mindset 3.0: 1) systems thinking and design (e.g. cradle-to-cradle); 2) consumer engagement (e.g. Villagereach); 3) new business models (e.g. Aravind Eye Hospitals); 4) 360° accountability (e.g. Transparency International); and 5) base-of the pyramid markets (e.g. the Danone and Grameen Bank partnership).

One of the leading think-tank organisations focused on the social enterprise space today is Volans Ventures, co-founded by John Elkington which, among its other activities, produces a roll call of 'The Phoenix 50' pioneers in the business of social innovation, nominated by entrepreneurs and other stakeholders.

3.15 Glocal CSR in Practice

I want to end this chapter with a few examples of CSR in practice – at global and local levels – from my own experience. The first is something that occurred when I was working for KPMG. We had been brought in by the global mining and metals company, BHP Billiton, to review their performance on Business in the Community's Corporate Responsibility Index. More specifically, they wanted to understand why they had performed so poorly, when they felt their CSR practices were strong. After digging into BITC's assessment questionnaire, we put our finger on something that was quite interesting. At the time, it should be explained, the BITC Index was a UK initiative, with the scorecard reflecting regional concerns accordingly. In particular, there were many questions on the emerging agenda of energy and consequently energy efficiency programmes scored lots of points in the Index.

So, what was the problem? Well, BHP Billiton was certainly not unconcerned about energy issues. After all, its new aluminium smelter in Mozambique was an energy-hungry beast. But it also happened to be located next to South Africa, which has some of the cheapest electricity in the world. As a result, energy efficiency was not their foremost priority in the region. By contrast, the epidemic of malaria in Mozambique was killing many of their workers and devastating their local communities. The company responded by developing a malaria control and treatment programme, which was highly effective. In fact, it was one of their great CSR success stories. The problem was that the BITC Index had not prioritised public health, so BHP Billiton – despite their laudable local approach – didn't get much credit for their CSR efforts on malaria. I hasten to add that BITC's revised Corporate Responsibility Index is today far more comprehensive and sensitive to glocality.

A second example is from a trip to Guatemala in 2008, where I had an opportunity to visit one of the local sugar plantations. They had kindly prepared a presentation on their approach to CSR and imagine my delight when I saw that they also have a CSR Pyramid. The interesting thing, however, was that it was not Carroll's CSR Pyramid. Economic responsibility was still at the base of the pyramid, but the next most important responsibility was to the families of their employees. The third tier was community responsibility and, rather intriguingly, the apex of the pyramid was engagement in responsible national policy development. Was theirs right and Carroll's wrong? Of course, they were both right. That is the beauty of glocality. It is not an 'either-or' mentality, but a 'both-and' approach. The other interesting observation is that they had formed a co-operative of farms. Individually, they were too small to justify a CSR programme, but collectively, it made sense.

This brings me to my final example, which has to do with glocality through empowering SMEs to incorporate CSR. On a 2009 trip to Mexico, I became aware of some excellent work being done by the IDEARSE Centre at Anahuac University on CSR and SMEs. In response to a government-sponsored programme aimed at SME Growth Acceleration, IDEARSE put together an approach for supporting the businesses' growth through the implementation of a CSR business administration model that would develop competitive advantages for the companies. Built into their business training programme, therefore, were six elements for SME development: self-regulation, stakeholders, human rights, environment, labour and social/community impact. Working with the supply chains of big brands like Sony, Coca-Cola and Cemex, IDEARSE have taken more than 70 SMEs through the programme, with stunning results. On average across the six CSR dimensions, the SMEs improved from a score of 23% to 43%, while simultaneously showing average annual sales growth of 30%.

All of these examples show that it is not only imperative, but entirely possible, to adopt the CSR principle of glocality. Without it, companies risk being branded as cultural imperialists. But more tragically, they risk failing in their CSR efforts, because they have not struck the magic balance between global principles and local application.

Discussion 3.6: Social entrepreneurship and Glocality

1. What characteristics do social entrepreneurs need to be successful? Can social entrepreneurship be taught?
2. Other than the examples given above, can you think of any other social entrepreneurs? What are their stories?
3. Glocality is often about the dilemma of balancing global and local priorities? Can you think of any good CSR examples?

CHAPTER 4: IMPLEMENTING CSR

This chapter starts going beyond the 'why' to the 'how' of CSR. In the pages that follow, I explore seven critical dimensions in which 'shapeshifting' (i.e. transformation) needs to occur in order to create sustainable and responsible companies. To make things more fun and interesting, I use the metaphor of elephants and lions, as I did in my book, Beyond Reasonable Greed (Visser 2002). Elephants are used as symbols of sustainable and responsible companies, i.e. those with good CSR, and lions represent unsustainable and irresponsible companies, i.e. those with bad CSR or no CSR. The seven elements where CSR implementation needs to take place are in relation to: values, vision, work, governance, relationships, communication and services.

4.1 Values: It's in his Kiss

Values are exactly what they say they are – a reflection of the things we value. They are not motherhood and apple pie statements in annual reports, or candyfloss principles framed on the boardroom wall. If you want to know what values a lion lives by, the answer lies not in his well-groomed mane or his charming smile; as the rock 'n roll classic goes: 'It's in his kiss!'

In other words, companies' values are betrayed by their actions, not their words or their spin-doctor's marketing material. And an unreformed lion will never be a convincing elephant, no matter how real his mask looks or how much grey makeup he applies. It is only by behaving like an elephant, not by looking like one, that companies start to shapeshift. If you watch a pride of lions at a waterhole in a game park, it is likely you will see them refusing to allow any other animal near to it – even (or maybe especially) if the day is extremely hot and the animals are getting thirsty and tired. It is clear that the lions' intention is to weaken their potential prey to the point that they are much easier to catch later on.

This is perfectly logical for a predator, but not the behaviour of an elephant. This waterhole scene perfectly mirrors the principle of exclusion widely prevalent in today's economies. As farmers merge and expand their land to compete in current world markets, no longer being afforded the protection by the state they used to have, so less land is available for the smaller farmers. Of course, this exclusionary principle applies in any field where large companies are gobbling up the market by trading on their economies of scale. The end-result is a small number of asset owners surrounded by a property-less, unemployed, highly resentful proletariat.

Have you heard that analysis before? It comes straight from Karl Marx, albeit that his ideology is politically incorrect to espouse.

Unfortunately, a lot of companies still embody values of exclusion. Many big corporates are, in fact, anti-competition? Profit maximisation rests on domination and monopoly control. Hence, alive and well in a wide variety of boardrooms are the principles of self-preservation, paranoid secrecy, cold-blooded rationality, materialistic greed, egotistical empire building, distrustful stakeholder relationships, organised pack-hunting, strict don't-step-out-of-line hierarchies and inequitable class and gender divisions.

This may sound overly like a Disney caricature of the evil antagonist. But if you step back and think about the corporate environment and the way in which managers behave and acquisitions happen, it starts to feel uncomfortably true. Don't get me wrong. I am not saying that business is the root of all evil, or that business people are devils in disguise. I am part of the scene myself. What I *am* saying is that the economy and business have adopted the lion persona so completely that the life of hunger and hunting and killing has come to feel perfectly natural. You see, the lion is not cruel; it is just being what it is – a carnivore. The difference is that business is not genetically programmed to be a predator. Neither are the people who make up companies.

Of course, many pension funds and other investors argue that, given the current rules of the game, they want their investments to behave like carnivores because that way they get the best returns. They would be horrified if the CEO got up at an annual general meeting and announced he was going to give half the growth in earnings towards fighting the war against HIV/AIDS. For this very reason, we need multi-level shapeshifting. A lonely elephant has little if no chance of beating the lions, especially if the odds are stacked against her. The tragedy is that most people spend their childhood being taught to become elephants – to be kind, considerate, gentle, generous, trusting, fair, friendly, selfless and cooperative. Then they get snatched away from their supportive family environment and find themselves in the clutches of a more ruthless master – the economy, the company, the boss, the bank. Very quickly, they unlearn their homemade values. They are taught to distrust their caring instincts and to forsake their former beliefs as feeble naivety. They are shown how dangerous and unfriendly the world is, full of hungry competitors and harsh conditions. They are bullied into 'getting tough' in order to survive.

In fact, I believe that most people - even people like General Electric's former CEO 'Neutron Jack' - are elephants at heart. One thing Jack Welch did, which you simply don't see from other CEOs, was to handwrite thank-you notes to his employees when he thought they'd done something special. Most CEOs only communicate with staff lower down if they're in for a roasting. Sadly, the majority of management take off their elephant masks as they leave home in the morning and put on their lion masks. It may not feel natural or comfortable; but it is expected. When in lion country, pretend to be a lion or you may get spotted and end up as someone else's lunch!

Keeping up our feline façade is only possible because we find ways to dissociate ourselves from our harmful actions. We trick ourselves into thinking that decisions – like sacking people in the interests of efficiency, refusing a charity request or killing off a piece of nature – are not personal. We rationalise that we are pawns on the chequer-board of the economy, the international markets, the shareholders, the budget, the performance appraisal form, or the corporate bonus system. Hence, while dishing out pain to others, we go on to accept a healthy salary increase and additional perks for ourselves. Then we feed on another course of equally self-serving illusions – like the idea that managers are more valuable than workers; or that only those who create the wealth should share in the spoils; or that there have to be winners and losers; and if there were no material incentives, who would work?

Elephant companies do not allow their people to hide behind convenient corporate masks. They do not profess values that they do not believe in or practice. Instead, they make it uncomfortable to think or act like a lion. Not by writing warm fuzzy value statements, or by throwing the rulebook at transgressors. Instead, they use two old-fashioned, tried and tested techniques – leading by example and applying collective moral pressure.

Take America's popular ice-cream chain, Ben & Jerry's Homemade Inc., for example. Since equity in the workplace was one of their fundamental values, the founders insisted on a top to bottom salary ratio of 7:1. Although the arrival of a new CEO in 1995 pushed up the ratio to 14:1, this was still commendably egalitarian compared with the rest of corporate America where CEOs were earning on average 85 times more than their employees (today it is more like four times that ratio). Staff diversity was another value, but not just on paper. By the mid-1990s, the number of minorities employed at Ben & Jerry's was 3%, almost double the 1.8% that made up the Vermont population. Three per cent of professionals and managers were also from minority groups, including the CEO. The percentage of women in senior and professional positions was 40% and the company paid senior women 37.5% more than the national average.

Giving is another instance in which Ben & Jerry's put their money where their values are. In one year they committed as much as 7.5% of pre-tax profits in donations to charity, compared with around 1% for the U.S. food and manufacturing sector as a whole. Seeking to live up to their social responsibility values, Ben & Jerry's have also invited a succession of social responsibility experts over the years to publish an independent commentary on the company's social performance.

Another great example of elephant values in action is Brazil's largest marine and food-processing machinery manufacturer, Semco. Under the innovative leadership of company president Ricardo Semler, Semco lives and breathes three fundamental values – democracy, shared prosperity and transparency. These values are based on the notion of giving employees control over their own lives. 'We hire adults,' says Semler (1993) in his autobiography *Maverick*, 'and then we treat them like adults.' Putting these values into practice has resulted in some serious corporate shapeshifting. For starters, the councillors (equivalent to what lion companies call executive directors) take it in six-month turns to act as CEO in cycles that overlap, rather than coincide with budgetary cycles. Associates (lower level employees) often earn more than coordinators (managers) or partners (divisional heads) and can increase their recognition and rewards without having to be part of line management.

All Semco employees attend classes to learn how to read and understand 'the numbers' and each and every one receives the accounts for their division each month. Staff are also given access on request to any other company information, including everyone else's salaries. 'If people are embarrassed by their salaries,' reasons Semler, 'that probably means they aren't earning them.' Semco has a similar open-house attitude to information leakage into the market. 'After all, why worry about yesterday's news?' Semco has done away with hourly pay and now everyone gets a monthly salary, which they are allowed to participate in setting themselves. Semco distributes a half-yearly salary market survey and says: 'Figure out where you stand on this thing. You know what you do; you know what everyone else in the company makes; you know what you need; you know what's fair. Come back on Monday and tell us what to pay you.' Those that belong to unions have their salaries negotiated collectively. Furthermore, each division in Semco has a separate profit sharing programme. Twice a year, they put aside over 20% of the after-tax profit on each division and decide – by simply majority vote – what to do with it. In most units the decision has ended up being one of equal distribution among all the workers in the division. Hence, the person who sweeps the floor gets as much as the division's partner.

Of course, corporate values seldom exist in isolation from broader cultural values. It is hardly surprising that modern capitalist enterprises display the Leonean values when the Western culture that produced them embodies such a conquering ethic. For this very reason, non-Western cultures may be on the brink of a renaissance as their more elephant-oriented values become increasingly valuable. This contrast is nowhere more pronounced than between the so-called Western or Northern countries and those of the South or East. For example, the culture of the West/North is highly focused on individual performance and rewards hierarchical authority and rational decision-making, while the East/South's emphasis is more about social harmony and cohesion, participative decision-making, creative expression and motivation.

The American Dream of rags-to-riches through individual hard work and personal achievement a powerful symbol of the West/North's lion values. In business, most of us operate under these values every day, so they will not be explored further. But consider the alternatives. In Japanese culture, there is the concept of *wa*, which stresses group harmony and social cohesion and *ringi* (meaning root-binding), which describes a bottom-up approach to decision making. This outlook on life translates into business practices that value consensus and unity of purpose, service and loyalty to a larger whole (the company, the country, the world), and cooperation between individuals and groups in the workplace. An objection may be made here that we praised Japan to the skies for these values in the 1970s and 1980s as they conquered the world's markets with their zero-defect cars, TVs, VCRs and music players. Then the wheels came off in the 1990s and they're still off. But one shouldn't confuse the good characteristics I am talking about with the deficiencies that have caused the Japanese economy to crash – an inflexible attitude towards structural changes and an emphasis on copycatting Western technology rather than doing original research and development.

In Africa, there is the widespread value of *Ubuntu*, which is based on a proverb meaning 'a person becomes human through other people.' Zimbabwean business leader and author, Lovemore Mbigi (1997), speaks of 'emancipating the spirit of *ubuntu* by building a culture based on tolerance, respect, human dignity and solidarity.' Similarly, South African executive, Reuel Khoza (2012), describes *ubuntu* as the philosophy of 'I am because you are; you are because we are.' It is a concept, he says, 'which brings to the fore images of supportiveness, cooperation, and solidarity, that is, communalism.'

According to Mbigi, *ubuntu* is supported by a host of related socio-cultural ideas from the African heritage such as *illima* (a cooperative effort in plowing), *inquina* (hunting as a team) and *ukudla* (sharing food). Similarly, there is the practice of *ukisisa* or 'cows never die'. According to this principle, when a poor person in the community is identified, their dignity is protected by someone who is better endowed with cattle-wealth asking the poor person to care for one of his or her cows. This transaction in turn provides the destitute member with milk and wealth in the form of one or two calves, after which the original cow is 'borrowed back'. The practical application of such elephant-friendly values in business is a golden thread that runs through the remainder of this chapter.

Discussion 4.1: Values

1. How would you describe the values that are reflected by the majority of companies in your country or city? Are they elephant-values or lion-values?
2. What would you choose as the top 3 values that are most important for practicing genuine CSR?
3. Can you describe an organisation (other than those cited above) that fully embraces the elephant-like values of sustainability and responsibility?

4.2 Vision: A Jumbo Quest

Shapeshifting seldom happens in countries or companies without visionary leadership. Like the revolutionary philosophers and scientists of centuries past, somebody has to be able to step outside of the parochial present and see the bigger picture of the future. And like those historical reformists, today's innovative leaders walk a tightrope between being recognised and celebrated as a visionaries and being regarded as crackpots to be locked up or heathens to be burned at the stake.

The great thing about creating a sustainable future is that it is an inspiring ideal: something that, like the elephant, is bigger than ourselves – a little frightening, somehow magical, an exciting challenge at the very least. And in today's barren desert of materialism and secularism, people are crying out for something inspirational, even sacred, to quench their thirst for meaning. Sustainability is that oasis shimmering on the horizon. It is what I call the 'big calling', the hunger for something to believe in, the eternal yearning to make a positive difference.

Often, this profound revelation is accomplished through partaking in a 'vision quest'. The vision quest is a sacred ritual common to many ancient indigenous cultures. It is performed at critical times in the life of an individual, such as entering adulthood, choosing a vocation or becoming an elder. Likewise, the vision quest can apply at a community level, when a tribe are seeking peace, needing rain or changing their leadership ranks. The traditional process goes something like this. The questers leave the safe environment of their community and travel to a remote, isolated place. Alone in this wilderness environment, as they fast and pit themselves against the elements, they begin to face their psychological fears and emotional demons. These invisible trials prepare their consciousness to receive a vision. The revelation may come as a sign, a symbol, a dream or a vision. It may manifest as a cloud shape or an animal messenger or simply a 'thought-quake'. When the questers return, the diviner and the elders help with the interpretation of their visions and what new meaning it heralds for the life of the individual and the community.

With the era of sustainability looming as a new stage in the life of business and nations, companies and countries need to go on their own vision quest. This could take many different forms: a personal Damascus-type experience by the CEO or President, perhaps catalysed by his or her children or grandchildren; demands for a policy response to a major strategic change such as clearer evidence that carbon consumption should be constrained; or a paradigm shift in the wake of a crisis such as the terrorist attack on New York on September 11, 2001.

Interface, a Fortune 1000 company and the world's largest producer of contract commercial carpets, is a good example of the potency of discovering an inspiring vision. In 1973, Ray Anderson left an executive position with a well known US carpet manufacturer and risked his life savings and the investments of good friends to found his own company, which became Interface. By 1994, the company was already extremely successful but it began to hear a strange rumble in the wind – enquiries from customers about the environmental impacts of Interface's products. Interface, like many companies have done before and after, stood on the cusp of a strategic decision. They could ignore the rumbling, believing it to be a bit of harmless corporate indigestion (which is to be expected with a growing appetite for profits). Or they could listen more carefully. After all, it might be an approaching tidal wave! Then again, it could also be a form of intelligent communication like the infrasonic language of elephants on the horizon. Needless to say, Anderson heard the call - if somewhat reluctantly at first.

He commissioned the company's research department to come up with an environmental policy. They in turn asked Anderson, as CEO at the time, to launch the environmental task force by giving them an environmental vision. Anderson recalls that he didn't want to make that speech because he had no vision other than compliance with the law. Then he came across Paul Hawken's (1994) book, *The Ecology of Commerce*, and felt its message – as he put it, 'like a spear in the chest'.

Anderson claims that 'in a heartbeat' he had found the vision he was looking for, together with a powerful sense of urgency to implement it. He saw that business was part of the problem *and* part of the solution. And he had the courage to say: 'Someone has to take the lead! Why not us?' Anderson offered the task force a vision: to make Interface the first name in industrial ecology worldwide through substance, not words. And he gave them a mission too: to convert Interface into a 'restorative enterprise'. First, Interface would attain a state of sustainability, and then it would become restorative by putting back more than the company takes from the Earth by helping others to reach sustainability - even competitors. How he translated this vision into practice is dealt with in a later section of this chapter.

The provocative vision of Anita Roddick, founder of the international cosmetics company The Body Shop, is another example of how shapeshifting can be catalysed. 'As far as I am concerned,' she said in her book *Business As Unusual*, 'the business has existed for one reason only – to allow us to use our success to act as a force for social change, to contribute to the education and consciousness-raising of our staff, to assist development in the Third World and, above all, to help protect the environment. What we are trying to do is to create a new business paradigm, simply showing that business can have a human face and a social conscience' (Roddick, 2001).

She explained that for The Body Shop the business of business is to keep the company alive and breathlessly excited; to protect the workforce; to be a force for good in society and only then to think about the speculators. She believed that if companies are in business solely to make money, you can't fully trust whatever else they do or say. She saw business as a renaissance concept, where the human spirit comes into play. 'It does not have to be drudgery; it does not have to be the science of making money,' she said. 'It can be something that people genuinely feel good about, but only if it remains a human enterprise.'

And how do you ennoble the spirit when you are selling something as inconsequential as a cosmetic cream? Roddick believed that you do it by creating a sense of holism or spiritual development, of feeling connected to the workplace and the environment and of forging relationships with one another. It's how to make Monday to Friday a sense of being alive rather than a slow death. How do you give people a chance to do a good job? By making them feel good about what they are doing. The spirit soars when you are satisfying your own basic material needs in such a way that you are also serving the needs of others honourably and humanely. 'Under these circumstances,' she added, 'I can even feel great about a moisturizer.'

Of course, her detractors will argue that she had to step down from pole position in the company precisely because she wasn't business-like enough in conducting the company's affairs. They will point to the very disappointing performance of the share price over some of the company's history. And they will gloat over the fact that her downfall was brought about by the supermarket chains that she derided. They may even accuse her of selling out to big business when she agreed for The Body Shop to be taken over by L'Oreal. Yet, there is no denying that she left an indelible mark on the corporate world.

In South Africa, the Spier company is another example of visionary elephant-like leadership. Set in the idyllic landscape of Stellenbosch in the Western Cape, Spier had operated as a wine farm for three centuries before the 90 hectare estate was bought by businessman, Dick Enthoven. Having led an extremely successful career in South Africa's mainstream business sector, Enthoven wanted to leave a legacy, to give something back. Transforming Spier became the centre-point of his vision quest. 'In 150 years from now,' said Enthoven, 'I want people to look back and say that they did a good job.'

The way this vision unfolded in practice is a colourful story full of inspiration. It started with Enthoven embracing the cultural heritage of the area. Spier set about restoring the old Cape-Dutch historical buildings on the estate that date back to 1680, and turning these into conference and restaurant facilities. Next, a hotel complex named The Village was constructed, drawing on the Cape's Malay influences for its architectural style and on ecological principles for its design. An open-air amphitheatre was also built and an Arts Trust started to develop and showcase local talent.

One of Enthoven's key concerns in the Spier project was 'the restoration of equity in a society that has been distorted by social engineering' (i.e. apartheid). For this reason, former farm labourers were given an ownership and management stake in the vineyards and vegetable farming enterprises. In addition, Spier embarked on establishing an off-site eco-village, which incorporates schools, offices, craft workshops, an arts venue, a community centre and homes for almost 150 local families.

There have been various ecological reforms at Spier as well. With 140 hectares of land set aside for organic farming, it is now one of the largest commercial organic farms in South Africa, cultivating both vegetables and vines. Spier has also formed a subsidiary called Green Technologies, which acquired the South African licence for an environmentally-friendly waste treatment system called the Biolytix

Filter. The installation of this Biolytic Filtration system at The Village on the Spier estate is the first of its kind on this scale in the world.

The vision around which Enthoven has been building Spier's renaissance is now classic triple bottom line thinking, underpinned by a set of inspiring values, including 'being custodians of culture; financial viability and economic sustainability; unexpected pleasures; places of the soul; sustainable resource use; community building; and learning for development.' As 'airy-fairy' as these values may sound, Eve Annecke, the Spier executive responsible for implementing them in all operations, can certainly not be accused of living with her head in the clouds. 'We are not on some sort of moral trip here,' she says. 'We're dealing with practical technologies and looking for better ways of doing things. We learn as we go and we face contradictions all the time: what good is organic farming when women are subject to regular abuse at home, or when babies are born with foetal alcohol syndrome? We live in a violent society. We are not pretending to solve all the problems but we are acknowledging that the problems exist and we work at resolving them where we can.'

Adrian Enthoven, chairman of Spier Holdings and a director of Biolytix, sums up their philosophy as follows: 'Our view is not purely altruistic. The whole world is moving in this direction – towards ecological sustainability. Economic imperatives are driving it, and economics relies on social sustainability. These three issues are inextricably linked and this is why, at Spier, we call for accountability in terms of the triple bottom line: financial viability, social equity and ecological sustainability.'

There are numerous other examples of companies that have experienced successful vision quests involving sustainability. Ryuzaburo Kaku, former chairman of the Canon group of companies, speaks for all of these pioneers when he muses that, in the highest stage of evolution of a corporation, 'a global consciousness emerges and the corporation sees itself contributing to the whole of mankind.' This is founded on the Japanese philosophy of *kyosei* – living and working together for the common good. Jumbo visions like these act like sprinklings of magic dust in the business of shapeshifting. They work not because they intellectually convince us, but because they emotionally engage us and spiritually inspire us. They work because we are all, as humans, on a vision quest for meaning in our lives.

Discussion 4.2: Vision

1. Many people and companies have had grand visions. What makes some inspire collective action and achievement, while others remain in the heads or on the boardroom walls of their creators?

2. Can you give an example of a company (other than those cited above) that has created a sustainability vision that has transformed the company's actions?

3. Can an organisation develop a compelling vision without a visionary leader? How much is vision an individual quest, versus a collective imagining?

4.3 Work: An Elephants Playground?

Having a leader's inspiring vision is one thing, but it is like whistling in the wind unless people in the workplace are able to express their own inherent magic – their creativity and imagination, their values and passions. As Anita Roddick (2001) once said, 'People become motivated when you guide them to the source of their own power.'

And yet lion companies don't seem all that interested in the personal magic of their employees. The problem is that magic is, well, a bit unpredictable (and a tad scary too). It cannot be reliably channelled in service of the almighty buck. And it usually involves a lot of flaky intuition and gooey emotions. After all, how can hunting be efficient if it is subject to the whims of a muse or constantly distracted by feelings of compassion for the other animals? No, when employees are at work, they must be constantly reminded of their mission: that they are lions hunting down prey – be it customers, market share, profits, or anything that glitters. They must focus on the corporate mission, the sales objectives, the quarterly review. Time is money. Therefore, they must be strongly discouraged from spending any work-time on socialising, resting, playing, eating, or attending to personal matters. They must do those things after hours (as if life after work doesn't really take place in real time).

The ideal employee of the lion company is one who arrives at work (early), checks in his or her personal life at the door, and goes straight into profit-making overdrive. It helps with the focus if they can switch off their feelings as well, since work is a place for rational individuals. And as for creativity and intuition, it's not that they are bad as such. It's just that they are so difficult to control, and they don't translate easily into data tables and bar charts. If the truth be told, they're just not very macho.

There is a problem of course – humans! We are not machines or computers. In fact, we almost insist on being unfocused. And, as a general rule, we are not very rational either. We have emotions, not to mention all our distracting demands – no work on weekends, big chunks of idle leave, irresponsible bouts of illness and pension payments when we become worn out. That's why lion companies have ingeniously invented a multitude of bribery mechanisms (incremental salary increases, incentive bonuses, pretentious job titles, offices with a door and even a view) and behavioural rules (policies, procedures, systems). In return, of course many employees of lion companies adopt their own version of lion-like behaviour. When they go to the office, they 'go to war' with all their rivals. Or they work to rule. Or they chisel extras out of their travel and expense accounts on the basis that if the company is going to be a predator, they can be too.

Elephant companies, on the other hand, do something that is almost unimaginable. They accept humans as humans. They don't try to turn us into machines. In fact, they encourage us to express all aspects of our human-ness. For example, they realise that we function according to natural rhythms, not artificial clock time – we all have cycles of productivity over the course of a day. We are also remarkably good at multi-processing and multi-tasking: it stimulates us and keeps us from getting tired, bored and unproductive.

In an elephant work environment, there is no fussing about start times and end times, or being in the office versus working at home. There is no need to feel guilty about attending to the odd 'distraction'. Employees don't build up stress as they do in lion companies where various bits and pieces of life are being neglected – like family and household chores and personal banking. Don't get me wrong: elephant companies do not offer a licence for slackness and corruption. By treating their staff as responsible adults, people apply their codes of conduct to themselves that are probably stricter than the external rules would be. They feel a sense of duty. They have self-discipline. Thus, it is often hard to tell 'work' apart from 'personal' or 'fun' or any other lifestyle choice in an elephant company, whereas lion companies prefer to put us in boxes.

Elephants' fuzziness is very frustrating to a lion manager of course. Elephants seem to just mosey around all day, nibbling a bit of this, dusting a bit of that, chatting to some friends here, splashing around in a mud hole there. They are not focused on the prey at all. Look at all that time they take for family bonding, for having fun in the water, for catching up with the gossip from passing friends. There's none of the stress of being a hunter. Mind you, they don't starve. In fact, they seem to do very well despite not being obsessed about food. Mmm, interesting! One CEO of an elephant company has Walt Disney mementoes all around his office which he calls his play-room. In particular, he has a large effigy of Mickey Mouse next to his desk. This is to remind all the important people that come to see him that he is head of a Mickey Mouse company that wants to have some fun!

Semco allows its employees to control their own working conditions. Time clocks have been eliminated, and people come and go according to their own schedules – even on the factory floor. The result is greater spontaneous coordination between workers, and more people who can now do several jobs. Interestingly, although they set their own schedules and targets (or perhaps because they do), they tend to work longer hours to meet them. The success of this 'factory floor flexi-time' is summed up by one of Semler's comments: 'When we introduced flexible hours, we decided to hold regular follow up meetings to track problems and decide how to deal with abuses and production interruptions. That was years ago, and we haven't yet held that first meeting.'

So, working like an elephant is not about becoming completely scattered and ineffective. It is about being flexible, discovering the most appropriate times to work and play and socialise, or to do a combination of these. When we reconnect with our natural rhythms and apply them to our work, we play to our own individual strengths. At the same time, we work out ways to find a harmonious blend with each other's natural cycles. This increases, not decreases, our productivity. The reason is that we are not spending vast amounts of energy fighting our own natural tendencies. At the moment, most of us in lion workplaces feel obliged to persevere with rolling rocks up a hill in the morning, even though we know that in the afternoon the landscape will be flatter and the rocks will feel lighter. Shapeshifting will mean sloughing off some of the lion's control-freak habits, trusting others more, and having a less regimented environment.

Being human at work is also about being able to be ourselves – our whole selves. Lion companies take their cue from neo-classical economics and assume that people are 'free rational utility-maximizing individuals'. 'Professionalism in management is regularly equated with hard-headed rationality,' noted the Tom Peters and Robert Waterman duo of In Search of Excellence fame (Peters & Waterman, 2004). 'The problem with the rationalist view of organising people,' they went on to say, 'is that people are not very rational.' To fit Frederick Taylor's old model of scientific management or today's organisational charts, man is simply designed wrong or, of course, vice versa according to how you argue it. 'In fact, if our understanding of the current state of psychology is even close to correct, man is the ultimate study in conflict and paradox.'

The successful performance of split-brain surgery in the 1960s and 1970s seems to confirm this view, as well as to lend further insight. In treating 25 patients for severe epilepsy, doctors found that not only can the two hemispheres of our brain operate independently, but they also seem to control essentially opposite functions. While the left brain is associated with rational and intellectual engagements, the right brain is oriented towards intuitive and creative processes. Canadian business professor, Henry Mintzberg (1976), was the first to spot the implications for business which he set forth in an article in the Harvard Business Review called 'Planning on the Left Side and Managing on the Right'. 'The key managerial processes,' he remarks, 'are enormously complex and mysterious, drawing on the vaguest of information and using the least articulated mental processes. These processes seem more relational and holistic than ordered and sequential, and more intuitive than intellectual; they seem to be most characteristic of right-hemispheric activity.'

This theme of duality and balance is one that the ancient Chinese understood well and is represented in their Tai Chi symbol, which depicts the flow of opposites within a greater whole. Contained within the circular symbol, the one extreme (*yang*) represents masculine, active, competitive and rigid characteristics, while the opposite (*yin*) encapsulates the feminine, passive, cooperative and flexible aspects. Lions are *yang*; elephants are *yin*. And most of today's companies are *yang* companies, praising 'hard' qualities like rationality and assertiveness, and pooh-poohing 'soft' traits like intuition and compassion.

It is not difficult to diagnose whether your company is a lion or an elephant. Just count the number of times words like 'love' and 'caring' and 'morality' crop up in management meetings; or how often people feel comfortable enough to cry at the office. Former head of chemical giant ICI once said that the word 'love' was as threatening in business as talking about an unexpected liability on the balance sheet. Author and former Fortune 500 company director, James Autry (1992), makes the same point in his inspiring book, *Love & Profit*. Feelings are seen as a weakness in the testosterone-dominated corporate world. One chairman was reported to have asked a colleague why one of his managers had left the business to join the church. His colleague replied: 'Long-term promotion prospects.' It hadn't occurred to the chairman that there might be life after the company!

For lions, displaying toughness is all-important. And toughness means dominating meetings and markets, intimidating suppliers and competitors, controlling situations and people. Toughness means showing intellectual superiority and aggressive ambition and not letting emotions cloud your judgement. Elephants, on the other hand, are led by matriarchs. Emotions are openly displayed within the herd – be they affection, grief or delight. Extrasensory perception is constantly relied upon. Nurturing intimate relationships is all-important.

Trying to turn complex, variable humans into rational, predictable machines has left many people feeling like prisoners, trapped in their jobs, unable to be who they really are. Certainly, given the choice, it is not how they would choose to spend their life. But there's the mortgage to think about, the school fees, the parents' expectations. Even beyond that, so many people I talk to experience feelings of existential crisis in their work.

One thing that would help with the existential crisis in business would be a switch from the present focus on 'jobs' to the old idea of 'vocations'. A job is something you do to earn money to get by. It is a means to an end. Thus, people often end up 'living for the weekend' or counting down the days to their retirement. A vocation, on the other hand, is a life pursuit that you do out of a sense of calling, a feeling of being uniquely suited for performing a certain kind of work. Mythologist Joseph Campbell talked about 'following your bliss' (Campbell & Moyer, 1991). How many people can use that word – bliss – to describe their work?

You may think that I am spiralling off into a dream world here, an idealist's fantasy. But stay with me. Pursuing a vocation should not be mistaken for some kind of hallucinatory happiness trip, free of all cares, worries, stresses or difficulties. In many ways, following your bliss is more difficult, because it entails soul searching, tenacious endurance, constant questioning, facing fears, shrugging off securities and stretching every fibre of your being. The difference is that it feels like a personal quest, a freely chosen path, a journey with a purpose. Intuitively, we are all searching for this Holy Grail in our careers, hobbies or voluntary work.

The experiences of Victor Frankl (2006), outlined in his book *Man's Search for Meaning*, provide some insight into this heartfelt yearning of ours to make something meaningful of our work. Frankl, a trained psychiatrist, survived four Nazi concentration camps, and noticed that people can endure the most trying and horrific circumstances if they can discover and nurture a sense of personal meaning. When there is something to believe in, the human spirit triumphs over physical hardship or emotional trauma. The 'something' can be anything – the achievement of a personal goal, the development of a particular skill, the creation of something unique or beautiful, or the pursuit of a spiritual quest. But the essential thing is that it is a personal belief. No one can tell you what should inspire you or motivate you. No one can brainwash you into discovering meaning in your work. No one can pre-select your vocation for you. Of course, the lion economy makes the pursuit of vocations very difficult. Round people are put in square holes because nobody consulted them about their true desires. Hence, once again, the need for multi-level shapeshifting.

Discussion 4.3: Work

1. What tasks in the workplace are most suited to right-brain thinking and what requires more left-brain orientation?
2. Describe what a truly caring workplace would look like. How would it differ from an uncaring workplace?
3. What is the link between the pursuit of CSR and the search for meaning or purpose in life by employees?

4.4 Governance: Council of the Animals

Governance is a word that lions don't like much. It smacks too much of giving away power. Or sharing supper. Lion directors prefer the freedom of making all their decisions in secret councils or while they're on the run, with no justification needed and no recourse back to them. Why should they consult beyond their colleagues in the inner sanctum on whether to swallow up another company, or shut down an operation and retrench thousands of workers? These are strategic matters that only the board can decide on. The pride rules.

Lions want power and autonomy – not for their own sake, they are quick to add, but because they need to make things happen and fast. Opportunities and threats come and go at cheetah-like speed, whether they are stock market fluctuations, competitor tactics, product innovations or customer fashions. Markets are like the gun-toting Wild West. Fastest on the draw stays alive and lives to chew another roll of tobacco. Not to mention pocketing a bit of the 'ole booty' along the way. Doing business is a verb, not an adjective; it is active not passive. Feline companies pounce in the twitch of a whisker.

In other words, if the lion king has his way, business is a monarchy, not a democracy. The CEO rules by divine right, issuing edits from his royal court of directors. And what good is it being a powerful lion king if you have to explain your every action to the masses? Or account for the origin and size of your obvious opulence? Lion kings exist to rule over their subjects; to direct their destiny and control their lives – their daily tasks, their dress code, their beliefs and their lifestyle. The people must be made to serve with unquestioning loyalty and contribute towards the overheads of running the royal court. And if they disobey, the long arm of the 'paw' will catch up with them.

To question a lion's choice of prey or hunting style is to invite getting your head bitten off. Lions expect everyone to trust their feline instincts and appetite-driven judgements unreservedly. After all, no lion ever caught an antelope (or conquered a country, or captured a market) by asking the buffalo for advice, or sitting around a thorn tree discussing it with the warthog, or asking permission from the rhinoceros. And those who would criticise the laws of the jungle are invited to reserve their irritating chatter for the monkeys; maybe they will listen.

This starts to get down to the heart of the governance debate, namely the dual issues of control and transparency. You don't need to ask a lion who should be in charge. But if you are a springbok or a zebra or a giraffe, you may want to have a say in the way that the bushveld is run. In particular, you may want to question the lion's right to kill off whomsoever he pleases, whensoever he pleases. Or his right to fatten himself and his pride, while the rest of the animals are starving during a drought. Or to be the growling censor of any information put out by the company on how it is run. Extracting facts is like extracting teeth – difficult when it's the lion's mouth you're trying to get them out of!

However, the seeds of a popular revolt have been planted, from the anti-WTO demonstrations in Seattle in 1999 to the Occupy movement of 2011. The demonstrations grow despite the predictable response of security forces. The frustration and anger about the unhealthy power balance in the world has boiled over (with increasing violence) in hundreds of cities around the world. Quite simply, the gap is getting too wide between the rich and the poor countries and between the rich and the poor within countries. For their part, the corporate lions participate annually in noble-sounding debates at the World Economic Forum, licking their paws and knowing full well that they will never be called upon to implement any resolutions. They will be free to go on as they please.

Companies have become more powerful than governments. Yet, the millions whose lives they affect have little or no say in what they do. The public do not choose which companies are allowed to exist and operate in their communities, nor do they elect the directors and managers. Yes, they do buy the company's products and services as consumers and are free to switch from one company to another. But, as I've emphasised already, the 'invisible hand' of the market exerts limited pressure. The only real accountability that business has is to itself and its lion-leaning shareholders. If, as a result of corporate actions, national economies go into crisis, or communities suffer, or the environment is degraded, it is rare for shareholders to question company directors. The share price has to drop for that to happen. The shenanigans at Enron in 2001 would never have become public if Enron had not gone bust as a result.

But the world is shapeshifting to some extent. Elephant activists are trumpeting their concerns loudly enough for the lions finally to be taking notice. Over the past two decades, for example, numerous corporate governance codes have emerged, which require companies to give a more transparent account of how their business is being run and the impacts on the various stakeholder groups. One of the most progressive is South Africa's King Report, which even makes explicit recommendations on sustainability reporting and social and ethical accountability.

Shapeshifting goes beyond putting ticks into boxes, however. At the end of the day, it is once again about values and behaviour. Companies that perpetuate the widening gap between rich and poor in their own payroll profile are always going to fall into the lions' camp. Companies that persist in managing from the top down will never turn their fangs into tusks. And companies that only create partnerships that benefit themselves may learn to purr, but they will never lose their roar. Elephant companies, on the other hand, embrace the principles and practices of good governance with passion. They worry less about controlling and more about caring and sharing. They volunteer; they don't grudgingly concede.

In order to implement governance at a practical level, shapeshifting needs to occur in at least three areas: company incentive systems, decision-making processes and communication methods. In exploring these issues, it is instructive once again to contrast Western and Southern cultural dynamics. For example, in traditional African culture, it is socially undesirable and inappropriate to behave so as to 'stand out from the crowd' in the way that individual achievement is promoted in Anglo-Saxon culture. The reason is that such behaviour may destroy vital social cohesion in a community by creating destructive competition or undermining the respected role of the elders in the tribe.

This is not to say that individuals are not encouraged to master areas in which they display a particular aptitude or natural gift. On the contrary, skilful specialisation, whether as a healer, artist, hunter or leader, has always been a key element in enabling communities to survive and thrive. But the context for this achievement is carefully managed, through strict social rules, in order to ensure that it enhances the common good and maintains cohesion of the unit. Contrast this with the stereotypical reward system in the West that tends to be based on individual merit regardless of what it does to the rest of the team.

Cashbuild is a pioneering South African company that showed how elephant thinking could be put into practice in business long before corporate governance had become a catchphrase. For instance, in the 1980s they revised their performance appraisal system so that they were geared to rewarding team achievements whilst also rewarding individual contributions to the improvement of the functioning of the team as a whole. In this way, the poor and mediocre performers were encouraged to raise their standards, in contrast to the situation where higher performers lower their standards to maintain their identification with the group.

According to former Managing Director of Cashbuild, Albert Koopman (1994), replacing reward and punishment systems with systems based on peer recognition and rejection makes good business sense. For example, under Cashbuild's old reward/punishment system, the company could never reduce employee absenteeism and lost hours to a figure below 15% despite repeated warning letters and disciplinary procedures. Then, when they used the peer group concept by simply placing red marks next to late or absent employees' names on a publicly displayed chart (with no management reprimand), lost hours immediately dropped to 1%.

Cashbuild also introduced other innovative practices. They held extensive 'sharing' sessions among employees, aimed at deepening understanding of diverse histories, cultures and values in the workplace. They removed the power imbalance in management-labour relations through the empowerment of shop steward committees and other representative councils. And once a year, the company held a three-day communal gathering – The Great *Indaba* – during which every employee had the opportunity to make his or her views on Cashbuild and its leadership heard. This sharing approach resulted in consensus being reached more quickly on key decisions. In the one year, it took a mere 35 minutes to conclude wage negotiations.

The Brazilian company Semco also shows how to take democracy seriously in the workplace. The company does not hire or promote people until they have been interviewed and accepted by all their future subordinates. Twice a year, subordinates evaluate their immediate managers and everyone in the company fills out an anonymous questionnaire about corporate credibility and top management competence. In addition, all important decisions are made collegially – sometimes even by a company-wide vote.

Of course, given the latest advances in computer networks which allow for real-time feedback, it is considerably easier to implement workplace democracy. But the battle-scarred lions have to let go of their control first. The great elephant leader and former South African president, Nelson Mandela (1994), gives some clues to this new governance style in his autobiographical *Long Walk to Freedom*. He recounts his childhood memories of how tribal meetings allowed for full participation by every Thembu person of the region, without interruption or intervention by the regent chief. He reflects on how these early experiences influenced his own approach to governance as follows:

'As a leader, I have always followed the principles I saw demonstrated by the regent at the Great Place. I have always endeavoured to listen to what each and every person in a discussion had to say before venturing my own opinion. Oftentimes, my own opinion will simply represent a consensus of what I heard in the discussion.' Mandela always remembered the regent's axiom: a leader is like a shepherd. He stays behind the flock, letting the most nimble go on ahead, whereupon the others follow, not realizing that all along they are being directed from behind.

Discussion 4.4: Governance

1. What are the implications of the Occupy (Wall Street) movement for corporate governance?
2. In what ways do you think the abuse of power by leaders can be prevented or moderated?
3. Can you identify any companies that embody good governance practices? What makes them different?

4.5 Relationships: Walking Gently as Giants

Elephants are highly sociable creatures. They move in large herds, which usually comprise of more than one family group. They protect, care for and even suckle each other's young. In the dry season, several herds will often join together or remain in infrasonic contact, almost as if camaraderie helps them face the harsh elements of nature. A lot of their time and energy is spent cultivating and nurturing relationships in the herd, whether by frequent rumbling dialogue, playing together or intimate caresses with their trunks. It is clear that building bonds of family and friendship is at least as important as feeding. In the wider context, they have no natural enemies and many of their actions are symbiotic in nature, such as digging water holes, fertilising ingested seeds and making vegetation accessible to other species.

In terms of our metaphor, lions also have relationships although they tend to see their opposite numbers more like self-serving acquaintances. Team building in the pride is important for effective hunting. Cubs will be looked after, so long as they are effective predators. But friendship does not extend much beyond the family. After all, other prides are competitors chasing after the same food. And other species are either competitors or prey, or accomplices. When mixing does occur, it is usually brief and unemotional with survival in mind. For the lion, procreation is hardly a romantic affair – wham, bam and not even 'thank you, ma'am'. And as for relationships with other creatures, well, who can trust a lion? No matter how smoothly he purrs, there is always the chance of you being 'friend today, food tomorrow'.

In business, the dynamics have been the same. Companies have cultivated relationships only from pure self-interest – mostly with shareholders, financial analysts, customers and suppliers. And usually, these interactions have been a pure power play – wining and dining the influential few, while ignoring the rest or pressuring them into conformance. The idea of genuine dialogue with communities, NGOs and government for the sake of enduring symbiotic relationships, rather than as a short-term bargaining tactic, is still somewhat unpalatable for most companies. With their quarterly eye on skittish profits, spending time and energy on building long term friendships without any immediate reward seems a costly indulgence.

But the game is changing. To survive in the sustainability era, companies have to move beyond their aggressive, competitive tendencies. They need to learn to be not only sociable, but genuinely concerned about the perspectives and wellbeing of all of their stakeholders. Brandenburger & Nalebuff (1997), in their book of the same title, call this transition *Co-opetition*, while Wheeler & Sillanpää (1997) talk about *The Stakeholder Corporation* and Hawken, Lovins & Lovins (1999) refer to *Natural Capitalism*.

Companies ignore this friendly advice at their own peril. Stakeholders, if maltreated, can bite back and even the most macho multinational lions can find themselves bleeding. Already, the casualty list of high profile companies is long – BP, Dreamworks, Green Cross, Intel, McDonald's, Monsanto, Nike, Proctor & Gamble, Shell, Texaco and Walmart, to mention but a few. Encouragingly, however, the list of 'branded' stakeholder-oriented shapeshifters is also growing, including the likes of 3M, AT&T, Body Shop, Canon, Electrolux, Hewlett Packard, Levi Strauss, Reebok, Unilever, Volkswagen and Volvo.

Employees are such core stakeholders to business that transgressions on this front are almost unforgivable. Texaco found this out when a racism scandal in 1996 lost its shareholders more than $1 billion in market capitalisation on the day the news broke and ultimately cost the company $115 million in a legal settlement of a suit filed on behalf of 1,400 employees. Likewise, Walmart and Nike sustained heavy reputational damage when they were caught employing cheap child labour in Third World countries. It didn't help Nike's public relations nightmare that it paid Michael Jordan $20 million a year to endorse their products, while paying its Indonesian subcontractors annual wages of less than $1,000.

A similar tale of employee neglect can be told about the asbestos mining industry. Companies like Turner & Newall (T&N) and Cape plc argued for years that the health risks to their workers were acceptable. The courts, however, are starting to side with former employees who are the victims of the occupational disease, asbestosis. T&N has already paid out more than £350 million over ten years to meet the claims of its former employees, and Cape plc recently reached a settlement agreement of £22 million to compensate the families of a group of former South African miners. One has to wonder whether other mining companies, as well as nuclear energy utilities and chemical companies, may suffer a similar fate in the elephant landscape of the future?

In contrast, Reebok, who has developed a reputation for taking a public stand on social issues, pledged to fight exploitative labour practices. It called on activists to alert it to any abuses that were occurring and began requesting all its vendors for certification that they are complying with codes of conduct, such as those of the International Labour Organisation. Levi Strauss has gone even further. In Bangladesh and Turkey, where children were working for contractors and providing their family's only source of income, Levi's actually paid the contractors to keep the children in school until they were 14. In areas where it felt it had less influence, like China, Levi's took the tough commercial decision to withdraw from the country until its human rights record improved.

In recognition of the importance of its employees, American telecommunications giant AT&T introduced alternative measures of performance that include 'people value added', alongside 'customer value added' and 'economic value added'. Likewise, Swedish insurance company Skandia began to quantify its hidden assets by producing reports that place a financial value on its 'intellectual capital'. Meanwhile, Volkswagen is trying to balance the reliance on 'shareholder value' with the concept of 'workholder value'.

Customers are another major stakeholder group, which all companies pledge to look after. But the evidence does not always agree. Take tobacco companies for instance, who at one point swore before Congress that they believed that cigarettes are not addictive (despite overwhelming evidence to the contrary). They are not so bold since the landmark court case in which Grady Carter was awarded $750 000 in damages for the loss of a lung following cancer surgery. This was one of the first in a string of liability claims against tobacco companies in 1996, resulting in losses in share value of billions of dollars (the value of British American Tobacco suddenly dropped by £3 billion alone).

Banks also have a notoriously bad track record with customers by failing to provide financial services to those that need them the most – the poor and socially marginalized population. Yet banks like the Los Angeles Community Development

Bank, the South Shore Bank of Chicago (before it closed in 2010), the Caja Labora in Spain, and the Grameen Bank in Bangladesh have shown that financial services can be made accessible to all customers, not just the lucrative 'high net worth' sector. Others, like the Cooperative Bank in the UK, VanCity in Vancouver, Citizens Bank in Tokyo and the Triodos Bank in Europe also show that customers' money can be made to 'work' for various sustainability causes, such as investing in community development and promoting renewable energy.

Suppliers are another key stakeholder group and proactive engagement with the supply chain is going to become critical for elephant companies of the future. Early adopters of this new reality were the Body Shop, the Cooperative Bank, Traidcraft and Ben & Jerry's. More recently, companies like Unilever, Sainsbury's, Volvo and Nortel have joined the party. Unilever, which sells several ranges of fish products, was an early adopter of the WWF-developed international labelling scheme for sustainable fish production, whereby its suppliers all need to be certified by the Marine Stewardship Council. This is a sister organisation to the highly successful certification scheme of the Forest Stewardship Council.

UK retailer Sainsbury's is also starting to scrutinise supplier relationships, insisting on 'dolphin friendly' tuna, organic vegetables and no animal testing. In the car manufacturing sector, Volvo has added environmental care as the third of its core values that suppliers need to embrace, the other two being safety and quality. Telecommunications company, Nortel, emphasises partnerships with its suppliers in tackling the environmental impacts of its production chain. This 'shared savings' approach is being used to achieve a reduction in use of chemicals in Canada and minimization of waste in the UK.

The European Business Network for Social Cohesion is dedicated to walking gently as giants. The network, comprising a coalition of more than 300 businesses including household names like British Telecom, Philips and Kellogg's, was established in 1995 to counteract the negative impacts of the global economy. They are a forum devoting their time to finding creative solutions that will help to avert redundancies, encourage employee reskilling, facilitate the reintroduction of laid off employees into the workforce, and protect vulnerable economic groups. The UK's Business in the Community is a similar initiative.

Early research by Harvard professors, Kotter & Heskett (1992), confirm that taking care of stakeholders is good for the traditional bottom line as well. They compared the 11-year records of large, established companies that gave customers, employees and shareholders equal priorities with those that always put their shareholders first. It turned out that the more stakeholder-sensitive companies grew sales four times faster, created eight times as many jobs, improved the share price eightfold and experienced greater net income growth. In other words, shapeshifting from a lion into an elephant is not the same as being condemned to starvation. Elephants have a healthy appetite; they just aren't obsessed with food to the exclusion of everything and everyone else.

Discussion 4.5: Relationships

1. All organisations exist in a web of relationships. What makes a stakeholder-oriented organisation different?
2. Which are the most important stakeholder groups for your organisation, or university? How did you prioritise these?
3. Should good stakeholder relationships be voluntarily self-regulated (e.g. through codes of practice), or should they be government regulated?

4.6 Communication: The Rumble in the Jungle

Lions don't communicate much except by roaring to intimidate others or purring with self-satisfaction. Likewise, modern companies have grown accustomed to speaking to stakeholders only on a 'need to know' basis – telling whom they want, what they want, when they want. Usually, this 'strategic conversation' coincides with a time when the company needs something from its stakeholders, such as support (or the absence of visible protest) to proceed with a new development.

Elephant communication is quite different. It is more like dialogue: an on-going, two way, interactive process which involves listening as much as talking, and includes non-verbal as well as verbal exchange. Elephant companies are far less opportunistic when it comes to communicating with stakeholders. The reason they enter into dialogue with their employees, or communities, or environmental NGOs, is the fact that these entities are interconnected in some way – they are interested in, concerned about, or affected by the company's operations.

Elephant companies believe that the time when something goes wrong, or when they are *required* to consult – like when there is an accident, or downsizing, or a new project – is precisely the wrong time to begin communicating with stakeholders. By then, it is way too late. A symbiotic relationship already needs to be in place, one that has been nurtured over many years. To enable this 'getting to know you and trust you' process to bloom, there need to be all kinds of forums and feedback mechanisms that keep companies' finger on the pulse of stakeholders' issues and concerns.

Attitude is also critical. Even having all the right communication tools may not be enough if these are only used to further predetermined company interests. Lion companies see stakeholders – whether they are labour unions or green activists – as irritating beasts trying to curtail their appetite or cramp their hunting style. Hence, the feline communication strategy is usually to roar louder than the stakeholders and frighten them away or drown out the sound of their complaints. Failing this, other popular tactics are to ignore the stakeholders, discredit them, or hire a lion lawyer to hunt them down and eat them in the courts.

The elephant company's *modus operandi* is quite different, mainly because they believe that stakeholders actually have something valuable to say. In fact, the fresh perspective that stakeholders bring could turn out to be a gift-wrapped opportunity. If they are saying that it is unacceptable to injure workers, or choke communities with pollution, or sell products that clog up the rivers, maybe that means that there is a market for safer, cleaner products? After all, stakeholders are customers too. It is not that stakeholders are always right and companies are always wrong. Rather, the point is that companies and stakeholders are inextricable interconnected. Their destinies are so meshed together that there is no 'them' and 'us'. All are part of one living system. Therefore, working out the solutions to any dilemma – like the classic 'jobs versus environment' debate – becomes a cooperative effort among all stakeholders.

How different the actual world is! Often in the corporate sector's dealings with stakeholders, you feel you're in a crèche with babies babbling past each other or crying with frustration when nobody understands what they are trying to say. At one end of the table companies bawl out phrases like 'economic value added', 'gross margin on sales' and 'real return on capital employed', while at the other end, activist NGOs return the fusillade with terms like 'social justice', 'intergenerational equity' and 'ecological sustainability'. In the end, each baby is left stomping its feet or wailing its heart out.

Any adult will understand that the missing ingredient is a common language that begins to construct a common outlook. Concepts like the triple bottom line, internalising externalities, stakeholder accountability, corporate governance and sustainable development are early attempts to develop a vocabulary that everyone can understand. But they still sound like jargon that will all too soon become unfashionable and forgotten. That is why we suggest a healthy dose of getting back to basics. Let's start by calling things what they are. Companies either 'care' about their stakeholders or they simply 'use' them for their own selfish gain.

Infants soon learn the important concepts in life – sharing and being selfish, playing and fighting, hurting and helping, being nice and being spiteful, laughing and crying. And what we try to teach children is to be like elephants, not lions.

Becoming mature means learning that you can't always have things your way, and that harming others is unacceptable behaviour. The title Robert Fulham (1988) chose for his book, *Everything I Ever Needed To Know, I Learned In Kindergarten*, says it all. So why not make these ordinary, everyday terms the basic language of companies too? Are companies sharing or being selfish? Hurting or helping?

In the same vein, the ingredients of effective communication are good, basic common sense. Be open. Share information. Not just the good stuff, but also the bad and the in-between. And not just the boring facts; also the hopes and dreams, the passions and emotions. Talk about the serious things (so-called hard facts) when they need talking about. But don't forget to share the lighter moments as well. Don't tell lies (or even bend the truth). And once there is a track record of honesty, trust what others say. Also, create rituals for dialogue, spaces for talking and listening – the proverbial coffee table (or fireside) chat.

Within the organisation, make sure your sustainability staff is singing from the same hymn sheet as line management. So often, a chasm develops between the two, with the environmental brigade perceiving the production guys as unrepentant polluters, while the operations managers see the 'tree-huggers' as clueless do-gooders who know nothing about production realities, yet inexplicably have the CEO's ear. On the other hand, don't make communication so rigid that it all sounds like propaganda from a central source. Leave some latitude for personal opinions.

There are no shortage of lion-like companies who mistake 'telling' for 'dialogue' and have been getting backchat from angry stakeholders ever since. McDonald's and Shell have become celebrated examples. When a small group of London activists published a pamphlet entitled What's Wrong with McDonald's, the company was quick to bear its fangs and lash out with its claws by instituting legal action. But McDonald's tough-guy approach bit back – the company found itself in court for 314 days with all its dirty washing being aired for the curious public to see. The resulting tide of discontent from disgruntled stakeholders spawned websites devoted entirely to McDonald's alleged sins on every possible subject.

Shell's fallout with stakeholders over its proposed sinking of the Brent Spar oil platform in the North Sea, as well as it alleged complicity in human rights abuses and environmental impacts in Nigeria, were a wake-up call for the company. Faced with widespread consumer boycotts and worldwide anti-Shell activist campaigns, the company was forced to re-examine its old approach of doing business. It shapeshifted its strategy towards the triple bottom line of sustainability and embarked on the most comprehensive stakeholder communication process ever attempted by a multinational.

Shell's public relations effort, reportedly costing $20 million a year, resulted in a programme of public reporting that was considered by many to be best in its class at the time. In addition to disclosing a host of externally verified environmental data, they began to listen and share the feedback they were getting from stakeholders. For example, in one People, Planet & Profits report, they quote the input they have received from the United Nations Environment Programme, the World Resources Institute, the World Conservation Union, Harvard Business School and the Ethics Resource Centre.

In addition, they have gone further by recognising that public opinion is as important as 'expert' input. Their early sustainability reports were sprinkled with quotes – the good, the bad and the ugly – from individuals that had responded to the 'Tell Shell' campaign. Senior executives read and discussed these comments as an important indicator of people's feelings on issues of concern to Shell, industry and society at large. Shell is still some way off regaining the trust of many of their stakeholders (especially in Nigeria), but at least they have heard the 'rumble in the jungle' and started to embed the dialogue process into their business.

Fortunately, the next generation of elephant wannabes can learn from McDonald's and Shell's trial-by-fire. They can choose the easier route by following in the footsteps of the elephant pioneers that have gone before them. For instance, the Body Shop's Values Report still stands as a world-class benchmark on measuring stakeholder accountability and disclosing stakeholder performance. Similarly, they can take inspiration from companies like Sbn Bank with their ethical accounting process, or Skandia with their Intellectual Capital report, or Electrolux with their environmental reports based on The Natural Step framework.

There are also numerous do-it-yourself guides that have emerged in recent years. If taken seriously, for example, the Accountability 1000 standard on Social and Ethical Accounting, Auditing and Reporting and the Global Reporting Initiative's Sustainability Reporting Guidelines can take companies a long way down the road of stakeholder engagement. Beyond these basic frameworks, however, technology-enabled interactive stakeholder feedback and real-time public reporting on the web are already looming large on the horizon.

Stakeholder communication is one of those areas where many companies are going to be unveiled as lions all dressed up as elephants. The true test of authenticity will not be in the letter of the glossy brochure, but in the spirit of the dialogue. Stakeholders will refine their extrasensory perceptions and develop a sixth sense about which companies are hiding something or bluffing and which are genuinely trying to listen and address real concerns in good faith. Elephant-like companies will do what comes naturally – be friendly and caring and compassionate.

Discussion 4.6: Communication

1. How effective have the GRI's Sustainability Reporting Guidelines been in creating a credible communications framework?
2. How might communications strategies and methods vary for different stakeholder groups? Give examples.
3. How could companies use the spread of social media and online tools to improve their stakeholder communications?

4.7 Services: The Genius of Nature

Products and services will need to shapeshift radically in a sustainable world. It will no longer be acceptable or successful to follow the lion's approach of producing 'widgets' and flogging them to a market brainwashed by advertising, whilst ignoring the damage they cause along the way. The new generation of elephant products and services will focus on adding value over their entire life cycle. In so doing, they will incorporate design characteristics inspired by the genius of nature. In fact, many products will become obsolete as they are replaced by 'leased benefits' instead.

The life cycle approach is one of the rules of the game in an elephant economy. Under this approach, companies are accountable for their products and services from 'cradle to cradle'. There are various manifestations of this new philosophy, including life cycle assessment (LCA), eco-efficiency, supply chain integrity and take-back schemes. LCA is an important tool that can assist companies to quantify the net impacts of their products and services, from raw material sourcing through to final disposal. Although LCA remains a complex and controversial methodology, standards such as ISO 14040-43 can serve as a useful guideline for the uninitiated.

Eco-efficiency is perhaps a less daunting way in which companies can begin to implement life cycle principles. The term was first used by the Basel-based researchers Schaltegger and Sturm in 1990. But the idea that actions preventing pollution and avoiding waste pay off financially pre-dated this by at least 15 years. For instance, the U.S. based consumer goods manufacturer 3M initiated its Pollution Prevention Pays (3P) program in 1975. In the first year, it achieved more than $800 million in savings from 4 000 3P projects. Dow Chemicals launched a similar initiative called Waste Reduction Always Pays (WRAP).

Von Weizsäcker, Lovins & Lovins (1995) coined the term *Factor Four* in a book of the same title. The concept refers to doubling resource efficiency (put another way halving material intensity) and halving waste outputs, thereby effectively reducing the environmental impacts by a factor of four. Seen from a business perspective, this creates the capacity to increase production within a fixed constraint of resources and sinks. The authors cited numerous examples of factor four achievements and now others are even promoting the notion of 'factor ten'. *Natural Capitalism* by Paul Hawken, Amory Lovins and L. Hunter Lovins. is required reading for understanding this exploding new discipline.

Another manifestation of life cycle principles is the increasing number of product take-back schemes that are being implemented either voluntarily or through legislation. As the word suggests, this involves companies taking back their products at the end of their useful life and either reusing, recycling or disposing of them. In the European Union, for example, five manufacturers – Motorola, Ericsson, Nokia, Alcatel and Panasonic – began by jointly implementing voluntary take-back schemes. Rank Xerox is another example: as early as 1995, the company recovered 80,000 (two thirds) of the photocopiers disposed of in Western Europe, with savings on virgin raw materials exceeding £50 million and the avoidance of disposal costs for over 7,000 tons of material.

One company that has taken the life cycle principles to their natural conclusion is U.S. carpet manufacturer Interface, under the inspiring leadership of the late Ray Anderson. Central to Anderson's vision of Interface as a 'restorative company' was the concept of the Evergreen Lease, converting the carpet as a material product into a service. Now known as Evergreen Service Contracts, the programme gives clients the option to lease the services (functionality, colour, design, aesthetics) of a modular carpet system, without taking ownership or liability for on-going maintenance and the ultimate removal for reclamation or recycling at the end of the carpet's useful life. Anderson was able to re-define Interface from being a carpet manufacturer into a provider of sustainable floor-covering services. Surely this product leasing approach is a glimpse of the future?

This leads us on to the emerging discipline of supply chain integrity. While eco-efficiency, take-back schemes and product leasing are mainly aimed at the environmental elements of life cycle accountability, supply chain auditing begins to address social impacts as well. Companies like the Body Shop and Traidcraft pioneered the idea of checking the ethical practices of their suppliers and actively engaging in fair trade practices. Following their embarrassing episode of being implicated in using sweatshops in Vietnam, even Nike got the message and began to do audits on labour practices in its factories worldwide. In the elephant landscape of the future, scrutiny up and down the supply chain is going to become standard operating procedure.

These are some tools and techniques that will be useful in shapeshifting products and services. However, the biggest shapeshift probably has less to do with new methods or models, and more to do with inspiration. I am referring to the potential for products and services to be inspired by the 'genius of nature'. Nature is the ultimate benchmark for a service-oriented system. Every ecological process is highly tuned to the needs of its benefactors, and every species is intimately aware of its connectivity and is constantly adapting to the conditions of its environment. Every detail of the universe, from the macro cosmic to the micro sub-atomic levels, embodies incredible feats of intelligent design.

There are efficiencies in nature that are only dreamed about by today's industrial engineers. Nature offers a multitude of lessons for business and an endless supply of inspirational design features for products and services. Already, today's eco-engineers are making design breakthroughs by studying termite hills and prairie dog burrows for improving air-conditioning systems. Sharks and owls provide insights into cutting down noise pollution from aeroplanes, and so the list of biomimicry possibilities goes on: wasp nests for more robust urban design and construction; octopuses and butterflies for dynamic camouflage technology; leaves for photosynthetic solar energy cells; and lobsters for more mobile extra-terrestrial exploration vehicles. The possibilities are endless.

Elephants themselves are a prime example of intelligent design. Their trunks are an inspiration for multi-functionality, serving as hand, nose, mouth, voice and radar all in one. Their ears can detect infrasound as low as 14 Hertz and are a highly effective air- conditioning mechanism as well. Their tusks are used for digging, stripping bark and self-defence. Their feet are padded and cushioned to create unbelievable stealth and agility. And their vast wrinkled skin protects them against the ravages of sun, rain, snow and parasites.

Importantly, nature-inspired products and services are usually oriented towards the triple bottom line. It goes without saying that, in nature, ecological integrity is an inbuilt system condition because every output is an input; waste equals food. However, social harmony is also inherent in maintaining viable ecosystems, as nature relies on symbiotic relationships of mutual interdependence. In addition, due to the efficiencies that nature has refined over billions of years, its designs are more likely than not to minimise resource consumption and turn waste into by-products. Once again, I am re-emphasising the need to search for new images and metaphors to serve as positive visions of the future. It is clear that we need to shapeshift beyond the Industrial Age, which has anyway been a dated symbol for the past four decades. And, while most would agree that we are well into the Information Age, which has the potential to usher in the elephant world of interconnectivity, some are already looking beyond it.

American futurist, Hazel Henderson (1988), claims that 'the Information Age is no longer an adequate image of the present, let alone a guide to the future. It still focuses on hardware technologies, mass production and economic models of efficiency and competition, and is more an extension of industrial ideas and methods than a new stage in human development.' Henderson points to a growing realisation by humanity of its dependence on nature, and more precisely, on light from the sun. Beyond the mushrooming ecological movement and the call for sustainable development, she draws support for her theory from the recent phenomenal growth in leading edge technologies that do nothing more than attempt to mimic the genius of nature. Examples of these include artificial intelligence technologies, biotechnologies, energy technologies and lightwave technologies / phototronics. Reflecting on these developments, Henderson talks about a 're-patterning of the exploding Information Age into an emerging Age of Light.'

Which metaphor endures in the next 50 years is not so important as the fact that its basic characteristics will reshape the way that companies do business. What is clear is that the landscape of our future will be vastly different from the present, and that the ability to understand the complex web of relationships that are woven around and within companies will be critical to surviving and thriving. This is something that will be impossible to achieve if business clings to its self-centred, 'drive into the future by looking into the rear-view mirror' approach. The metamorphosis will necessarily require business to assume a more open, compassionate and intuitive identity. This is what corporate responsibility ultimately means: the ability to respond to the needs of stakeholders, to the limits of the Earth, to the impacts of business processes on others, and to the magical potential that is inherent in people and nature.

Discussion 4.7: Services

1. What is the difference between 'cradle to grave' and 'cradle to cradle' design?
2. Can you think of examples of products that are 'closing the loop' of production and consumption, i.e. being designed to be endlessly recycled?
3. Interface's Evergreen Lease scheme has been far less successful than they hoped it would be. Why do you think this is the case?

CHAPTER 5: LEADERSHIP FOR CSR

This chapter is based on research that was conducted with the University of Cambridge Programme for Sustainability Leadership (CPSL 2011) and a paper written jointly with Polly Courtice, Director of CPSL (Visser & Courtice, 2011).

Through our research, we wanted to create a clearer understanding of the nature of sustainability leadership and how it can contribute to transformational change. We do this by locating sustainability within the leadership literature, defining the concept of sustainability leadership, and presenting a model of sustainability leadership in practice. The model was tested with a sample of senior business leaders and refined in line with their feedback. The model presents insights on sustainability leadership in three areas: context, individual characteristics, and actions.

The model of sustainability leadership that we have developed was corroborated by interviews with the following business leaders, conducted in 2010: Neil Carson, CEO of Johnson Matthey; Ian Cheshire, CEO of Kingfisher; Jeffrey Immelt, CEO of General Electric; Philippe Maso, CEO of AXA; Jan Muehlfeit, Chairman of Microsoft Europe; Truett Tate, Group Executive Director: Wholesale, for Lloyds Banking Group; José Lopez, Executive Vice President: Operations and GLOBE of Nestle; and Sandy Ogg, Chief Human Resources Officer for Unilever. The chapter and the model are illustrated by extensive quotations from these interviews.

5.1 Definitions and Theories of Leadership

De Vries (2001) reminds us that the Anglo-Saxon etymological root of the words lead, leader and leadership is laed, which means path or road. The verb means to travel. Thus a leader is one who shows fellow travellers the way by walking ahead. He also suggests that leadership – which focuses on the effectiveness of strategy – is different to management – which deals with the efficiency of operations.

Ian Cheshire (2010), CEO of Kingfisher, says 'leadership is about getting people to go where they wouldn't have gone on their own.' Rather more flamboyantly, management guru Tom Peters (1989) suggests leadership is about 'discovering the passion, persistence and imagination to get results, to be able to find the Wow factor and to be able to think the weird thoughts necessary to learn and thrive in a disruptive age.'

The element of transformational change in Peters' definition makes it particularly relevant to sustainability. Visser & Courtice (2011) have a working definition of leadership, as follows:

> A leader is someone who can craft a vision and inspire people to act collectively to make it happen, responding to whatever changes and challenges arise along the way.

In addition to definitions, there are also various theories on leadership and while it is not our intention to provide an exhaustive review of these, they do set a frame for sustainability leadership. Hence, we can distinguish three main approaches to understanding leadership:

1. The Trait/Style school, which focuses on the characteristics or approaches of individual leaders (McCall & Lombardo, 1983; Tannenbaum & Schmidt, 1973);
2. The Situational/Context school, which focuses on how the external environment shapes leadership action (Hersey & Blanchard, 1999; Vroom & Yetton, 1973); and
3. The Contingency/Interactionist school, which is about the interaction between the individual leader and his/her framing context (Fiedler, 1971; De Vries, 2001).

To these can be added the rather more practical tenets of leadership as described by Goffee & Jones (2009):

1. Leadership is relational. It is something you do *with* people, not *to* people. Put simply, you cannot be a leader without followers. Like all relationships, it needs to be monitored and cultivated.
2. Leadership is non-hierarchical. Formal authority or a title doesn't make you a leader. Leaders can be found at all levels.
3. Leadership is contextual. You need to size up and tap into what exists around you and then bring more to the party.

5.2 Defining Sustainability Leadership

These definitions and theories provide the background for understanding sustainability leadership, which has emerged as a topic in its own right in recent years. According to a survey of 766 United Nations Global Compact (UNGC) member CEOs (Accenture & UNGC, 2010), 93% of CEOs see sustainability as important to their company's future success. But this begs the question: what do we mean by sustainability leadership? Visser & Courtice (2011) offer the following simple definition:

A sustainability leader is someone who inspires and supports action towards a better world.

The Sustainability Leadership Institute (2011) offers another definition, suggesting that sustainability leaders are 'individuals who are compelled to make a difference by deepening their awareness of themselves in relation to the world around them. In doing so, they adopt new ways of seeing, thinking and interacting that result in innovative, sustainable solutions.'

Based on a review of the leadership literature and our experience in working with senior leaders on sustainability, we take the view that sustainability leadership – or more precisely, leadership for sustainability – is not a separate school of leadership, but a particular blend of leadership characteristics applied within a definitive context. If it is to be aligned with a mainstream school of leadership at all, the Contingency / Interactionist school is probably most relevant, as the context – comprising the sustainability challenges facing the world and our aspirations for a more sustainable future – calls for particular types of leadership and is manifested in key areas of action.

Sandy Ogg (2010), Chief Human Resources Officer for Unilever, explains this contingency approach when he says, 'I don't think there's any difference between the character or timeless elements [of leadership], whether you're leading sustainability or whether you're leading for profit. But when it comes to the differentiators, why is it that Paul Polman [CEO of Unilever] stands out? It's because he understands the context and he understands leading with empathy in a multi stakeholder environment.'

Interestingly, a number of business leaders felt that the need to differentiate sustainability leadership from leadership in general may be a necessary, but temporary phenomenon. For instance, Ian Cheshire (2010) believes that 'sustaining the [sustainability] agenda and really embedding it in the organisation is the unique current set of challenges on a 10 year view. Beyond that, hopefully it becomes much more business as usual.'

Similarly, Neil Carson (2010), CEO of Johnson Matthey, says: 'This is like the quality revolution that we had in the eighties. What happened was companies either died or they got quality. One day this is going to be the same for sustainability. But there's an interim period where that's only true for some companies. So you've probably got ten years or maybe longer of there being a need for it to be pointed out that there is sustainability leadership and that it's important.'

Drawing on both the theory of leadership and the practice of sustainability by leaders, Visser & Courtice (2011) designed and tested a Sustainability Leadership Model – depicted and described below – which has three components: the external and internal context for leadership; the traits, styles, skills and knowledge of the individual leader; and leadership actions. None of these elements is unique to sustainability leaders, but collectively they encapsulate a distinctive set of characteristics and actions in response to sustainability challenges.

The sustainability leadership that we observe in practice and describe below is geared towards bringing about profound change, whether in our political and economic systems, our business models and practices, or in the broad social contract with stakeholders and society. Hence, the leadership model we have developed is implicitly about creating change.

Discussion 5.1: Leadership and Sustainability

1. What are the characteristics of a 'good' versus a 'bad' leader? Can you give examples?
2. How are leaders affected by their context? How might a leader in a time of crisis differ from a leader in a time of stability?
3. Do you think our global sustainability challenges call for a different type of leadership? If so, explain what you mean.

5.3 A Model of Sustainability Leadership

In our model, context refers to the conditions or environment in which leaders operate, which have a direct or indirect bearing on their institutions and on their decision-making. This context is broadly divided into the context that is external to their institution and over which they may have a lesser degree of influence (e.g. ecological, economic, political, cultural and community contexts), and internal to their institution or sector, over which they are generally assumed to have higher levels of influence (e.g. the organizational culture, governance structure or role of leadership).

Many business leaders are conscious of the role of context. For example, Jeff Immelt (2007), CEO of General Electric says, 'The most important thing I've learned since becoming CEO is context. It's how your company fits in with the world and how you respond to it.'

Similarly, José Lopez (2010), Executive Vice President Operations and GLOBE of Nestle, explained that 'the context is that sustainability processes in place today are not trending in the right direction. As a matter of fact, poverty is going up, the world is not moving on essential things like waste, like emissions and utilisation of resources. So with that realisation, companies incorporate in their vision and mission what they are in business for, and then that gets enacted by continuous improvement processes that they carry out. What is important is the context. When you look at the "creating shared value" approach you don't have any more, in the case of Nestlé, just a "making money" kind of context.'

Figure 5.1: The Cambridge Sustainability Leadership Model

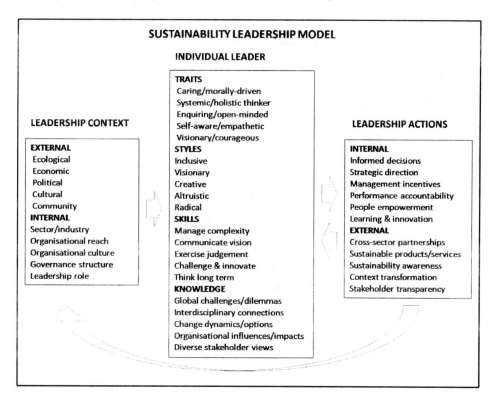

Understanding the sustainability leader requires that we appreciate their traits, styles, skills and knowledge. It is a combination of these that make the individual leader unique. For example, when asked, 'How would people in Unilever describe you as a leader?' Paul Polman (2009), CEO of Unilever, said: 'I hope that the word integrity comes into that. I hope the word long term comes into that. I hope the word caring comes into that, but demanding as well.'

Individual sustainability leaders are unlikely to embody all of the traits, styles, skills and knowledge in our model. Rather, they need to draw on what is appropriate or fitting to their own personality and circumstances, so as to be most effective in addressing sustainability challenges. Furthermore they will seek to develop these qualities in others, building teams that bring as many of the required elements to bear, and in effect enabling a form of distributed leadership to exist within the organisation (Center for Excellence in Leadership et. al, 2007).

Doppelt (2010) cites the case of Interface, which focuses more on team structure than on individual leaders. He writes, 'Some are entrepreneurs, some are team builders, some are competitors, some are commanders, some are safety orientated and some are creators. Few people excel in all these areas. The entrepreneur is the antithesis of those who are safety orientated. The commander is the antithesis of the team builder. While no single person may have all these attributes, they are all needed for Interface to achieve its potential.'

5.4 Traits of Sustainability Leaders

There are any number of ideal leadership traits. For example, Kouzes & Posner (2007) argue that good leaders are honest, forward looking, competent, inspiring and intelligent. In a globalising world, Morrison (2000) emphasises the importance of leaders developing competencies tailored to their company.

We believe the sustainability leader typically embodies a number of traits, by which we mean distinguishing attributes, qualities or personal characteristics which are generally seen as being enduring. Below, we define each trait and give an illustrative quote from a sustainability leader.

Caring / morally-driven

Sustainability leaders care for the well-being of humanity and all other forms of life, as well as being guided by a moral compass. According to Jan Muehlfeit (2010), Chairman of Microsoft Europe:

'We're at the crossroads. Adam Smith spoke in his *Wealth of the Nations* about profit and care, saying that the first thing we do is take care of ourselves, but the second thing we do is take care of others. By care, I don't only mean care about other people, but also care about society and care about nature.'

Systemic / holistic thinker

Sustainability leaders have the ability to appreciate the interconnectedness and interdependency of the whole system, at all levels, and to recognise how changes to parts of the system affect the whole. According to Jeffrey Immelt (2010), CEO of General Electric:

'In time periods of relative stability, you don't need to be a systems thinker [but] we're in a period now of great volatility. So the type of people that ultimately are going to lead at sustainability (and one of the reasons why it's so tough) is that it really requires a new generation of systems thinkers to make it work. That's why some of these issues are so hard to solve because they really require forward systems thinking, solutions orientation.'

Enquiring / open-minded

Sustainability leaders are always actively seeking new knowledge and diverse opinions, questioning received wisdom, including being willing to have one's own opinions challenged. According to Philippe Maso (2010), CEO of AXA:

'It is about looking outside [and staying] permanently engaged. There is a community activity which brings you a lot of information, but it's also about talking and making sure you get enough challenge on what you do. Our children are looking at the world differently. If we are going to be in power in the next 10 or 20 years, we need to make sure we can respond to this demand properly.'

Self-aware / empathetic

Sustainability leaders have high levels of emotional intelligence (the ability to understand their own emotions and those of others), sincerity, personal humility and reflexiveness (the ability to see their own place in and influence on a situation). According to Ian Cheshire (2010), CEO of Kingfisher:

'Real leadership is about greater and greater self-awareness and being more and more authentically yourself. Then you can use that knowledge or that mastery to put together and drive better teams – because you're more clear about who you are, what your impact is, what you have to offer and what you don't have (and therefore you need). And by association that implies the humility to listen and be aware as opposed to being on broadcast and an egomaniac, which I think is the traditional model of CEOs.'

Visionary / courageous

Sustainability leaders bring inspiration, creativity, optimism and courage to bear in the role, driven to produce results and possess the ability to balance passion and idealism with ambition and pragmatism. Sandy Ogg (201), Former Chief Human Resources Officer for Unilever, asks:

'Do we have the courage to put up a magnetic north out there for our company in an environment where everything changes every day? It's absolutely necessary. You have to have the courage to say, 'You know what, I don't necessarily know the end destination, but I know it's going to look something like this and we're going that way. That's one thing I love about Paul Polman. He says, 'Listen, I may be wrong, but I'm not confused.'

5.5 Styles of Sustainability Leaders

We make a clear distinction between traits of individual leaders and their style, i.e. the manner and approach which they use to provide direction, to motivate people and to implement plans. Lewin, Llippit & White (1939) carried out leadership decision experiments and identified three different styles of leadership: autocratic, democratic and laissez-faire. Other popular styles of leadership that have been identified and studied include charismatic (Musser, 1987), participative (Coch & French, 1948; Vroom & Yetton, 1973), situational (Hersey & Blanchard, 1999), transactional (Burns, 1978; Adair, 1984; Drucker, 1993), transformational (Bass, 1990), quiet (Collins, 2001) and servant leadership (Greenleaf, 2002).

One particularly influential model was Blake & Mouton's (1968) Managerial Grid, which concluded that leadership styles were all essentially varying combinations of concern for people and concern for tasks. Similarly, the sustainability leader typically draws on a combination of number of styles, as illustrated below.

Inclusive

Sustainability leaders are collaborative and participative, building commitment through dialogue and consensus, democratic approaches, coaching, and a culture and structure that provides peer support, encouragement and recognises achievement. According to Ian Cheshire (2010), CEO of Kingfisher:

'Leaders actually lead through teams. The idea that you have a superstar leader is just nonsense. The whole aspect of selecting, developing and managing teams as the core challenge of leadership is something I feel particularly strongly about. A great definition of leadership is about getting people to go where they wouldn't have gone on their own. If they can get there on their own then they don't really need a leader. Equally, you can't always be dragging them in the opposite direction to where they want to go. It's about the leader and the followers working together to get to certain outcomes.'

Visionary

Sustainability leaders bring passion and charisma into the mix, focusing on challenging and transforming people's perceptions and expectations, and motivating them to transcend narrower forms of self-interest. According to Sandy Ogg (2010), Former Chief Human Resources Officer for Unilever:

'There's so much going on now in the world that if you don't have amplification and time compression, then it doesn't rumble. So I call that 'leading big'. If you've got something meaningful and important that you want to do, have the courage to lead big. You can't let it drool or dribble out into an organisation like ours and expect to have any impact. People are just too busy, there's too much going on. I think that the thunder is important too because people have to feel a message that is linked to emotion.'

Creative

Sustainability leaders are good at playing the role of designer, architect, innovator, game-changer and transformer of the system. According to Jeffrey Immelt (2010), CEO of General Electric:

'There is an inquisitiveness and a problem solving, or just a curiosity and a willingness to see things through other people's point of view. When I hear that Bill Gates is working on malaria, I get the sense that maybe it can be solved. That gives me great hope because he's going to apply tremendous resources and a headset for solutions that allow some of these big problems to be solved.'

Altruistic

Sustainability leaders transcend self interest and focus on the collective or the good of the whole, which is often characterised as servant leadership. According to Jan Muehlfeit (2010), Chairman of Microsoft Europe:

'Bill Gates is absolutely the model for people in Microsoft – especially with what he is doing with Africa in terms of the education, what he is doing in India. It is a very good example of a leader because he is basically saying, 'I will spend my money on the big issues that this planet is having.' For me personally – I've been with the company for 17 years – it's a huge role model for what to do to change the world for the better.'

Radical

Sustainability leaders practice highly visible leadership, characterised by taking risks, acting like a revolutionary, campaigner, crusader or activist and challenging of the status quo; often referred to as missionary leadership. Anita Roddick (2001), Founder & former CEO of The Body Shop International encouraged leaders to:

'Be daring, be first, be different, be just. If you think you're too small to have an impact, try going to bed with a mosquito.'

Discussion 5.2: Traits and Styles of Sustainability Leaders

1. Do you agree that there are distinctive traits and styles associated with strong CSR/sustainability leaders?
2. Are there any CSR/sustainability leaders (other than those cited above) who embody one or more of the traits identified in the Cambridge model?

3. Are there any CSR/sustainability leaders (other than those cited above) who embody one or more of the styles identified in the Cambridge model?

5.6 Skills of Sustainability Leaders

A survey of business and sustainability leaders in the UK (Isos MORI, 2010) found that 99% recognise that developing the skills that will be needed for a sustainable economy is important to the future success of the UK economy, while 70% believe that the gap in skills for a sustainable economy will become one of the most pressing challenges facing UK businesses in the next 5 years. At the same time, only 15% think that developing the skills needed for a sustainable economy is well-established or partly established in UK businesses in general (as compared with 48% for their own organisation).

The skills for sustainability leadership, as per our model, are introduced below.

Manage complexity

Sustainability leaders are good at analysing, synthesising, and translating complex issues, responding to risk, uncertainty and dilemmas, recognising and seizing opportunities and resolving problems or conflicts. According to Philippe Maso (2010), CEO of AXA:

'Sustainability is a complex thing to conceive and everyone who comes with too simplistic views [is] not effective, because reality would prevail at some point in time. You have to accept that there is a huge complexity of knowledge and the way we frame it. You need to be quite sure you are pushing in the right direction. There is a quantum of uncertainty that needs to be not too high, so you can really have positive actions.'

Communicate vision

Sustainability leaders practice sharing a vision and facilitating dialogue that inspires action and creates shared meaning (active listening, emotional intelligence, reflection) and creating conditions that encourage learning from experience. According to Ian Cheshire (2010), CEO of Kingfisher:

'The key thing for leadership agendas is the ability to genuinely communicate – which is actually a two way process of genuinely listening well and communicating well. Because in some pure sense we don't actually build anything with our hands; all we do as leaders is communicate. We basically get things to happen through communication. I do think that A-grade leadership is very hard to do without good communication skills. You can go so far if you're technically gifted but not terribly good at communication. Communication is most critical and most difficult in increasingly complex organizations.'

Exercise judgment

Sustainability leaders make good and decisive decisions in a timely fashion, including prioritising, making difficult choices and handling dilemmas. According to Sandy Ogg (2010), Former Chief Human Resources Officer for Unilever:

'How do you solve any big problem? You break it down. Let's go to Indonesia. Let's get specific. Let's talk about the supply chain and what is it that you can do there? That's probably something that we can solve. If you think it all the way through, you can have a plan in Indonesia of two or three things which, if we focus on it and pay attention to it, we can have a business that's 3 billion.'

Challenge and innovate

Sustainability leaders are adept at imagining possible solutions/futures or alternatives, thinking outside the box, and bringing creativity into thinking and practice. According to Neil Carson (2010), CEO of Johnson Matthey:

'Until everybody on the whole planet gets sustainability there's a real competitive advantage in moving in this direction aggressively. The more competitive the individual leader is in terms of natural inclinations then the more quickly they'll latch on to sustainability.'

Think long term

Sustainability leaders use visioning strategic planning and long term thinking, seeing the whole, while not discounting the future. According to Truett Tate (2010), Group Executive Director: Wholesale, for Lloyds Banking Group:

'To be credible in the sustainability space there needs to be a clear demonstration of a vision of 50 to 100 years from now. Sustainability must have a longer term vision and must be able to articulate that. '

5.7 Knowledge of Sustainability Leaders

The Ipsos MORI (2010) survey on the skills required for sustainability leadership in the UK found that middle managers, and function heads especially, need sufficient knowledge about sustainability to translate it into successful business strategies, as well as effective and persuasive communication using clear and accessible language.

The most important areas of knowledge for sustainability leaders are introduced below.

Global challenges and dilemmas

Sustainability leaders understand social and ecological system pressures and the connections between these systems and political and economic forces. According to Jan Muehlfeit (2010), Chairman of Microsoft Europe:

'The first challenge is inclusive globalisation. The other global issue is the gap between the rich and poor, the inequality gap. The other one has to do with the emerging markets, because 20 years ago we had one billion people in the western style of capitalism, today it's probably 3 to 4 billion. That's where I think leadership needs to go, to be much more aware of those global issues. What the business leaders need to do is to create a bigger picture and also to be much more connected to the big global challenges.'

Interdisciplinary connectedness

Sustainability leaders understand the relevance and interconnectedness of the physical sciences, social sciences, technology, business and other disciplines. Jeffrey Immelt (2010), CEO of General Electric, asks:

'How do you develop leaders for this time period of volatility we live in today? One of the things that we are quite keen on is what we call systems thinking. It's people that can integrate between technology, market needs, public policy and so on. You have to integrate many things all at the same time.'

Change dynamics and options

Sustainability leaders understand how complex systems work and the range of options for promoting beneficial change in them, e.g. financial markets, policy options and trends, technology options, consumer behaviour and attitudes, organisational dynamics, change models and metrics. According to Neil Carson (2010), CEO of Johnson Matthey:

'What could easily happen is that when taking small steps to start with, they become large bounds later. Intuitively, I'm a practical being and I think that there's no other way of doing it, you can't go from 0 to 60 miles an hour in one bound. My instinct is that we've probably got 10 or 20 years, but also that things can accelerate once you get started. Businesses will lead consumers along this path, they'll start to get engaged and then governments will follow in the end.'

Organisational influences and impacts

Sustainability leaders understand an organisation's full impact (footprint), finding and developing opportunities for value creation and new markets. José Lopez (2010), Executive Vice President: Operations and GLOBE of Nestle, asks:

'Why did Greenpeace to drop their campaign against Nestle? It's been achieved by putting on the table a very technical view of the issues we are talking about. We've demonstrated that we have a logic, a path and a process that drives continuous improvement into topics of high concern, which in this case is deforestation. What matters is not that we agree on how the world should look at the end of all that and who should be in charge and how should people behave and so on, but that we agree that what we are doing truly delivers improvement and betterment of the sustainability of nature.'

Diverse stakeholder views

Sustainability leaders appreciate different world views and belief systems, both within communities and across geographic, cultural and political divides, and how to incorporate these appropriately. According to Philippe Maso (2010), CEO of AXA:

Through technology and the evolution of our mentality, we ask leaders to be much more capable of engaging in a web of relationships. We know the difference between being an influencer versus being a commander or controller. The stakeholder-orientation is seen in a new breed of people which is emerging everywhere who have been trained in doing things differently and can carry messages that are very difficult to get across and require a very specific attitude, which is a rare but increasingly recognised skill.

5.8 Characteristics of Sustainability Leaders

In the CPSL (2011) report, entitled A Journey of a Thousand Miles: The State of Sustainability Leadership 2011, we also present a simplified and synthesized version of the model presented in this chapter (above), in which we propose seven key characteristics of sustainability leadership, including: systemic understanding, emotional intelligence, values orientation, compelling vision, inclusive style, innovative approach; and long term perspective. These are illustrated briefly below by further quotations from leaders.

Systemic, interdisciplinary understanding

José Lopez (2010), Executive Vice President Operations and GLOBE of Nestle, insists that 'one of the elements that will really get us going in this sustainability fight is the elimination of the root cause for unsustainable behaviour, unsustainable business morals, unsustainable practices and so on. The ability to see the root cause of those things will set companies apart. They have to do with the profound thinking that you have and the processes of how you invest money and how you train your people and how you develop resources.'

Emotional intelligence and a caring attitude

Jan Muehlfeit (2010), Chairman of Microsoft Europe, observes that 'over the next ten years, the only way individuals, organisations and countries will succeed and compete will be through the ability to unlock human potential.' He believes that 'as a leader for the future, you would need to distinguish between motivations; you can motivate people's hands or their brains but you can't motivate their hearts – it takes real inspiration.'

Values orientation that shapes culture

Truett Tate (2010), Group Executive Director (Wholesale) for Lloyds Banking Group, believes there is a 'personal, almost spiritual commitment that needs to be epitomised in someone who is going to be successful in this sustainability space. So, a morality, a spirituality [which has] a great coupling with [having a] longer term vision.' He adds that their credibility must come from 'the way that they behave and interact with the world. They epitomise interconnectedness. They understand community [in the sense of] communion with facets of the world around us.' Hence, although not everyone would characterise their actions in terms of spirituality, a values-based approach is critical.

A strong vision for making a difference

Ray Anderson (2009), CEO of Interface, is well known for his vision to make Interface the first truly sustainable, zero-impact, or 'restorative' company in the world, which their performance metrics suggest they are on-track to reach by 2020. He calls on 'our people, our customers, our suppliers, our communities and our owners … to learn and believe in a new and better way to be more profitable, and to reach for significance beyond success – a higher purpose for us all.' Hence, CSR leaders are able to effectively communicate a compelling narrative on how their organisations can contribute to creating a better world.

An inclusive style that engenders trust

For Ian Cheshire (2010) 'the job of the leader is to create conditions for other people to succeed and to do that in a sustainable way so that the business endures. You might be technically brilliant, you might even be a great communicator, but unless you can genuinely put together a diverse and effective team and then manage it for performance, you're not actually an effective leader.' Speaking about sustainability, he says: 'If we've decided that this is our playing field and this is our agenda and our view of where we want to go, how do I then mobilise people around this agenda? How do I get the right teams together on the right topics? How do I sustain the level of interest in this going forward? How do I make it become a business as usual part of the DNA as opposed to forcing it through?'

A willingness to innovate and be radical

Jeffrey Swartz (2010), CEO of The Timberland Company says, 'Future capabilities will be very different, and will put a premium on lateral thinking and cross-functional, collaborative problem solving.' For Timberland, this includes not only designing cradle-to-cradle products like their Earthkeeper 2.0 boots, but also responding to challenges by Greenpeace and working with their Brazilian supplier Bertin to support the deforestation moratorium (meaning they will no longer source cattle from protected areas of the Amazon). Hence, CSR leaders recognise that complex problems require creative solutions.

A long-term perspective on impacts

Neil Carson (2010), CEO of Johnson Matthey, believes that 'companies think much longer term than governments and good companies think much longer term than bad companies.' He makes the point that in terms of sustainability, long term thinking is especially important for leaders of sunset industries. 'If you're into coal mining and turning coal into heat and power, then you've got to think of the long term. You're not really a coal miner, you're a power supplier. You can look at ways of making things more efficient. Then you can look at ways of sequestering the CO_2. You can make all these plans ahead of time and move in the right direction. And our experience is that the employees will really react very well to those kind of long-term plans. You get more out of the employees than you might expect if you embark on such a journey.'

Discussion 5.3: Skills and Knowledge of Sustainability Leaders

1. Are there any CSR/sustainability leaders (other than those cited above) who embody one or more of the skills identified in the Cambridge model?
2. Are there any CSR/sustainability leaders (other than those cited above) who embody one or more of the types of knowledge identified in the Cambridge model?
3. Choose a strong sustainability leader. How many of the seven key characteristics outlined in 5.8 above do they seem to embody? Give examples to support your claims.

5.9 Actions of Sustainability Leaders

According to the Accenture & UNGC (2010) survey, CEOs believe that execution is now the real challenge to bringing about the new era of sustainability. Leadership action is particularly important, because the gap between sustainability aspirations or imperatives and actual performance remains wide. For example, IBM's (2009) sustainable enterprise survey of more than 220 senior executives worldwide showed that 60% believed CSR had increased in importance over the previous year.

Yet, there continues to be a significant gulf between the sustainability goals companies are setting for themselves and what they are actually doing to attain them. Hence, 'walking the talk' remains the real test. As Polman (2009) says, 'you cannot talk yourself out of things you've behaved yourself into.'

The individual leaders and the actions they take have a self-evidently reciprocal relationship, each having the potential to impact and change the other. Typical internal (company-wide) actions include:

- Making informed decisions;
- Providing strategic direction;
- Crafting management incentives;
- Ensuring performance accountability;
- Empowering people; and
- Embedding learning and innovation.

In addition, sustainability leaders typically respond to the challenges and opportunities of sustainability through the following external (stakeholder-related) actions:

- Fostering cross sector partnerships;
- Creating sustainable products and services;
- Promoting sustainability awareness;
- Transforming the operating context; and
- Ensuring transparency.

In order to illustrate the importance of actions for sustainability, we highlight a number of cases in below. These show that although each company is far from reaching the goal of sustainability, leaders have taken important concrete steps along the journey.

5.10 Sustainability Leadership at General Electric (GE)

Jeffrey R. Immelt is the ninth chairman of GE, a post he has held since 7 September 2001. He has been named one of the 'World's Best CEOs' three times by *Barron's*, and since he began serving as chief executive officer, GE has been named 'America's Most Admired Company' in a poll conducted by *Fortune* magazine and one of 'The World's Most Respected Companies' in polls by *Barron's* and the *Financial Times*.

Despite these accolades, GE has not escaped criticism by financial analysts and sustainability activists. The way in which Immelt has responded to these criticisms is the real story of sustainability leadership.

Speaking at the Prince of Wales's Business and Sustainability Programme London Lecture in 2010, Immelt set out four pillars of a competitive society: education, affordable healthcare, financial systems that promote entrepreneurship, and clean energy. In particular, he emphasised that a clean energy future – one that is sustainable, that emphasises energy security, that drives competitiveness and job creation and that reduces pollution – represents 'the biggest opportunity that we will face in the next decades, and we have to grab it and we have to lead in this regard.'

Hence, Immelt has unapologetically linked GE's commercial strategy with their sustainability interests. This is most evident in their Ecomagination programme, launched in 2005 and carefully aligned to GE's overall mission of 'imagination at work'. Immelt backed this programme up with bold targets – such as increasing revenues from sustainable products to $25 billion by 2010 – and substantive investments to ensure innovation, including doubling R&D spend in the area to $1.5 billion by 2010. Ecomagination is clearly about making GE money and is an unapologetic investment in future profitability. Even so, Immelt believes that 'it's happening before it has to. It's leading by example.'

In a related project, in July 2010, GE announced a $200 million open innovation challenge that seeks breakthrough ideas to create a smarter, cleaner, more efficient electric grid, and to accelerate the adoption of more efficient grid technologies. The money will be invested globally into promising start-ups and ideas. 'Innovation is the engine of the global effort to transform the way we create, connect and use power,' Immelt said. 'This challenge is about collaboration and we are inviting others to help accelerate progress in creating a cleaner, more efficient and economically viable grid. We want to jump-start new ideas and deploy them on a scale that will modernize the electrical grid around the world.'

Another key to Immelt's success as a sustainability leader is his inclusive approach. He believes that 'Enron and 9/11 marked the end of an era of individual freedom and the beginning of personal responsibility. You lead today by building teams and placing others first. It's not about you.' One of the ways GE demonstrated this collaborative approach in the market was to partner with Walmart and help them to sell 100 million energy-saving compact fluorescent light bulbs (CFLs), thereby creating a tipping point in consumer purchasing habits. Success meant that total sales of CFLs in the U.S. would double, saving Americans $3 billion in electricity costs and avoiding the need to build additional power plants for the equivalent of 450,000 new homes.

It is to Immelt's credit that he has made these strategic investments in sustainability despite the company's stock value having halved over the past decade, and enormous pressure from market analysts to focus on GE's quarterly profits. This is the mark of a true sustainability leader – not only viewing the world systemically and thinking long term, but also investing accordingly. It is no wonder that, under Immelt, GE is still ranked as a top 10 global brand by *The Financial Times* and *Business Week*.

5.11 Sustainability Leadership at GlaxoSmithKline (GSK)

According to the CEO survey by Accenture & UNGC (2010), 72% of CEOs cite 'brand, trust and reputation' as the main factor that has driven them to take action on sustainability issues. Certainly, this seems to be the case in the pharmaceuticals industry, where they have suffered a serious crisis of trust over the past 10 years. This was triggered in 2001 when 39 of the largest international pharmaceutical companies took the South African government to court over plans to introduce legislation aimed at easing access to AIDS drugs, arguing that it would infringe their patents and contravene the Trade Related Aspects of Intellectual Property Rights (TRIPS) agreement.

Tens of thousands of people marched in protest all over the world, and 300,000 people from over 130 countries signed a petition against the action. Eventually, following public pressure, as well as objections from the South African government and the European Parliament, 'Big Pharma' dropped the case. Justin Forsyth, Oxfam Policy Director, said at the time, 'This court case demonstrates how powerful drug companies are bullying poor countries just so they can protect their patent rights on life-saving medicines.' Fanning the flames of public discontent, John le Carré's 2001 book, *The Constant Gardener*, and the 2005 film adaptation depicted drug companies as corrupt profiteers. As *Mail & Guardian* journalist Qudsiya Karrim reported for *Inside Story* in 2010, 'The past decade has been a public relations nightmare for big pharmaceutical companies – and deservedly so.'

This was the turbulent milieu into which Andrew Witty stepped as CEO of GlaxoSmithKline (GSK) in 2008. Believing that 'to be a successful and sustainable business, we must fulfil our social responsibilities and build trust with our stakeholders', early in 2009, Witty announced a major reform in their corporate policy on drug affordability and accessibility. GSK cut its prices for all drugs in the 50 least developed countries to no more than 25% of the levels in the UK and U.S.

and made drugs more affordable in middle-income countries such as Brazil and India. In addition, they committed to reinvest 20% of their profits into hospitals and clinics in the least developed countries.

Going even further, Witty launched a radically new initiative on opening access to intellectual property through the donation of a number of patents to a 'Pool for Open Innovation against Neglected Tropical Diseases'. Explaining this move, Witty said, 'I think it's the first time anybody's really come out and said we're prepared to start talking to people about pooling our patents to try to facilitate innovation in areas where, so far, there hasn't been much progress.' GSK may not yet have won the battle for the hearts and minds of its stakeholders, but at least some critics are being cautiously supportive. 'He is breaking the mould in validating the concept of patent pools,' said the head of Oxfam's medicines campaign, Rohit Malpani. 'It is a big step forward. It is welcome that he is inviting other companies to take this on and have a race to the top instead of a race to the bottom.'

Some of the business benefits have been rather immediate. For instance, in the Philippines, a 60% price cut in the cancer vaccine Cervarix increased sales by around 600%. Time will tell whether these short-term concessions – which in some ways undermine the commercial viability of their Research and Development investments – will prove sustainable in the long term. What Witty has recognised, however, is that without the trust and support of your key stakeholders, there is no long term to contemplate.

5.12 Sustainability Leadership at Skanska, Unilever and IBM

Skanska CEO, Johan Karlström, believes, 'What is green today will be vanilla tomorrow. To be a leader you have to aim for deep green.' For Skanska, this means taking bold action. The company uses carbon footprinting tools to benchmark the carbon emissions of building projects and to help identify low-carbon project options.

The results speak for themselves. In Stockholm, they have built apartments that are twice as energy efficient as the average, while in New York, Skanska's work as a contractor on the 32nd floor of the Empire State Building has resulted in reductions in energy consumption of 57% and water use of 40%, while 80% construction waste was recycled.

When Unilever CEO Paul Polman recently launched their Sustainability Living Plan, it seemed to confirm something Chief HR Officer Sandy Ogg (2010) told us about 'leading big'. For Unilever, this means seeking to double the size of the company, while halving the environmental footprint of their products, sourcing

100% of their agricultural ingredients sustainably by 2015 and helping a billion people out of poverty.

According to IBM CEO, Samuel J. Palmisano, a smarter world – by which he means a more instrumented, connected and intelligent global society – is also a more sustainable world. 'In the post-industrial age that we have now entered,' he says, 'the relevant struggle is not nature vs. industry, but systemic vs. fragmented.'

For example, using IBM integrated solutions, Cosco, a global shipping firm in China, reduced its distribution centres from 100 to 40, lowering its logistics costs by 23% and its CO_2 emissions by 15%. Palmisano emphasises that 'the most important factor in achieving this kind of progress is not technology. It's leadership. Because just as complex, interdependent systems demand new kinds of technology, they also require new forms of management.'

Discussion 5.4: Sustainability Leadership Cases

1. Do you think G.E., GSK, Unilever, Skanska, Unilever and IBM are good sustainability leadership cases?
2. G.E. is a company that is sustainable in a literal sense that it has existed for more than 120 years. What do you think is the secret of its longevity?
3. GSK was investing in long term R&D in order to develop life-saving drugs, but it was criticised by activists when it could not offer these at affordable prices. What is their new business model, and is it more sustainable or less sustainable?

5.13 The Paradox of CSR Leadership

One of our most compelling and persistent findings is that sustainability leadership is fraught with paradoxes. As the competitive landscape shifts and global challenges evolve, companies that were lauded in the past as sustainability leaders may be discredited in the present. Similarly, today's targeted villains may end up being tomorrow's sustainability heroes and vice versa. There are a number of reasons for this state of flux in CSR leadership:

Sustainability is aspirational – No company, or society, has achieved sustainability. The goal of sustainable development is an ideal state that we are striving for. By definition, companies will fall short of the mark and be exposed for their inadequacies.

The context is dynamic – Our global challenges are part of a complex, living system, which is constantly changing. Companies that do not innovate and adapt to match the evolving context will be left behind, while others will emerge as new leaders.

Perceptions can change – The sustainability agenda is driven as much by emotions and perceptions as by factual realities. Society's views on issues – like nuclear energy and GMOs – can change, and with it the perceived sustainability performance of companies.

Sustainability is a learning process – As our understanding of sustainability challenges and solutions improves, so too do our expectations of companies. Companies in their turn need to constantly renew their sustainability learning, or be left wanting.

We can illustrate this paradox of CSR leadership by putting the spotlight on a number of companies (BP, Monsanto, Walmart and Nestle). The purpose is not to name and shame, but rather to emphasise the dynamic and complex nature of sustainability leadership. Besides, far from representing an underperforming minority, these examples are typical of the prevailing majority on the corporate sustainability landscape.

One classic case is John Browne's leadership of BP from 1995 to 2007. At the time, Browne was widely credited not only with resurrecting the company's financial fortunes, but also for turning BP from being a target for NGO criticism to being hailed as a leader on sustainability.

One landmark action was in 1998 when Browne threw down the gauntlet to BP and the oil industry, promising to cut emissions from its own operations by 10% from 1990 levels by 2010, which was more than the average Kyoto Protocol country targets and certainly more than any other major oil company had committed to up until that time. In fact, they achieved the target four years later, eight years ahead of the target and at no net cost to the company.

Other applauded actions were BP's investment in renewables and the implementation of an internal greenhouse gas emissions trading scheme. And yet today, after a spate of accidents like the Texas City oil refinery explosion in 2005 and the Deepwater Horizon oil well blowout in 2010, as well as key strategic actions like investment in the Alberta tar sands, BP's sustainability reputation is severely tarnished and Browne's perceived legacy as a sustainability leader has been brought into question.

Nestle is another case in point. In 1977, they became the target of a boycott campaign that still exists today, in which they were accused of aggressively marketing baby milk formula in Africa as an alternative to mother's breast milk. Despite Nestle stating that it its infant formula is only targeting mother's who cannot produce their own milk, the company continues to draw criticism that it is in violation of a 1981 World Health Organization code that regulates the advertising of breast milk formulas.

Today, Nestle's sustainability approach goes under the guise of a strategy for creating shared value, which focuses on specific areas of the company's core business activities – namely water, nutrition, and rural development – where value can best be created both for society and shareholders. They are investing heavily in all of these areas and attracting praise from many sustainability advocates. Nevertheless, this did not prevent Nestle's Kit-Kat brand from being the target of a Greenpeace campaign in March 2010, which accused the company of aiding and abetting rainforest destruction through their Indonesian supply chain. Greenpeace later called off the campaign.

Another example of the paradox of sustainability leadership is Walmart. When Harold Lee Scott Junior took over as President and CEO of Walmart in 2000, *Fortune* magazine described the company's public image as being that of a 'rapacious behemoth'. Scott commissioned a review of Walmart's legal and public relations problems, and it was not a pretty picture. A discrimination lawsuit had been certified as a federal class action, new stores were blocked by activists in Los Angeles, San Francisco and Chicago, and the company had just forked out millions to regulators for air and water pollution infringements.

Speaking at the 2007 London Lecture of HRH The Prince of Wales's Business and the Environment Programme, former CEO, Lee Scott reflected on how hurricane Katrina in 2005 had 'brought out the best in our company ... In the aftermath of the storm, we asked ourselves: How can we be that company – the Walmart we were during Katrina – all the time? Sustainability became a big part of the answer.'

Taking action, Scott announced three radical goals: 1) to be supplied 100% by renewable energy; 2) to create zero waste; and 3) to sell products that sustain people and the environment. Already, we see the 'Walmart effect' of scalability in action in three areas: more sustainable fish, cotton and lightbulbs.

Another case full of contradictions is Monsanto. When Monsanto began manufacturing the chemical pesticide DDT in 1944, it was seen by many as a saviour of the agricultural industry, dramatically increasing food yields. But years later – and following the scientific work of Rachel Carson (1962), author of the highly critical *Silent Spring*, and others – DDT was banned as a highly toxic contaminant, and Monsanto was stereotyped as a dangerous and polluting business.

Similarly, when the company pioneered genetically modified crops in the 1980s, including the creation of drought-resistant strains that could help alleviate poverty, they expected to be lauded as sustainability pioneers, yet found themselves targeted by environmental and social activists for creating farmer dependency and allegedly reducing crop resilience. Despite selling 90% of the USA's GMO seeds, the EU placed a moratorium on all GMO crops.

5.14 Distributed Sustainability Leadership

These paradoxes of sustainability leadership are more the rule than the exception. This is inevitable in a global context that is so dynamic and with sustainability challenges that are so complex. Hence, our research should be considered against this backdrop of uncertainty, ambiguity and apparent contradiction. Hence, while the characteristics of leadership, and its application to sustainability, may be fairly durable and unchanging, the examples of sustainability leaders in practice are anything but constant.

In the final analysis, sustainability leaders realise that their task is, ultimately, about survival. Ogg (2010) says, 'This is what Paul Polman has been very, very clear about. This is not some aspirational dream to help us to try to recruit the best people in the world. At the end of the day this is a survival issue. We will not get the right to grow, and even worse, will not have the right to be in business, if we create a big environmental disaster. The world won't put up with it. There's too much awareness and amplification. You think about the impact a blogger can have when they choose to amplify their message.'

Ultimately, given the scale and urgency of the challenges, CSR leadership needs to be bold leadership. It also needs to be collaborative leadership – leaders acting together at all levels of organisation and society. Many of the CSR leaders that we spoke to emphasised the importance of collective action. James Smith (2010), Chairman of Shell UK, told us that his view of leadership is not based on a hierarchical model but on the notion of a network – i.e. that the leadership is not invested in one person. Smith concedes that many CEOs do base their leadership on the cult of personality and cause things to happen, but their success is short lived. Sustainability leadership, by contrast, 'is about cultivating good people for sustainability to be delivered.'

Hence, while individual leaders at the apex of organisations are critical change agents for sustainability, finding CSR leaders or champions throughout our communities, government departments and companies, is also essential. Some call this approach 'distributed leadership', which MIT Professor Deborah Ancona

(2010) says is 'where junior leaders act when local needs arise and as organizational imperatives demand.'

We all have the potential to be CSR leaders, whatever our area of practice, whatever our role and whatever our level of seniority. We also conclude from our research that – given the paradox of CSR leadership – the success or otherwise of the CSR leader (whether individual or organisational, hierarchical or distributed) must rest with the performance of the company. Ultimately, CSR leadership must be judged by the success of our actions – and whether we inspire and support others to follow our vision and passion for a better world.

Discussion 5.5: Paradoxes of Sustainability Leadership

1. Do you believe BP and Monsanto's poor public image on sustainability is justified? What could they do to reverse stakeholders' perceptions?
2. Can you think of any examples (other than those cited above) of companies that we perceived as sustainability leaders and are now seen as laggards? What about laggards who are now seen as leaders? What caused the changes?
3. Which is more lacking in your company or city or country: central, top-down leadership on sustainability, or bottom-up, distributed leadership?

CHAPTER 6: CSR AND CHANGE

6.1 Creative Destruction

One of the key theories on innovation is creative destruction. The concept is most associated with Joseph Schumpeter (2008), following his 1942 book Capitalism, Socialism and Democracy, in which he described creative destruction as 'the process of industrial mutation that incessantly revolutionizes the economic structure from within, incessantly destroying the old one, incessantly creating a new one ... [The process] must be seen in its role in the perennial gale of creative destruction; it cannot be understood on the hypothesis that there is a perennial lull.'

The idea, of course, is much older. In Hinduism, the goddess Shiva is simultaneously the creator and destroyer of worlds. In modern times, the German sociologist Werner Sombart described the process in 1913, saying 'from destruction a new spirit of creation arises; the scarcity of wood and the needs of everyday life ... forced the discovery or invention of substitutes for wood, forced the use of coal for heating, forced the invention of coke for the production of iron.' Even Marx and Engels had a go at describing the process in their Communist Manifesto, stating that 'constant revolutionizing of production, uninterrupted disturbance of all social conditions, everlasting uncertainty and agitation distinguish the bourgeois epoch from all earlier ones. ... All that is solid melts into air.'

The idea of melting solids is very similar to the metaphor used by sustainability and social enterprise thought-leader, John Elkington (2008), to explain the disruptive changes going on in the world. When I interviewed him, he said: 'What happens in an earthquake? The land becomes thixotropic; what was solid suddenly becomes almost semi-liquid. I think we are headed towards a period where the global economy goes into a sort of thixotropic state. Key parts of our economies and societies are on a doomed path really, and I think that's unavoidable. I think we're heading into a period of creative destruction on a scale that really we haven't seen for a very long time, and there are all sorts of factors that feed into it – the entry of the Chinese and Indians into the global market, quite apart from things like climate change and new technology.

As to what this means for business, Elkington believes that 'all of these pressures are going to mobilise a set of dynamics which are unpredictable and profoundly disruptive to incumbent companies, so some companies will disappear. I think most companies that we currently know will not be around in fifteen to twenty years, which is almost an inconceivable statement. But periodically this happens and there's a radical bleeding of the landscape. We'll find this sort of reassembly going on. Over a period of time we're going to have some fairly different products, technologies and business models coming back into the West, and I think it's going to be quite exciting, but very disruptive.'

We see all kinds of examples of creative destruction in corporate sustainability and responsibility. For virtually the whole of the 20th century, the biggest companies in the world were the oil and motor giants – companies like Exxon, BP, General Motors and Toyota. But the 21st century, with growing concerns over energy security and climate change on the one hand and the rising geo-political and economic power of the East on the other, are ushering in a new era. Already in 2006, the richest man in China was reported to be Shi Shengrong, CEO of the solar company Suntech, and the richest women, Zhang Yin, made her fortune from recycling. By 2009, it was Wang Chuanfu, founder of BYD, which manufactures batteries and electric cars.

A 2010 report published by the Pew Environmental Center found that in 2009, China invested $34.6 billion in the clean energy economy, while the United States only invested $18.6 billion. In June 2010, China also launched their own Clean Tech Index. The U.S. is fighting back. Venture capital investment in renewable energy, electric cars, energy efficiency, and other green technology jumped to $1.5 billion in the United States in the second quarter of 2010, a 64% spike compared with the same period in 2009. Green tech investment in the U.S. has now returned to the record levels of the third quarter of 2008, before the global economic collapse.

This explosive growth was brought home to me when, at an event of Women In Sustainability Action (WISA) in Shanghai where I was speaking in June 2010, I got talking to a supplier of wind turbines to Europe. Simply put, he cannot keep up with the demand. He is turning customers away because there is already a 12 month lead time of orders in the pipeline. Even Germany, an early leader in the clean-technology space, can no longer compete with China in this sunrise industry. It is no coincidence that while Obama's energy reform bill was scuppered by the U.S. Congress, Malaysia created an Energy, Green Technology and Water Ministry. And while the British company BP was virtually brought to its knees by the Gulf spill, in May 2010, the Korean company Samsung unveiled an eye-watering investment plan to 'future-proof' the company by sinking $21 billion into its green technology and healthcare businesses. It claimed that the investment would generate $44 billion in annual sales and 45,000 new jobs by 2020.

6.2 Change Management

There are many different approaches and models for change management in organisations. Rather than trawl through them, here I want to focus on just three that I have found most useful. The first is Richard Beckhard and David Gleicher's Formula for Change: D x V x F > R. This means that three factors must be present for meaningful organisational change to take place. These factors are:

D = Dissatisfaction with how things are now;

V = Vision of what is possible; and

F = First, concrete steps that can be taken towards the vision.

If the product of these three factors is greater than R (Resistance), then change is possible. I have seen CSR change efforts fail for all four reasons. Deep-seated resistance often exists because the benefits of the status quo accruing to those in power are considerable. CSR initiatives, especially if they are integrated into the core business, are often seen as extra burden. For instance, an operations manager of a plant really does not want the extra hassle of collecting emissions data for a CSR report, or subjecting his staff and facilities to an audit.

Most often, I think, the dissatisfaction that we may feel with the state of the world or a company's actions is not widely enough shared. Jonathon Porritt (2005), author of Capitalism as if the World Matters, has had many years in the sustainability game (he started the UK's Green Party and chaired the government's Sustainable Development Commission, among other things). He told me: 'Looking at people all over the world today, [in the] rich and poor world, they are not remotely close to a state of mind that would call for anything revolutionary. There's no vast upheaval of people across the world saying, "This system is completely and utterly flawed and must be overturned and we must move towards a different system." There isn't even *that*, let alone an identification of what the other system would look like.'

Likewise, on creating a compelling vision, Porritt concludes that 'we have not collectively articulated what this better world looks like – the areas in which it would offer such fantastic improvements in terms of people's quality of life, the opportunities they would have, a chance to live in totally different ways to the way we live now. We haven't done that. Collectively we've not made the alternative to this paradigm, this paradigm in progress, work emotionally and physically, in terms of economic excitement. We've just not done it.' Taking first steps is something companies are generally much better at, especially picking the so-called 'low hanging fruit'. But the reason these steps so often don't get beyond the pilot or peripheral stage is because the other two factors – dissatisfaction and vision – are not strong enough.

A second model I find helpful was developed by a colleague from Cambridge University, Professor Charles Ainger. He created a matrix of organisational change, with one axis showing a spectrum from top-down commitment to bottom-up passion, and the other plotting discipline and compliance processes through to creativity and innovation through imagination.

Hence, *top-down processes* (reinforcement systems) may include objectives, goals, targets, track-records, measurements, rewards and penalties, while *bottom-up processes* (skills for change) include manuals, standards, procedures, learning, skills, IT and knowledge management systems, protocols, quality management, audits and workshops. On the other hand, *top-down imagination* (a purpose to believe in) includes vision, mission, purpose, strategy and values, while *bottom-up imagination* includes culture, behaviour, inspiration, awareness, stories, meaning, understanding, demonstrations, pilots and trials. Hence, if you are engaging in a CSR change effort, you should ensure that you are working effectively in all four quadrants to raise the chances of success.

Discussion 6.1: Creative Destruction & Change Management

1. What do you think is the most powerful force for creative destruction in the world today? How might it change the business landscape?
2. Think about a change effort that failed in your city, or country or organisation. Using Beckhard and Gleicher's Formula, what was missing?
3. Think about a change effort that was successful in your city, or country or organisation. Using Ainger's Organisational Change, explain how each quadrant was fulfilled.

6.3 Leadership for Change

Jim Collins (2001), author of *Built to Last* and Good to Great, reminds us that companies which went from being 'good' to 'great' did not rely on revolutions, dramatic change programmes or wrenching restructurings: 'Rather, the process resembled relentlessly pushing a giant flywheel in one direction, turn upon turn, building momentum until a point of breakthrough, and beyond.' In some collaborative research with Polly Courtice, Director of the University of Cambridge Programme for Sustainability Leadership, we identified a number of key change processes that are required for sustainability to be advanced.

At a macro level, leaders need to change the prevailing values, culture, incentives, rules and resources. Today's leaders appear to be aware of this crucial role, with 54% of CEOs in a survey by Accenture & UN Global Compact (2010) believing that a cultural tipping point on sustainability is only a decade away – and 80% saying it will occur within 15 years.

At the organisational level, leaders can catalyse change for sustainability through various actions, including innovation, empowerment, accountability, closed loop practices and collaboration. This includes implementing structures and processes for good governance, transparency and stakeholder engagement. But accountability does not have to be all about formal controls. Collins (2001) believes great leaders foster a culture of discipline, saying: 'When you have disciplined people, you don't need hierarchy. When you have disciplined thought, you don't need bureaucracy. When you have disciplined action, you don't need excessive controls.'

Sustainability leaders often adopt principles of cradle-to-cradle production as a way to foster change, thereby internalising externalities and extending these principles to the supply chain. For example, Motorola demonstrated lifecycle thinking in mobile phones, with the launch of the world's first carbon neutral mobile phone – MOTO W233 Renew – early in 2009.

Sustainability leaders also build formal cross-sector partnerships, as well as innovative and inclusive collaborative processes such as Web 2.0 style social networking. Flowers (2008), co-author of Presence (Senge et al., 2005), poses this challenge as a question, saying, 'We know a lot about heroic action because that's in the past of leadership. But how do you have leadership in groups across boundaries, multi-nationally?'

At the human level, leaders catalyse change for sustainability through envisioning, inspiring, empowering and supporting. Sustainability leaders provide a compelling vision, encouraging long term thinking, making strategic investments and promoting intergenerational equity. Immelt (2010) says that 'every leader needs to clearly explain the top three things the organization is working on. If you can't, then you're not leading well.'

According to Robert Greenleaf (2002), true empowerment requires servant leadership. He explains that 'The servant-leader is servant first. It begins with the natural feeling that one wants to serve. Then conscious choice brings one to aspire to lead. The best test is: do those served grow as persons; do they, while being served, become healthier, wiser, freer, more autonomous, more likely themselves to become servants?' Collins (2001) also emphasises the people aspect of change. Good-to-great leaders, he says, 'first got the right people on the bus, the wrong people off the bus, and the right people in the right seats – and then they figured out where to drive it.'

Sustainability leaders also focus on creating a culture and structure that provides peer support and encouragement and recognises achievement. As Immelt (2010) puts it, 'Today, it's employment at will. Nobody's here who doesn't want to be here. So it's critical to understand people, to always be fair, and to want the best in them.'

6.4 Wheels of Change

Another way to think of change in a structured way is using Bob Doppelt's (2010) 'wheel of change', taken from his book Leading Change Towards Sustainability. All organisational change, he argues, comprises seven steps: 1) change the dominant mindset; 2) re-arrange the parts of the system; 3) alter the goals of the system; 4) restructure the rules of engagement; 5) shift the flows of information; 6) correct the feedback loops; and 7) adjust the parameters. Doppelt also reminds us that change is like an iceberg, where the most important parts are below the surface. What we usually see are events (crises, daily issues). What makes change really effective is when we change what we cannot see, like patterns of behaviour (trends, recurrences), systemic structures (policies, relationships, norms), mental models (thinking, perspectives, assumptions) and visions (underlying values, beliefs).

Another 'wheel of change' is Peter Senge's (2003) concept of the learning organisation, popularised in his book, The Fifth Discipline. He described the five interrelated disciplines as follows: 'Systems thinking [the fifth discipline] needs the disciplines of building shared vision, mental models, and personal mastery to realise its potential. Building shared vision fosters a commitment to the long term. Mental models focus on the openness needed to unearth shortcomings in our present ways of seeing the world. Team learning develops the skills of groups of people to look for the larger picture that lies beyond individual perspectives. And personal mastery fosters the personal motivation to continually learn how our actions affect our world.'

In a follow-up book, Learning for Sustainability, Senge (2006), together with co-authors from the Society for Organisational Learning, apply the fifth discipline model to sustainability. In particular, they emphasise connecting the 'inner' and 'outer' work that needs to be done: 'Connecting the inner changes in how we manage and lead with the outer effects our organisations have on larger systems; connecting the inner changes in mental models and personal visions with the outer changes in management culture; and connecting the inner changes in who we are as human beings with how we act and interact.'

In seeking to create change for sustainability, Senge and his colleagues once again emphasise the interconnected nature of all change processes, and the critical role of business: 'There has never before been a time when the social, ecological and economic conditions that challenge political leaders in any one part of the world have been so interwoven with what is occurring in so many other places. This phenomenon has arisen through the ever-growing web of interconnectedness spun by institutions, especially multinational corporations. Collectively, these organisations determine what technologies are created and how they are applied around the world: which markets develop and which are largely ignored. These institutions determine who benefits from the world economy and who does not.'

Given the interconnectedness, the key to change, Senge believes, is collaboration. To illustrate his point, at the MIT Sustainability Summit 2010, Senge asked the question: What would it take to get rid of disposable cups? Who would have to work together to eliminate disposable cups? The answers suggested include everyone from Starbucks and its competitors to paper manufacturers, food service providers, recyclers and municipal governments. To make real headway on really tough sustainability issues is a 'massive undertaking in collaboration'. What's more, the parties that need to collaborate often aren't naturally inclined to.

Senge concludes that a good-guy/bad-guy mentality can be a barrier to such collaboration. 'You've got to wake up and say "We're all part of the system". You know who is causing the destruction of species? You and me. You know who's causing the huge waste problems around the world? You and me.' Once you become more open-minded to this possibility, then you can look for collaborative solutions. 'Look for small steps of things you can do together with people with whom you traditionally would never have cooperated — and do something useful, no matter how small.'

Discussion 6.2: Leadership & Systems Change

1. What are the strengths and weaknesses of Greenleaf's servant leadership concept? Can you think of any business leaders that embody this approach?
2. Can you think of any examples of social, environmental or ethical behaviour changes that involved Doppelt's 'below the surface' processes?
3. Using Senge's approach to interconnectedness, explore what it would take (and who would have to collaborate) to eliminate all waste from the smart phones life cycle.

6.5 Theory U

The theme of collaboration was echoed by Otto Scharmer (2007) in his book, Theory U. Theory U, which was given a preview in Presence (Senge et al., 2005), explores a new way of creating change through leadership. The Presencing Institute declares that 'this time calls for a new consciousness and a new collective leadership capacity to meet challenges in a more conscious, intentional, and strategic way. The development of such a capacity would allow us to create a future of greater possibilities. We know a great deal about what leaders do and how they do it. But we know very little about the inner place, the source from which they operate. And it is this source that 'Theory U' attempts to explore.'

Theory U – or Presencing as it is also known – is depicted visually as moving down the one side of a 'U' and back up and out the other side. Essentially, it is a process of letting go assumptions, listening to others, being open to something new and unexpected emerging, and then testing the new vision through pilots, before rolling out the solution. According to Scharmer, presencing is an antidote to a prevailing feeling of powerlessness in the world, of being a victim of forces beyond our control. He told me that 'it actually goes all the way up, including to the boardroom levels where you are chased by Wall Street. For those in leadership situations in business or government, the demands are so enormous that this deeper space of reflection becomes one of the anchor points that you use every day to be more effective' (Scharmer, 2008).

Scharmer (2008) sees this as part of a bigger story, in which the way in which we can make change happen in the world is changing: 'If you look at the evolution of capitalism really, we have three coordination mechanisms that have evolved over the past 200 years: regulation and hierarchy; market and competition; and dialogue and stakeholder negotiations. We have these three, and often the debate in sustainability is, is it regulation or is it markets and innovation or is it stakeholder dialogue and negotiation? But that's what we are already doing, and it's not getting us the results that we need. What we need is more of these three plus a fourth one. The fourth one is disruptive, it's the radical jump that we as a macro system are about to do. We can see it in the area of sustainability and climate change on a small scale. It has to do with seeing and operating from the whole. It means that the coordination is not some kind of market mechanism; it's not somebody's regulation, it is what spontaneously happens.'

There are synergies between CSR 2.0 and Theory U, since the CSR 2.0 is about an approach to CSR that is disruptive and transformative. The alignment between these two models is explored in more depth by Van Lawick van Pabst & Visser

(2012), who conclude that 'the U-approach will address many of the barriers to adoption of CSR 2.0. CSR thus becomes a non-linear experiential journey where we learn to work through a transition state of emerging solutions instead of directly or incrementally moving to easy or obvious outcomes, based on previous practices.'

6.6 Mapping the Innovation Territory

Examples of social entrepreneurs like Taddy Blecher of CIDA and many others suggest that sustainability and responsibility innovation is alive and well and, if anything, growing rapidly. Consider what Danone has done with food fortification. Working with Muhammad Yunus's Grameen group in Bangladesh, the company set out to put enough vitamin A, iron, zinc and iodine into a 60 g or 80 g cup of yogurt to meet 30% of a child's daily needs. That proportion was beyond anything Danone had ever attempted. It took a year and dozens of tries to figure out how to do it without the nutrients reacting to one another and souring the yogurt.

The question remains: Is such innovation a random and unpredictable phenomenon, or is there some underlying rationale or theory that we can use to better understand and advance social and environmental innovation? In 2007, a joint Nordic project was launched to focus on CSR as a key innovation driver. The ambition was to develop a systematic approach to CSR-driven innovation to make SMEs break new ground on, for example, low-income markets or strengthening competitiveness by linking innovative solutions to key social or environmental problems. Inspired by the concept of corporate social innovation, social entrepreneurship is now being supported in Denmark by the government-funded Center for Social Economy.

In 2007, I did a research project with my colleagues at Cambridge University on sustainability innovation (Blowfield et al., 2007). In our attempt to 'map the territory', we derived a model that looked at the Enablers, Processes and Agents of sustainability innovation. There were a number of interesting findings.

First, of the four *enablers* of innovation that we identified – government, finance, technology and culture – most of the current efforts are focused either on finance or technology. For example, in the SustainAbility & Skoll Foundation (2007) survey of over 100 social entrepreneurs, 72% cited 'access to finance' as their primary challenge, and much of the report is dedicated to understanding this issue. Furthermore, many typical cases held up as innovation success stories – whether they be General Electric's Ecomagination programme or Vodafone's M-Pesa service – are almost inevitably technology solutions. The corollary of this finding is that the role of government and culture is being neglected. Government, by setting clear, long term policy targets on social and environmental issues like biodiversity, climate change or access to health and sanitation, can create an enabling environment that allows business to innovate. Likewise, fostering a corporate and national culture of innovation – of opportunity orientation rather than risk obsession – is a necessary precondition for innovation.

In the area of *processes*, of which we identified three – individual actions, management systems and tailored approaches – most of the focus has been on individual actions. This mirrored our findings for *agents*, where individuals get all the attention, rather than companies and non-business agents. Hence, the notion of a 'sustainability champion' or a 'social entrepreneur' trains our hopes on the creative, conscience-driven, business-savvy individual. This overlooks the important role of innovation within large companies – what the second in the SustainAbility & Skoll Foundation (2008) series of reports called 'intrapreneurship' – as well as the potential for NGOs like Water and Sanitation for the Urban Poor (WSUP) to be part of the innovative solution.

Volans Ventures (2009) has a different take on the process, which they see happening in 5 stages: 1) Eureka! in which the opportunity is revealed via the growing dysfunction of the existing order; 2) Experiment, a period of trial and error for innovators; 3) Enterprise, during which investors and managers build new business models, creating new forms of value; 4) Ecosystem, when critical mass and partnerships create new markets and institutional arrangements; and 5) Economy, when the economic system flips to a more sustainable state, supported by cultural change.

Another interesting finding from my Cambridge research was that most cited cases seem to be innovation processes specifically targeting sustainability issues, rather than efforts at embedding sustainability principles in core innovation processes. This is a fundamental distinction, because it means that most Research & Development (R&D) going on in companies – and hence most innovation – is not systematically integrating social and environmental criteria. As a result, much like CSR more generally, innovation is a peripheral, project or product specific activity, which is exactly what is preventing scalable solutions from emerging in the mainstream economy. Until CSR is built into every organisational process – and especially into strategic functions like R&D or new product development – we will always be playing on the fringes of the Age of Responsibility.

Discussion 6.3: Theory U and Social Innovation
1. Theory U presents transformative change as a deep psychological process of disruption. How could this be applied to CSR?

2. Research by Blowfield et al. (2007) suggests that government and culture are neglected enablers of sustainability innovation. Why do you think this is the case, and how could it be changed?

3. In an industry or sector of your choice, can you imagine what different innovations might emerge if sustainability was integrated into the core R&D function, as compared with R&D that is incorporated into the sustainability function?

6.7 We Are the Champions

What impact do individuals have on creating change through CSR? This was the topic of my PhD research, the research findings of which are set out in detail my book, *Making a Difference* (Visser, 2008c). In the following paragraphs and pages, however, I give a short summary of what I discovered, using quotations from the research interviews I conducted to illustrate the CSR Change Agents model that I derived.

Let's begin by what we know about individual change agents. Intuitively, we resonate with adages such as Gandhi's 'be the change you want to see in the world', or Margaret Mead's famous quote: 'Never doubt that a small group of thoughtful, committed citizens can change the world; indeed, it's the only thing that ever does.' But beyond these clichés, what do we really know about change in the context of CSR?

The first rich vein of research to mine is the concept of 'champions' within organisations. This goes back to the emergence of human resource (HR) champions in the 1980s. In the 1990s, firms started to apply the idea to environmental management and corporate social performance as well. So what is a CSR champion? Essentially, it is an individual who has the ability to translate a set of personal beliefs about creating a just and sustainable future into an attractive vision for their organisation or sector. Or put another way, they are masters at identifying, packaging and selling social and environmental issues to those in their business that have power and influence to address them.

CSR champions do not always have formal corporate sustainability and responsibility roles. They are often described as being action-oriented, enthusiasts, inspirers, experts, volunteers, communicators, networkers, sponsors, implementers and catalysts. They demonstrate that, contrary to popular belief, individuals have considerable discretion within organisations to pursue and promote agendas that they are passionate about. Crucially, however, they need a combination of knowledge and skills to be successful. For example, they need to be able to gather sufficient credible information to make a rational case for change. They need the ability to tell an emotionally compelling story about a more sustainable future. And they need enough political savvy and interpersonal skills to persuade others, especially leaders, to listen and take action.

Hence, to be effective change agents, CSR professionals need to act as champions. For example, one safety, health and environmental manager I spoke to talked about his role in convincing his organisation (a large chemical company) to phase out the use of various harmful substances, such as CFCs, PCBs and asbestos: 'To me it was a major achievement to convince the 30,000 colleagues of mine in the company to move out of this business before legislation hits us'. But this still doesn't tell us what motivates us to engage with the agenda in the first place. Talking to CSR professionals – by which I mean managers, consultants, academics and NGO representatives working on corporate social, environmental and ethical issues – the desire to create change recurs as a consistent theme, but the way in which they make change happen, and the satisfaction they derive as a result, differs considerably.

For some, as one might have guessed, values play an important role. In particular, CSR is seen as a way to align work with personal values. For example, one manager I interviewed said: 'It's the inner drive, it's the way I am put together, my value system, my belief system, it's my Christian belief, my ethical approach.' Another explained that it is important to have 'inspirational leadership and people who align with your value sets.' For many CSR professionals, their motivation also derives from the fact that sustainability and responsibility are such dynamic, complex and challenging concepts. 'The satisfaction is huge,' said one corporate responsibility manager. 'Because there is no day that is the same when you get into your office. It's always changing, it's always different.' Another reflected that CSR 'painted a much bigger picture' and is 'just as holistic as you want it to be. It requires a far broader vision.'

6.8 Types of CSR Change Agent

These two factors – values alignment and the CSR concept – were fairly cross-cutting motivators that I identified in my research. However, it was also possible to distinguish four fairly distinctive types of CSR professional, based on how they derive satisfaction from their work. In practice, every individual draws on all four types, but the centre of gravity rests with one, representing the mode of operating in which that individual feels most comfortable, fulfilled or satisfied.

Experts

The first type of CSR change agent is the Expert. Experts find their motivation though engaging with projects or systems, giving expert input, focusing on technical excellence, seeking uniqueness through specialisation, and pride in problem solving abilities. To illustrate, one Expert-type CSR professional said: 'There were a couple of projects that I did find very exciting ... It was very exciting to get all the bits and pieces in place, then commission them and see them starting to work.' Another Expert said: 'I usually get that sense of meaning in work when I've finished a product, say like an Environmental Report and you see, you know, I've really put in a lot and here it is. Or you have had a series of community consultations and you now have the results.'

Facilitators

The second type of CSR change agent is the Facilitator. Common themes among Facilitators are the derivation of motivation from transferring knowledge and skills, focusing on people development, creating opportunities for staff, changing the attitudes or perceptions of individuals, and paying attention to team building. For example, one Facilitator-type CSR professional said: 'If you enjoy working with people, this is a sort of functional role that you have direct interaction, you can see people being empowered, having increased knowledge, and you can see what that eventually leads to.' Another Facilitator explained that 'the part of my work that I've enjoyed most is training, where I get the opportunity to work with a group of people – to interact with people at a very personal level. You can see how things start to get clear for them, in terms of understanding issues and how that applies to what they do.'

Catalysts

The third type of CSR change agent is the Catalyst. For Catalysts, motivation is associated with initiating change, giving strategic direction, influencing leadership, tracking organisational performance, and having a big picture perspective. One Catalyst-type CSR professional claimed: 'The type of work that I'm doing is ... giving direction in terms of where the company is going. So it can become almost a life purpose to try and steer the company in a direction that you believe personally is right as well.' Another said: 'I like getting things changed. My time is spent trying to influence people. The real interesting thing is to try and get managing directors, plant managers, business leaders and sales guys to think differently and to change what they do.'

Activists

That is quite different from the fourth type of CSR change agent, the Activist. For Activists, motivation comes from being aware of broader social and environmental issues, feeling part of the community, making a contribution to poverty eradication, fighting for a just cause, and leaving a legacy of improved conditions in society. One Activist-type CSR professional said: 'It's also about the issue of being poor. It actually touches you. You see these people living in appalling conditions, the shacks, the drinking water is so dirty, or there's no running water at all – you see those kind of things, it hits you, and you think: What can you do?' Another confessed: 'I think my purpose here is to help others in some way and leave a legacy for my kids to follow. I could leave a legacy behind where I actually set up a school, a kids' school, or a campus for disadvantaged people, taking street kids out and doing something, building homes for single parents.'

6.9 Dynamics of CSR Change Agents

The different types find some resonance in the broader management and sustainability literature. For example, the Catalyst type clearly draws on a strategic role and applies it to sustainability, bringing in a lot of ideas from change management. Arguably, the Facilitator finds echoes in the servant leadership and sustainability management research. The Activist is probably best described in the work on social and environmental entrepreneurship and there are glimpses of the Expert in much of the more technical scholarship on environmental and quality management.

It is important to note that the typology is dynamic. In the same way that sources meaning in life can vary over the life cycle or other changing circumstances, there is ample evidence to suggest that CSR professionals' default types can change as well. For example, one CSR manager I interviewed seemed to have shifted from being an Activist to a Facilitator (moving from political activism to business training and lecturing); another, from Expert to Catalyst (from laboratory work to strategic policy advice) and yet another, from Expert to Facilitator (from a technical scientist to a team unit manager).

For some CSR change agents (but not all), their formal roles and their type are aligned, as in the examples cited above. Hence, there is a suggestion that either people are naturally attracted to roles that fit with their change-agent types, or that their roles shape the meaning they derive as certain types, or perhaps both. As one manager reminded me, 'In your career or in your work, the manager must be able to swing from the one type to the other.'

Another important influence is organisational context. For instance, one CSR professional made observed that the fact that the 'organisation dynamics of corporates require conformism to the organisational culture, which to a large degree requires maintenance of the status quo ... this makes it difficult for Activists.'

Career stage or life cycle is another important context. One CSR manager said: 'I think that one of the things that you have to bear in mind is how much individual flexibility you get in working environments. I think at an earlier stage in someone's career, no matter what their typology might be, they don't necessarily yet have the luxury of finding themselves in the position that gives expression to their preference.'

6.10 Applying the CSR Change Agents Model

Beyond simply improving our understanding of CSR change agents, there are several practical uses for the typology. The most obvious potential applications occur at an individual and team level, with benefits for CSR managers, managers of CSR teams and human resource managers.

For CSR managers, the typology acts as a prompt for individuals to reflect on their most natural type, or mix of types. This allows them to think about what sorts of roles they derive the most satisfaction from, and to consciously compare this to their formal role. If there isn't a natural fit between their type and their formal role, it may help to explain work frustrations or lacking motivation. As one CSR manager testified: 'It immediately helps me to understand some of the frustrations that I have with some of the areas.'

For managers of a CSR team, the typology helps to cast light on the mix of team members, from the perspective of their different sources of motivation. This can influence the way in which individuals are managed and allocated tasks, as well as the general management style adopted. For example, if there is a predominance of Experts, incentives that recognise quality may be far more effective than for a Catalyst loaded team, where tracking of strategic goals may be more motivational.

If the typology is used as a team-building exercise (i.e. where each individual's self-classification is shared among the group), mutual understanding, sensitivity and team dynamics may improve. The manager of a CSR team may also decide that there is merit in having a balance of all four types represented, which will in turn affect recruitment decisions.

Likewise, human resource managers may use the typology to assist in recruitment, either for targeting a particular type to fit the corporate culture, or a specific role or need in the organisation, or as a way to ensure a balanced distribution of types in the organisation or the sustainability team. It could also be invaluable in designing targeted recruitment campaigns and incentive packages for this niche of professionals. For example, an appeal to values and expertise may be more successful on average than promises of financial reward and job status.

Another link to human resource management is the potential of employee volunteering. Numerous surveys and studies show that there is a compelling business case for involvement in CSR issues generally and employee volunteering more specifically. The basic rationale is that engagement with sustainability improves employee satisfaction and motivation, which in turn enhances loyalty, commitment and productivity and reduces turnover.

However, my research suggests that companies also stand to gain a lot by going beyond the business case, i.e. by justifying their corporate sustainability activities on the basis of values – what some call the 'moral case'. My findings suggest that taking this position (in addition to, rather than instead of, the business case) would tap into a powerful source of motivation, namely the life satisfaction that CSR managers (and in all likelihood many other employees) derive from values alignment.

To conclude, there is a saying in Africa that there are two hungers – the lesser hunger and the greater hunger. The lesser hunger is for the things that sustain life – goods and services and the money to pay for them. The greater hunger is for an answer to the question 'why?' – for some understanding of what life is for.

It is my contention that CSR change agents have a fantastic opportunity to feed the greater hunger, by making a constructive difference and leaving a positive legacy. As existential psychiatrist Victor Frankl (2006) said, 'Each person is questioned by life; and they can only answer to life by answering for their own life.'

Discussion 6.4: CSR Champions & Change Agents

1. The concept of CSR champions suggests that change does not always come from the top. How do you think CSR champions can be more effective?
2. Which change agent type do you think you are, and why? (Expert, Facilitator, Catalyst, Activist)
3. What legacy would you hope to leave behind at the end of your career? i.e. what would you hope to have changed in your society, community, sector or organisation?

CHAPTER 7: CASES IN CSR

7.1 A Little World (ALW)

It is 2006 in the Seiling village of Aizawl District in Mizoram, India. Imagine, for the purposes of illustration, a woman in her 40s – let's call her Niroshini. She is wearing a beautiful purple sari and standing in a short queue. Despite her elegance, Niroshini is, by virtually any definition, poor. She earns $2.50 a day, or $912 a year. In her village, she is one of the fortunate few to have a steady job, sewing clothes. Even so, she has no property, no car, no official identity papers, no proof of address and – at least until today, 6 November 2006 – no bank account. She reaches the front of the queue, which is in the living room of her friend and neighbour, Indira. She is excited, but nervous, as she exchanges greetings and takes a seat at the simple desk.

Indira smiles reassuringly, picks up a mobile phone, and asks Niroshini to speak her name clearly into the receiver, thereby creating a voice imprint. Then she asks Niroshini to look into the lens of the phone and takes a head-and-shoulders photograph. Next, Niroshini is asked to place each of her fingers in turn on the glass lens of a small, handheld device, which is a biometric scanner that records her fingerprints. Finally, as she doesn't read or write very well, Indira helps her to fill in a one-page form, attesting to her name and address, which Niroshini has to sign. The whole process takes about 10 minutes. 'Congratulations!' says Indira, 'you have just opened your first bank account.' Niroshini shakes her head, incredulous. She doesn't know whether to laugh or cry, so she hugs Indira. 'Thank you, sister! Thank you!'

What just happened was the result of a six-year entrepreneurial journey by Anurag Gupta to create a viable method for banking and payments in the villages of India – a technology-enabled microbank that brings basic financial services to the some of the country's remotest and poorest communities. The case was first comprehensively described by Arora & Cummings (2010) and featured in *The Age of Responsibility* (Visser, 2011). It is an excellent example of social entrepreneurship. According to Duvvuri Subbarao, Governor of the Reserve Bank of India, only 40% of the Indian population have a bank account, 10% have life insurance coverage and less than 1% have non-life insurance. Furthermore, a mere 5.2% of Indian villages have a bank branch.

Gupta – like the more famous Grameen Bank founder, Muhammad Yunus – is not a banker. He qualified as an architect in the 1980s and started working in the remote villages of India as a 'barefoot architect'. Then, on 30 September 1993, the most devastating Stable Continental Region (SCR) earthquake in the world hit Latur in the state of Maharashtra, killing over 10,000 people. Gupta was deeply moved and spent the next few years working in the region, designing earthquake-resistant village houses. Indeed, if his story ended there, it would be a remarkable and inspiring tale. But Gupta is a true entrepreneur, always curious, always challenged, always innovating.

Towards the end of the 1990s, the Dot Com boom was sweeping the world and Gupta wanted in on the action. But being a social entrepreneur, he wondered how he could use the burgeoning ICT revolution to make a difference in the villages of India. The breakthrough idea came in 2000, when Gupta was on a visit to Belgium. Being self-employed, he had struggled to obtain a credit card from the banks in India. However, in Belgium, he discovered he could use a smart-card based electronic purse (e-purse) to manage his expenses during the week-long trip. Gupta immediately saw the potential of this offline micro-payment technology for carrying out small transactions in Indian villages. On his return, he registered a company called A Little World (ALW) to see if he could adapt and introduce the e-purse system to India.

Over the next few years, Gupta worked hard on bringing all the necessary players together in a partnership called the Zero-Mass Consortium, including companies such as Proton of Belgium, Gemplus International of France, Giesecke, Devrient and Infineon Technologies of Germany, and ERG Group of Australia. Meanwhile, the rapid rise of mobile phone technology changed their initial focus on smart-cards and instead they developed a P2P (person-to-person) payment product called mCHQ (later re-named mChek) as an application on mobile SIMs, in collaboration with Escotel and later with Airtel. Major Indian banks like ICICI Bank and SBI signed up for mCHQ in 2005, as did VISA.

Despite its success, Gupta was not convinced that mCHQ did enough to tackle financial inclusion. Then fortuitously, in 2006, the confluence of an important change in Indian banking legislation and a breakthrough in mobile phone technology gave him the means to realise his mission. As a result, he spun off mCHQ's technology and business assets into a separate company, and re-focused ALW on his original vision of financial inclusion. The legislative change was the introduction by the Reserve Bank of India of so-called 'Business Correspondent (BC) Guidelines', whereby non-profit making entities are allowed to function as intermediaries (BCs) of mainstream banks in rural areas. So Gupta set up a non-profit organisation called ZMF (Zero Microfinance and Savings Support Foundation) to act as a BC, supported by ALW as the technology partner.

Gupta was already focused on the mobile phone as the key enabler for his vision of micro-banking. By 2006, the new generation of mobile phones included NFC (Near Field Communication) capabilities that allowed easy, wireless connection to peripheral devices like printers and biometric scanners. This eliminated the need for prohibitively expensive, skills-dependent, battery-hungry laptops. However, they faced another problem. With the banks initially insisting that all transactions take place 'live' (in real time) online – and as connectivity is rather haphazard in the villages – transactions were extremely time consuming. 'All 600 people from a village would line up at once, losing a day's wage to wait in line,' recalls Gupta.

This problem was solved by the launch of Nokia's 6131 handsets. Gupta explains the significance of this breakthrough: 'Conventional devices can never meet an unconventional set of challenges. The offline transaction service was possible because the new Nokia 6131 phone that succeeded the earlier Nokia 3220 NFC had 2GB of available local storage on a micro-SD card. The new phone also had bluetooth. This encouraged us to combine the printer and fingerprint scanners (which were separate devices initially), and attach a serial bluetooth interface to the combination device to enable communications with the NFC phone.'

'We were struggling to find an affordable smart card' Gupta said. 'The new Nokia 6131 handsets gave us the most important breakthrough so far: the ability to eliminate smart cards altogether. Instead of the villager's biometric and account data being stored on expensive smart cards, which could be lost or damaged and were costly to replace, we started issuing plain plastic cards that were only used for photo and ID number verification and the mobile phone's memory held the villager's transactional and identification data. We could now hold up to 50,000 customers' data on a single mobile, in a securely encrypted database, thanks to the PKI level of security provided by NFC. The mobile had finally become a core banking branch in every sense.'

With all the pieces of the puzzle in place, the story of Niroshini (the formerly unbanked person) and Indira (the one-person village microbank) became possible. Working with and on behalf of the State Bank of India (SBI), ALW ran pilot projects in the unbanked rural areas of Aizwal (Mizoram), Medak (Andhra Pradesh) and Pithoragarh (Uttarakhand). Each pilot enrolled about 5,000 villagers for no-frills bank accounts, which allowed them to deposit, withdraw and transfer small amounts, as well as to take out microloans. Less than six months later, in April 2007, ALW also piloted the disbursement of government benefits (Electronic

Benefit Transfer, or EBT) through the microbanks and on behalf of six major Indian commercial banks.

The EBT innovation had profound effects. In one village, a women said: 'I used to get my payment from the post office with a delay of several weeks, sometimes months, after repeated trips. Now I get it here, much earlier, in my village.' And because it is an automated, electronic transfer that can only be paid to a fingerprint-authenticated individual, ALW is also cutting out corruption. After switching to the microbanking method, 10-15% of social security pensions remained unclaimed, suggesting the extent of 'phantom beneficiaries' that were defrauding the government before. The microbanks have other benefits too. Because ALW develops a credit history for rural villagers, they will eventually have access to credit at rates 2-3 times cheaper than what they would normally get from informal moneylenders and microfinance institutions. There is also huge potential for what a 2010 Allianz report calls microinsurance.

Four years after its launch, in 2010, ALW was on the tipping point of serious scalability, with 11,000 microbank branches operating in all states of India and serving 5.5 million customers. Part of the reason for its success has been Gupta's relentless pursuit of efficiency and low-cost options, so that today each microbank branch costs less than $85 a month to run and customers are only charged around 5 Rupees (10 cents) a month to use the bank's services. At the time when I interviewed him, in April 2010, Gupta expected ALW to become the largest micro-banking system in the world within 6 months and – pending capital injection of around $60 million – to have set up in 150,000 locations in India over the next 2-3 years.

Impressed? Believe it or not, Gupta is just getting started. He sees the branch network as an enabler to deliver all kinds of other essential services to India's rural poor. Already, he has innovated rechargeable LED light boxes to replace polluting and hazardous kerosene lamps, as well as enhancements to wood or cow-dung burning stoves, using a fan that halves cooking time, halves fuel requirements and almost eliminates the poisonous smoke. Future innovations include water filters, bicycles, televisions, spectacles, radios, medicines and textbooks.

To make all these products affordable, Gupta plans to use a lease-purchase model, whereby costs are divided into weekly instalments for 6, 12, 18 or 24 months, depending on the product. So, for example, a rural villager pays just a few Rupees for one-week's use of a rechargeable LED lamp. At the end of the week, they return it and pay the next week's instalment for an already recharged LED light-box replacement. Using a similar approach, villages will also be able to buy communal toilets, with monthly instalments of just 20 Rupees (40 cents) for a period of 5 or 10 years.

ALW's vision remains ambitious: To touch a billion people through innovative technologies and alliances at the bottom of the pyramid for delivering multiple financial and other services at the lowest cost through mainstream financial and other institutions. Having spent a little time with Gupta, I would not bet against his inspiring vision becoming a reality. ALW is a testimony to Gupta's creativity and to the power of using innovation – not only in technology, but also in partnerships and business models – to tackle some of society's most intractable social challenges.

Discussion 7.1: A Little World

1. What are the characteristics of Anurag Gupta that make him a successful social entrepreneur?
2. What can we learn from the case of A Little World about the role of technology in social innovation?
3. What are some of the benefits and risks of the lease-purchase model that Gupta plans to use for delivering socially beneficial products to the bottom of the pyramid (BOP) markets of India.

7.2 Anglo American

In South Africa, someone dies of AIDS every two minutes and almost one-in-three women aged 25 to 29 – and more than a quarter of men aged 30 to 34 – are living with the HIV virus. On average 17% of employees are infected with the virus. In the face of such a crisis, one positive example of business responsiveness is the multinational mining company Anglo American, which has been at the forefront of the war against the disease for nearly three decades. Their Group Medical Consultant, Dr Brian Brink, was there right at the beginning – in 1980 he was set the task of discovering the first black South African that had contracted the disease – and he is still battling the scourge.

Their great leap forward was in 2002 when Anglo decided to go beyond simple AIDS awareness programmes and to offer their employees free access to the life saving antiretroviral treatments (ARTs) that had become available. In a 2010 interview with the UK's *Telegraph*, Brink recalls: 'We decided to make the treatment available to all of our staff, despite the fact we didn't know what this would cost. Doing this was transformational and it solved a significant problem for the company – the fact that a lot of our staff were dying.'

Today, Anglo American has a much better handle on both the infection rates and the costs. The company estimates that approximately 12,000 of its 71,000 workforce are currently HIV positive. That is still a chronic situation, but compared with where they started – essentially training up two men for each job in the hope that one of them will survive – they have come a long way. The company spends 3.4% of its payroll of the HIV/AIDS programme, a figure that will probably go up as HIV positive employees survive longer. The only way to reverse the upward trend is by stopping the new HIV infections.

When Anglo American first committed to offer the ARTs, it was a time when no other company in South Africa was doing so and when the 'business case' had yet to be quantified. Nevertheless, Brink made the persuasive argument to top management that 'purchasing anti-retroviral drugs isn't a cost that's going to kill the company, it's a cost that's going to protect the company.' They were convinced – as much by the moral case as the intuitively sound economic rationale – and today the evidence proves that Brink was right.

The company calculates that the fully-accounted for cost of treatment is $126 per HIV positive employee. However, people on ART are more able to work. Therefore, absenteeism declines 1.9 days per employee per month, which saves of $96 a month. The use of healthcare services also declines, saving $87. Added to this is the fact that staff turnover and benefits payments are reduced, which saves a further $36 a month. At the individual level, the total savings of $219 per patient per month amount to approximately 174% of the cost of providing treatment.

So, in the end, giving out ART free of charge makes economic sense. But it required Anglo American to take that leap of faith, and to place responsiveness before short-term costs. The financial merits of the decision are clear in retrospect, but the commitment to provide free ARTs was proactive. The story is far from over, as this is literally a lifelong pledge by Anglo American. Furthermore, the company is now dealing with the added burden and complexity of an escalating drug-resistant Tuberculosis epidemic. At least it has the experience of tackling the AIDS crisis to draw on, but it just goes to show that responsiveness is not a once-off CSR tactic; it is a continuous and dynamic commitment to living the company's values.

Discussion 7.2: Anglo American

1. What can we learn from the Anglo American story on HIV/AIDS about 'the business case' for CSR?
2. What do you think a comprehensive HIV/AIDS corporate responsibility programme would have to include to be successful?
3. What was the role of values and leadership in Anglo American's response to the HIV/AIDS pandemic?

7.3 Big Pharma

In 2001, Oxfam launched a campaign called 'Cut the Cost', challenging the pharmaceutical industry to address responsible drug pricing.

In the same year, the Indian pharmaceutical company Cipla cut the annual price of anti-retroviral AIDS drugs to Médecins Sans Frontières (MSF) to $350, as compared with the global industry standard of $1,000, and the Western market price of $10,400.

Cipla also announced its intention to allow the South African government to sell eight of its generic AIDS drugs, the patents for which were held by other companies.

Consequently, MSF put pressure on the five major pharmaceutical companies involved in the UNAIDS Accelerating Access Initiative to match Cipla's benchmark. Merck's response was to cut the price of its HIV/AIDS treatments for developing countries, including offering Crixivan at $600 and Stocrin at $500. Pfizer in turn offered to supply antifungal medicine at no charge to HIV/AIDS patients in 50 AIDS stricken countries. Bristol-Myers Squibb announced that it would not prevent generic-drug makers from selling low-cost versions of one of its HIV drug (Zerit) in Africa. GlaxoSmithKline granted a voluntary licence to South African generics producer Aspen, allowing them to share the rights to GSK's drugs (AZT, 3TC and Combivir) without charge.

However, at the same time, in 2001, 39 of the largest international pharmaceutical companies took the South African government to court over plans to introduce legislation aimed at easing access to AIDS drugs, arguing that it would infringe their patents and contravene the Trade Related Aspects of Intellectual Property Rights (TRIPS) agreement.

The pharmaceutical companies eventually dropped the case following pressure from the South African government, the European Parliament and 300,000 people from over 130 countries who signed a petition against the action.

Here are some facts related to the case:

- Since 1981, 65 million people have been infected with HIV and 25 million have died of AIDS-related illnesses.
- In 2006, 4.3 million new infections were recorded, as were 2.9 million AIDS-related deaths—more than in any previous year.
- Today, more than 39.5 million people are living with HIV—half of them women and girls.

- Funding levels have increased from some US$ 300 million in 1996 to US$ 8.9 billion in 2006.
- In 2001, Anglo American estimated that the $4.5 million a year it cost to treat over 50,000 of its employees and their spouses would be offset from savings due to fewer death benefit payouts and less absenteeism.

Discussion 7.3: Big Pharma

1. Do you think pharmaceutical companies were acting irresponsibly by trying to protect their patent rights?
2. How have the pharmaceutical companies had to change their business model to cope with the pressure to supply cheap life-saving drugs in developing countries?
3. Can you think of any other industries where competition from 'generics' are an issue? How have they dealt with the challenge?

7.4 Big Tobacco

When it comes to using marketing spin to create an image of responsibility, the tobacco industry are past masters. For decades, as research on the negative health impacts of smoking piled up, the industry sponsored a campaign of disinformation and deception. Let's start with what we know about tobacco. According to the World Health Organisation (WHO), 'no other consumer product is as dangerous, or kills as many people. Tobacco kills more than AIDS, legal drugs, illegal drugs, road accidents, murder and suicide combined.' Of everyone alive today, 500 million will eventually be killed by smoking, and while 0.1 billion people died from tobacco use in the 20th century, ten times as many will die from tobacco use in the 21st century.

This is not simply a health issue, but also an economic crisis. According to 2001 figures, in America alone, smoking cost the economy $76 billion in health costs and lost productivity. Smoking-related diseases account for 6% of all health costs in the USA and, on average, a smoker takes 6.16 days of sick leave, as compared with 3.86 for non-smokers. One study showed that, of all the trash collected in the USA in 1996, cigarette butts accounted for 20%. There are indirect costs as well. Every year 1 million fires are started by children using cigarette lighters. In 1997, China's worst forest fire was caused by cigarettes and killed 300 people, as well as making 5,000 homeless and destroying 1.3 million hectares of land. In 2000, fires caused by smoking cost $27 billion and killed 300,000 people.

The debate about the ethics of industry-sponsored research and the practice of misdirection by Big Tobacco reached its zenith when, in 1994, the CEOs of seven of America's largest tobacco companies testified before the House Subcommittee on

Health and the Environment of Congress, all denying that cigarettes are addictive. They lied under oath.

Two years later, an investigative article in Vanity Fair entitled 'The Man Who Knew Too Much' told the true story of Jeffrey Wigand, a research chemist working for a tobacco company, who planned to go on the 60 Minutes TV show to expose the lies and deception of the industry, as represented by the CEOs that he labelled 'The Seven Dwarves'. The story was later turned into the 1996 movie, The Insider, starring Russell Crowe as Wigand, which was nominated for 7 Academy Awards (including Best Picture, Actor and Director) and 5 Golden Globes. Asked in an interview to separate fact from fiction in the movie, Wigand replied: 'Was I followed by an ex-FBI agent in the employ of Brown & Williamson? Yes. Was there a bullet found in my mailbox in January 1996? Yes. Did someone threaten to harm my family if I told the truth about the inner workings of the tobacco company I worked for? Yes. Did the tobacco industry attempt to undermine my integrity with a 500 page smear campaign? Yes.'

The industry took another public relations hit in 2005, with the release of another movie, Thank You for Smoking. It is a satirical comedy that follows the machinations of Big Tobacco's chief spokesman, Nick Naylor, who 'spins' on behalf of cigarettes while trying to remain a role model for his twelve-year-old son. Among the more amusing black humour scenes is one where Naylor and his friends – a firearm lobbyist and an alcohol lobbyist – meet every week and jokingly call themselves the 'Merchants of Death' or 'The MOD Squad'.

Of course, Hollywood represents the lighter end of a far more serious and significant anti-tobacco lobby that has built momentum over the past two decades. We have simultaneously seen a United Nations WHO campaign and numerous governments passing legislation restricting smoking in public places and banning nearly all forms of tobacco advertising. The tobacco companies themselves have been scrambling to regain their lost credibility and to present a more responsible face, seemingly with some success.

For example, companies like British American Tobacco (BAT) have engaged in extensive stakeholder consultation exercises and, since 2001, their businesses in more than 40 markets have produced Social Reports, many of which have won awards from organisations as diverse as the United Nations Environment Programme, PriceWaterhouseCoopers and the Association of Certified Chartered Accountants. BAT has also been ranked in the Dow Jones Sustainability Index, the FTSE Ethical Bonus Index and Business in the Community (BITC) Corporate Responsibility Index, and they funded Nottingham University's International

Centre for CSR. If these accolades and associations are to be believed, 'responsible tobacco' is not an oxymoron after all.

Discussion 7.4: Big Tobacco

1. Do you believe 'responsible tobacco' is an oxymoron? (a contradiction in terms) i.e. can a tobacco company be socially responsible given the impact of its products?
2. Do you think the way Big Tobacco acted to hide their knowledge about the negative health impacts of their products is unique to the tobacco industry?
3. What changes have tobacco companies made in the past decade to become more socially and environmentally responsible?

7.5 BP

When John Browne took over as Group CEO of BP in 1995, it was the same year that Shell was being heavily criticised for its proposed sinking of the Brent Spar oil platform in north Atlantic, as well as its alleged complicity with the Nigerian government in the execution of human rights activist, Ken Saro Wiwa. Browne would have taken special note of former Shell UK Chairman Malcolm Brinded's warning that 'the days when companies were judged solely in terms of economic performance and wealth creation have disappeared. For us, Brent Spar was the key turning point. It was a wakeup call, not only to Shell, but to the entire oil and gas industry, and to industry in general.'

Indeed, Browne would have been all too aware of a few skeletons in BP's own closet at that time. Most notably, the fact that between 1993 and 1995, BP's contractor Doyon Drilling was engaged in illegally dumping of hazardous wastes on Endicott Island, Alaska, injecting it down the outer rim of the oil wells. When BP learned of the practice and failed to report it to the authorities, it contravened the so-called U.S. Superfund legislation (the Comprehensive Environmental Response, Compensation and Liability Act). After a few years of legal wrangling, in 1999, BP agreed to a settlement of $22 million, which included a criminal fine of $500,000 (the maximum), $6.5 million in civil penalties, and BP's establishment of a $15 million environmental management system at all BP facilities in the U.S. and Gulf of Mexico engaged in oil exploration, drilling or production.

Another 'skeleton' was the allegations in 1996 of complicity in human rights abuses in Colombia. It was a seminal lesson for Browne, as he later recalled at an EIB Seminar on Business and Human Rights in London (4 June 2010): 'BP entered that country ... seeking a tantalising prize of rich resources amidst violent insurrection, a polarised society and dark undercurrents in politics ... Clearly, security was a challenge but we assumed we had the answer – a thick barbed wire fence with security personnel and, if necessary, the help of the Colombian Army. What we hadn't realised was that a fence keeps you in as well as others out ... BP's presence – in particular, the payment of an unfortunately named dollar-per-barrel 'war tax' – was viewed as giving tacit support to a brutal military regime in which human rights were being trampled underfoot ... For the first time I realised that the company's brand, its reputation, and ultimately its value, had been laid on the line because of our failure to fully appreciate our human rights responsibilities.'

Browne also inherited BP's membership of the Global Climate Coalition (GCC), a powerful lobby group created in 1989 shortly after the UN created the Intergovernmental Panel on Climate Change (IPCC). The GCC actively attempted to undermine emerging climate science and to derail international policy development. To his credit, Browne withdrew BP's membership in 1997. In a ground breaking speech at Stanford University, he stated that 'the time to consider the policy dimensions of climate change is not when the link between greenhouse gases and climate change is conclusively proven, but when the possibility cannot be discounted and is taken seriously by the society of which we are part. We in BP have reached that point.' As Petroleum Economist put it, 'BP had left the church.'

Within the space of a few years, step by step, Browne began to transform the image of BP. One of the great watershed moments was in 1998 when Browne threw down the gauntlet to BP and the oil industry, promising to cut emissions from its own operations by 10% from 1990 levels by 2010, which was more than the average Kyoto Protocol country targets and certainly more than any other major oil company had committed to up until that time. In fact, they achieved the target four years later, eight years ahead of the target and at no net cost to the company.

Browne seemed to doing and saying everything right and was slowly but surely becoming the darling of environmentalists that were desperate for signs of reform among the big brands. One crucial tool was public reporting. BP, having merged with Amoco at the end of 1998, issued their first Environmental and Social Report in 1999. In his CEO statement, Browne made encouraging statements like 'the environment is the primary challenge facing the industry' and 'there is no trade-off between our commercial and financial performance and our standards of care'.

To reassure the market analysts, he promised 'to apply to our performance in these areas with the same rigour we apply to the delivery and reporting of our financial performance – measuring, setting targets as part of an overall performance contract and reporting openly on how we have done, using independent, external auditing and verification processes wherever possible.' I can, to a certain extent, attest that these were not just flowery words, as KPMG had, during the time I was working for them, been helping BP to design an internal carbon emissions trading scheme – a progressive step for any company, let alone an oil major.

By 2000, Browne felt the company had earned enough public kudos to risk a major rebranding of BP. The company reportedly spent $7 million in researching the new 'Beyond Petroleum' Helios brand and $25 million on a campaign to support the brand change. When Browne justified the exercise by saying 'it's all about increasing sales, increasing margins and reducing costs at the retail sites', perhaps more people should have tempered their expectations. Certainly Greenpeace wasn't duped, concluding at the time that 'this is a triumph of style over substance. BP spent more on their logo this year than they did on renewable energy last year.'

Antonia Juhasz (2008), author of The Tyranny of Oil, is similarly sceptical, claiming that at its peak, BP was spending 4% of its total capital and exploratory budget on renewable energy and that this has since declined, despite Browne's announcement in 2005 of BP's plans to double its investment in alternative and renewable energies 'to create a new low-carbon power business with the growth potential to deliver revenues of around $6 billion a year within the next decade.'

Sceptics notwithstanding, Browne had earned his new title as the 'Sun King' and his reputation was not only being earned with green stripes. BP was also one of the first companies to declare their support for the Publish-What-You-Pay campaign. However, after BP decided unilaterally to publish the value of taxes paid to the Angolan government, the state-owned oil partner, Sonangol, accused the company of breaking confidentiality clauses in its agreements and threatened to terminate its contracts. As a result, under advice from Browne, the UK's Blaire government launched the Extractive Industries Transparency Initiative (EITI) in 2002 at the World Summit for Sustainable Development in Johannesburg to tackle the so-called 'resource curse' and ensure 'the verification and full publication of company payments and government revenues from oil, gas and mining.'

Success or failure is all about timing. If Browne had been a politician and had retired in 2003 after two four-year terms of office, he may still have been covered in glory, with his Sun King crown firmly in place. After all, he had turned BP into an oil major – perhaps even a competitor for Exxon Mobil – by creating a lean, mean, green machine. Instead, he hung onto power long enough to face the consequences of his own legacy of cost-cutting and rhetoric mongering. As a result, between 2004 and 2007, the proverbial chickens came home to roost. Browne was left tarred and feathered.

While Browne had clearly prioritised environmental issues from the start, he had reason to be less nervous about health and safety risks. The last really serious BP incident had been in 1965, when Britain's first offshore oil rig, the Sea Gem, had capsized, killing thirteen crew. But that complacency, if indeed it existed, all changed on 23 March 2005, when an explosion and fire at BP's Texas City refinery killed 15 workers and injured more than 170 others. An investigation into the accident by the Occupational Safety and Health Administration (OSHA) ultimately found over 300 safety violations and fined BP $21 million – the largest fine in OSHA history at the time.

The story did not end there. In 2007, in a separate settlement related to the explosion, BP pleaded guilty to a violation of the federal Clean Air Act and agreed to pay a $50 million fine and to make safety upgrades to the plant. Complying with the terms of the OSHA settlement was also a condition of the Justice Department agreement. Blast victims challenged the plea deal, arguing that the fine was 'trivial' in light of BP's $22 billion profits in 2006. Two years later, in 2009, OSHA imposed an additional $87 million in fines, claiming that the company had not completed all the safety upgrades required under the agreement and alleging 439 new 'wilful' safety violations. Predictably, BP announced its contestation of the fine.

A few months after the Texas City explosion, BP's Thunder Horse semi-submersible oil platform in the Gulf of Mexico almost became fully submersible after Hurricane Dennis hit. The rig had been evacuated before the storm, so no one was injured, and when the platform was re-stabilized, no serious damage had been incurred. However, during repairs, it was discovered by chance that the underwater manifold was severely cracked due to poorly welded pipes. While this was not the cause of the platform's instability, the rig's design engineer admitted that it could have caused a catastrophic oil spill.

In March 2006, BP was not so 'lucky', when it was found to be criminally liable for a corroded pipe on Alaska's North Slope that leaked 200,000 gallons of oil. In August of the same year, another leak appeared and the entire Prudhoe Bay operation had to be shut down. During the investigation, a federal grand jury subpoenaed records from a Seattle engineering firm that had been hired by Alaska to evaluate BP's pipeline-maintenance record and uncovered a draft report that was highly critical of BP, but somehow turned into a final report that was largely complimentary. Member of Congress, Rep. Jay Inslee, concluded that BP had made a 'wilful, conscious decision' to 'quash that information from the public.'

By the time of Browne's undignified exit into the wings of BP history in 2007, he was widely criticised for the dual crimes of 'greenwashing' and instilling a cost-cutting culture that was the root cause of BP's spate of safety and environmental incidents. Even the new CEO, Tony Hayward, a year before taking over, admitted that BP had 'a management style that has made a virtue of doing more for less.' In a twist of ironic fate, in June 2010 Browne was appointed efficiency czar by the new British coalition government and tasked with finding £6.2 billion ($9.9 billion) in spending cuts. Less than a month later, one of the first casualties was the government's Sustainable Development Commission (SDC), shut down on the same day that the agency released its annual report showing tens of millions of pounds worth of savings from cutting fuel, water, waste and other resources as a result of its actions in government.

After taking over, Hayward quickly showed that he was not one for green rhetoric. Less than six months into the job, he announced BP's plans to invest nearly £1.5 billion ($2.3 billion) to extract oil from the Canadian wilderness – the so-called Alberta tar sands. In fact, Browne had sold BP's interests in the tar sands in 1999, but claims that the tar sands represent the biggest stock of oil outside Saudi Arabia obviously proved irresistible to Hayward. This action earned it a Guardian newspaper headline as 'the biggest environmental crime in history'. In hindsight, they might have reserved that headline for the Deepwater Horizon spill a few years later. Greenpeace claims that it takes about 29 kg of CO_2 to produce a barrel of oil conventionally, but as much as 125 kg for tar sands oil. It also believes the production threatens a vast forest wilderness, greater than the size of England and Wales, which forms part of one of the world's biggest carbon sinks.

Two years later, Hayward's 'back to the petroleum' strategy gained momentum when BP announced that it had shut down its alternative energy headquarters in London, accepted the resignation of its clean energy boss and imposed cuts in the alternative energy budget – from $1.4 billion (£850 million) in 2008 to between $500 million and $1 billion in 2009. Bizarrely, Hayward used this occasion to stress that BP remained as committed as ever to exploring new energy sources. No wonder Grist journalist Joseph Romm responded with an incredulous rant: 'Seriously, they gut the program and claim it is "reinforcement" of their commitment. Perhaps BP stands for "Beyond Prevarication" or "Beyond Pinocchio".'

Today, all of this history – the story of Browne, of Hayward and of BP – appears like a dress rehearsal for the main event. I am referring of course to the catastrophic 2010 Gulf of Mexico oil spill. On 20 April, an explosion and fire on the

Deepwater Horizon drilling rig killed 11 workers and injured 17 others. The rig sank and the incident caused the wellhead on the ocean floor to start gushing oil. After numerous failed attempts, the oil flow was stopped for the first time with a temporary cap 87 days and 184 million gallons later. Time will tell whether this temporary fix – and the proposed permanent 'solution' in the form of relief wells – will prove conclusive.

Understandably, at the time of writing, estimates of the scale and consequences of the disaster still vary considerably, and will continue to change over time. However, on 17 July, the Guardian newspaper gathered the following numbers from the Associated Press and Friends of the Earth: $30 billion cost to BP (including a $20 billion damages fund); 444 sea turtles and 1,387 birds found dead; 572 miles of shoreline oiled; 2,700 square miles of visible slick; 83,927 square miles closed to fishing; 1.82 million gallons of dispersant chemicals applied; and a $336 million market value of the spilled oil. One number that is hard to forget is that BP's share price lost 50% of its value in 50 days. Not surprisingly, speculation was rife about whether the company would survive intact, or whether it would be taken over, merged or disaggregated.

The lawsuits also started coming thick and fast. By 16 June, it faced more than 225 lawsuits in 11 U.S. states. According to Bloomberg, investors in three states, including Louisiana and Alaska, sued BP's board of directors for allegedly causing more than $50 billion in shareholder losses by failing to implement safety policies that would have prevented the spill. In a separate class-action lawsuit in Florida, the company was accused of 'a pattern' of criminal acts including fraud. A month later, on 16 July, BP announced that it had already paid $201 million to more than 32,000 claimants, including fishermen, who received $32 million, and shrimpers, who received $18 million. In addition, about $77 million was paid for loss of income to a variety of occupations including deckhands and employees of seafood processing plants and other businesses.

At one point during the crisis it emerged that BP admitted using Photoshop to exaggerate oil spill command centre activity. The oil spill had become a story that will run and run, like a snowball changing shape, gathering weight and increasing destruction as it goes. Many questions for remain unanswered: Will BP's reputation recover? Will the sacrifice of Hayward be enough? Will this be the worst environmental disaster in history? Will we look back on the Macondo blowout as the inadvertent tipping point that ushers in a new low-carbon future?

Discussion 7.5: BP

1. What lessons about sustainability leadership can we learn from John Browne's story?
2. How do you think Hayward handled the Deepwater crisis better? Did he deserve to get fired?
3. Do you think the oil companies will help or hinder the transition to a low-carbon economy? Will they survive?

7.6 Cabbages & Condoms

On HIV/AIDS, one of the most remarkable stories of responsiveness comes out of Thailand, and makes the point that business responsiveness is not only the purview of large multinationals. This story is about the Population and Community Development Association (PDA) and its Founder and Chairman, Mechai Viravaidya. PDA is one of Thailand's largest and most successful private, non-profit development organisations. Among the many programmes and projects it runs is the quirkily-named Cabbages & Condoms restaurant in Bangkok, a social enterprise dedicated to raising awareness on family planning and HIV/AIDS.

Through PDA and his other activities, including serving as a Senator in the Thai government and Chairman of some of Thailand's biggest companies, Viravaidya has played a pivotal role in Thailand's immensely successful family planning program, which saw one of the most rapid fertility declines in the modern era. The rate of annual population growth in Thailand declined from over 3% in 1974 to 0.6% in 2005, and the average number of children per family fell from seven to under two.

Viravaidya was also chief architect in building Thailand's comprehensive national HIV/AIDS prevention policy and program. This initiative is widely regarded as one of the most outstanding national efforts by any country in combating HIV/AIDS. By 2004, Thailand had experienced a 90% reduction in new HIV infections. In 2005, the World Bank reported that these preventative efforts helped save 7.7 million lives throughout the country and saved the government over $18 billion in treatment costs alone. As a result of his outstanding work, in 1999 Viravaidya was appointed the UNAIDS Ambassador.

In 2010, as part of my CSR Quest world tour, I conducted an interview with Viravaidya and was most intrigued by his answers. I started by asking him what demonstrable impact social enterprises can make to society's problems, using Cabbages & Condoms as an example, to which he replied: 'We originally referred to the Cabbages & Condoms Restaurant as a "Business for Social Progress", which is commonly known as a social enterprise in the West. The profits from our restaurant directly benefit our NGO, the PDA. The impact has included promotion of family planning in Thailand, HIV/AIDS prevention through condom usage, poverty alleviation, and education in North Eastern Thailand. The restaurant has been a successful social enterprise, and we always encourage civil society leaders in Asia to set one up to help maintain financial sustainability, including with youth groups.'

What are the barriers to scaling up social enterprises like Cabbages & Condoms? 'The biggest hurdles to social enterprise,' said Viravaidya, 'are good ideas and funds for large-scale endeavours. It is best for new organisations looking at establishing a social enterprise to seek advice from the business community and start small.' Conscious of his extensive involvement in politics, I was curious on his view of government's role in enabling social enterprises to succeed. He said this varies from country by country. Whereas in the UK, the government is quite active in its support, the Thai Government currently plays no role in incentivising social enterprise. What's more, Viravaidya would like to keep it like that: 'The best thing they can do is to kindly stay out of the way.'

So why use business as the vehicle for responding to the needs of society? Why not just have a charity? 'We needed to ensure that the poverty eradication and education initiatives performed under our NGO had long-term sustainability and were not entirely dependent on outside donations,' explained Viravaidya. 'The social enterprises we have established have earned approximately $150 Million over 25 years and fund approximately 70% of our development endeavours. We would not have been able to accomplish half as much as we have without our social enterprises.'

Discussion 7.6: Cabbages & Condoms
1. What were key success factors in Viravaidya's impact on HIV/AIDS in Thailand?
2. What role do you think governments should play with respect to social enterprises?
3. Cabbages & Condoms made a small contribution to Thailand's fall in fertility rates. What other key ingredients do you think helped to achieve these results?

7.7 Cadbury

The early hours of 19 January 2010 marked the end of an era – the end of Cadbury's 186 years of independence, as it accepted the $21.8 billion takeover offer from American food giant, Kraft. A few days later, Todd Stitzer resigned as chief executive, leaving behind a legacy built up by Cadbury over nearly 200 years, with hints at more widely expressed fears that the takeover may sound the death knell for the family values that came to define the company. The business that Cadbury became – with annual sales in excess of $8 billion from operations in 60 countries, with 45,000 employees and with some of the world's most recognised brands, from Dairy Milk Chocolate, Flake and Creme Eggs to Clorets, Stimorol and Halls – is a far cry from where it all started.

The story begins in Victorian England when John Cadbury – one of Richard Tapper Cadbury's ten children – opened his first shop in 1824 in Birmingham, alongside his father's drapery and silk business. Cadbury's store sold tea, coffee, hops, mustard and the luxury commodities of cocoa and drinking chocolate, which he prepared by grinding cocoa beans from South and Central America and the West Indies using a mortar and pestle. Although cocoa and drinking chocolate had been available in England since the 1650s, the associated price tag ensured that they remained the preserve of the British elite.

Within this niche market, John Cadbury's product experimentation and flare for promotion ensured that his business flourished. His first advert, placed in the Birmingham Gazette, stated that 'John Cadbury is desirous of introducing to particular notice "Cocoa Nibs", prepared by himself, an article affording a most nutritious beverage for breakfast.' In 1831, he opened his first factory and by 1842 was selling sixteen lines of drinking chocolate and cocoa in cake and powder forms.

Not that we would have recognised those products by today's standards. For a start, they were sold in blocks, a little of which had to be scraped into a cup or saucepan and mixed with hot milk or water. More significantly, however, cocoa and drinking chocolate were balanced with potato starch and sago flour to counter the high cocoa butter content, with any number of other 'healthy ingredients' added for good measure. John Cadbury's son, George, later described the drinking chocolate as a 'comforting gruel'.

Business continued to prosper, not least due to the reduction in taxes on imported cocoa beans in the mid 1850s, introduced by Prime Minister William Gladstone. Cocoa and drinking chocolate was now within reach of the mass public. At the same time, Cadbury received a Royal Warrant as 'manufacturers of cocoa and chocolate to Queen Victoria'.

Despite his early commercial success, John Cadbury was not all about business. He grew up in the tradition of the Society of Friends, or Quakers, a nonconformist religious group formed in the 17th century. The Quakers became known in rapidly industrialising Britain for using business to achieve social aims, such as reducing poverty, tackling injustice, improving working conditions and encouraging temperance (abstinence or reduced dependence on alcohol). Cadbury was one of these conscience-driven business pioneers, alongside fellow Quakers like Joseph Rowntree, Samuel Tuke and Joseph Fry. In fact, many well known organisations claim a seminal influence by the Quakers, including Amnesty International, Barclays Bank, Carr's, Cornell University, Friends Provident, Greenpeace, Oxfam and Sony.

As a member of the Temperance Society, one of Cadbury's primary motivations for selling tea, coffee and hot chocolate was to provide a mass-market alternative to alcohol, which was widely regarded as an exacerbating factor, if not a root cause, of poverty and deprivation among the working classes. Cadbury also led a campaign to ban the use of child labour for sweeping chimneys and set up the Animals Friend Society, a forerunner of the Royal Society for the Prevention of Cruelty to Animals (RSPCA).

After retiring in 1861 due to ill health, Cadbury spent much of the remaining third of his life dedicated to civic and social work in Birmingham. However, his legacy did not end there. Many of his social reform ideas were taken up and extended by his sons, Richard and George, when they took over the business, aged 25 and 21.

In their first few years, the business nearly went under. In the end, however, a combination of technological changes and product innovation saved them. After visiting a competitor's factory (the Van Houten's) in the Netherlands, they introduced a new cocoa press that removed cocoa butter from the beans, leaving a more palatable essence that became the drinking chocolate we know today. The excess cocoa butter after pressing was made into 'eating chocolate', which soon became Cadbury's flagship product: dairy milk chocolate.

The Cadbury brothers are credited with introducing many of England's most progressive workplace practices. One of their most significant actions was to move their factory in 1879 from the grimy city of Birmingham to Bournville in the English countryside – to create a 'factory in a garden'. There, they provided workers with numerous facilities that exceeded Victorian standards of the day, including heated dressing rooms, kitchens, gardens, sports fields and swimming pools. The company even organised leisure outings and summer camps for employees.

Working conditions were also progressive. Cadbury was the first company in England to introduce the five-and-a-half day working week. They were also pioneers in providing medical and dental facilities, offering a pension scheme and shutting the factory on bank holidays. Initially, they provided houses for senior staff only, but George Cadbury's vision soon grew more ambitious. 'If each man could have his own house, a large garden to cultivate and healthy surroundings,' he reflected, 'then there will be for them a better opportunity of a happy family life.'

And so the Bourneville Village project was conceived: 120 acres of land near the factory was acquired in 1895 and houses built for Cadbury's workers and others in the area. The motivation was not only to provide affordable, convenient accommodation for employees, but also to prevent any less sensitive developers from acquiring the land and creating an urban sprawl. In 1900, Cadbury handed over the land and houses to a Trust, which still administers the real estate, separate from the company, but with Cadbury's managers as trustees.

Reforms continued throughout the 20th century, under the leadership of the Cadbury brothers and successive generations of the family. In 1905, 'works committees' were set up to deal with matters affecting employees, which became democratically elected 'works councils' in 1918. These councils had equal representation from management and workers and focused on working conditions, health, safety, education, training and social activities for employees. In 1969, the councils were unionised and the tradition of employee participation in labour relations continues to this day.

Not surprisingly, given their progressive track record on workplace issues, Cadbury also played a key role in addressing issues of fair trade and supply chain ethics. As far back as 1905, the Cadbury brothers stopped buying cocoa from São Tomé because of poor labour conditions. As a result, they helped found the cocoa industry in Ghana. A hundred years later, Cadbury launched its first Fairtrade labelled chocolate, which was the culmination of a whole raft of responsible supply chain management initiatives, including the Cadbury Cocoa Partnership (addressing child labour in Ghana and Cote d'Ivoire), the Roundtable on Sustainable Palm Oil (RSPO), the International Cocoa Initiative (ICI) and the Better Sugar Cane Initiative (BSCI).

Through these and various internal programmes, Cadbury set itself a 2010 target of 'sustainably sourcing' at least 50% of their key agricultural raw materials (cocoa, sugar, mint, palm oil, gum arabic, liquorice, hazelnuts, almonds and raisins). They also required all 3,000 key suppliers to acknowledge Cadbury's Human Rights and Ethical Trading (HRET) policy and to register on the Supplier Ethical Data Exchange network (SEDEX), a not-for-profit organisation that uses the latest technology to enable companies to maintain and share data on labour practices in the supply chain.

Prior to their takeover by Kraft, Cadbury's HRET policy was just one of nineteen corporate policies covering various aspects of responsible business practice, from environment, health and safety to marketing, ethics and stakeholder engagement. Beyond these internal commitments, Cadbury also made very public commitments to responsibility, for example as a signatory to the Courtauld Agreement, WRAP (Waste & Resources Action Programme), the UN Millennium Development Goals (via the Business Call to Action) and the UN Global Compact.

Cadbury regularly assessed their performance across all these numerous programmes by allowing themselves to be rated on Business in the Community's (BITC) Corporate Responsibility Index, the Dow Jones Sustainability Index, the FTSE4 Good Index and the Carbon Disclosure Project's Climate Change Leadership Index. They also used the Global Reporting Initiative's (GRI) G3 Sustainability Reporting Guidelines to produce annual Corporate Responsibility & Sustainability reports.

In one of these reports (2007/08), after consulting with over 400 different stakeholders, they concluded that the issues of most concern – i.e. with high potential impact on the company and high societal and investor interest – were food safety, health (including nutrition and obesity), financial performance, environment impacts and sustainable sourcing (plus 10 other issues rated lower).

Responding to the health issue, Cadbury introduced a 12 Point Nutrition Action Plan in 2004, and a No Genetically Modified Organisms (GMOs) policy in Europe (elsewhere they were 'guided by the customer' and clearly labelled whether products contained GMOs). In response to environmental concerns, Cadbury bought Green & Blacks (an organic chocolate company) in 2005 and launched a 'Purple Goes Green' initiative in 2007, with 'delivery tracks' across six dimensions: energy, packaging, water, transport, waste and effluent and hazardous materials.

All these are just a sample of the social, environmental, ethical and governance management initiatives that are described in their 100+ page Corporate Responsibility & Sustainability report. I expect that John Cadbury, and all the Cadbury generations that succeeded him, would have been justifiably proud of how the company turned out; and especially how its successive leaders and employees took a legacy of Quaker inspired values and built a multinational company with one of the most recognised and trusted brands in the world.

No wonder there was more than a hint of both pride and sadness in CEO Todd Stitzer's parting words. He might have quoted W.B. Yeats (although he didn't) as he handed over the keys to Kraft: 'I have spread my dreams under your feet. Tread softly because you tread on my dreams.'

Discussion 7.7: Cadbury

1. Cadbury was inspired by religious values. Do you think the increase in secularism in the world is having a negative impact on the emergence of values-driven business leaders?

2. There are two acquisitions in the Cadbury story – Cadbury taking over Green & Blacks, and Kraft taking over Cadbury. Other examples are the Body Shop being taken over by L'Oreal and Ben & Jerry's being taken over by Unilever. What impact do you think these takeovers have on the corporate responsibility of the companies involved?

3. Cadbury hints at issues of health and obesity linked to their products. How should companies in the food and drink business – including soda, confectionary and fast food companies – address these concerns?

7.8 CIDA Campus

An example of social innovation in Africa that has inspired me over the years is the story of the CIDA Campus in Johannesburg. When I was still working at KPMG, I met CIDA's co-founder and CEO, Taddy Blecher. He was a privileged white South African who qualified as an actuary and was earning a six-figure salary before he gave it all up to start a social enterprise. His motivation was seeing the extremity of need that surrounded him. 'South Africa today is a sea of youth, with no direction, no guidance. These kids roam around the townships, they grow up in shacks, in squatter camps. So it's actually a huge challenge in this country to try to pull the youth back.'

'Traditionally,' he said, 'people have always looked at Africa as a basket case and they've said Africans are not able to do it for themselves. So when they are sick, we send medicines and when people are starving to death, there's a food drop somewhere, and the food disappears or it goes rotten. As far as we're concerned that's a superficial way of thinking about development. Africans have genius; they have the ability to create for themselves. And it was really around that philosophy that we decided to create the first free University in South Africa. We wanted to prove that it was possible to take a child off the streets who had come through a very disadvantaged education and turn them into a chartered accountant, turn them into a merchant banker, a stock broker, a Java programmer. Because if we could prove that it was possible, we could take the country forward into a new reality.'

CIDA Education Manager, Sandra Musengi explains that 'CIDA is unique in that our students run the campus itself, and obviously that helps us to cut down a lot of costs. We've got our cleaning services, we've got your basic operations. By having our students run the campus, they start to understand basic principles of management, basic principles of operations. As a result, by the time they go out into the workplace, they have already acquired a certain level of skills.' In fact, they leave not only with these skills, but also with a social entrepreneurial mindset. 'When we come to CIDA, we are all from different backgrounds, but something makes us one,' explains Musengi. 'We have this will, we have this drive, we have this passion of wanting to bring change.'

Beyond relying on the students to run the campus, CIDA relies on voluntary contributions from guest lecturers and business suppliers. 'We've had to find a way of getting materials, teachers, money, making it accessible,' says Blecher, 'so that we could reinvent this paradigm of university.' Today, CIDA has thousands of graduates earning tens of millions in salaries this year. 'That's going back to families that had absolutely nothing,' reflects Blecher. 'So we're creating a human chain, it's a human network. And I do believe we could change Africa and the developing world if we could create a human network where everybody's holding hands. It's only really selfishness that stops us from building stable, decent societies.'

'This is really what CIDA is trying to do is be a life raft that pulls people out of the majority of the population to the other side of the river where there is employment and opportunity. And as we pull them, they pull everybody else behind them and that's really what our model is.' And Blecher's vision for the future? 'If we get the support, and people adopt these ideas, we could open up universities, colleges, vocational schools and relevant high schools right across the whole of Africa for next to nothing and they could be fully self sufficient.'

Discussion 7.8: CIDA Campus

1. What can we learn from the CIDA Campus case about the critical success factors of social enteprises?
2. What characteristics does Taddy Bletcher have that make him an ideal social entrepreneur?
3. Education is often regarded as a 'public good' that governments should provide or subsidise. Why did CIDA Campus use the 'private' sector to achieve its objectives?

7.9 Coca-Cola

Coca-Cola received its wake up call to the CSR 2.0 principle of circularity in 2002, when residents of Plachimada, a village in India's southern state of Kerala, accused the company's bottling plant there of depleting and polluting groundwater. Two years later, the local government forced Coke to shut down the plant. In 2006, their situation got worse when a New Delhi research group found high levels of pesticides in Coca-Cola and PepsiCo's locally produced soft drinks, resulting in several Indian states banning their products. Coke denied any wrongdoing, claiming that bore-hole water fed farming was mainly responsible for lowering the water table and that the pollution claims were unsubstantiated. However, the public perceptions battle had already been lost.

Speaking to Time magazine in 2008, Jeff Seabright, the company's vice president of environment and water resources, admitted that Coke had mishandled the controversy. 'If people are perceiving that we're using water at their expense, that's not a sustainable operation,' he says. This realisation resulted in a serious shift in Coke's strategic positioning of its CSR towards tackling water as priority number one. 'It's great that companies used to hand out checks for scholarships or to clean up litter,' said Seabright, 'but increasingly the real relevance is using the company's core competence to address issues that are of societal concern.' And for Coke and the communities in which it operates, the concern is water.

About 2.4 billion people live in water-stressed countries, according to a 2009 report by the Pacific Institute. Water demand in the next two decades will double in India to 1.5 trillion cubic meters and rise 32% in China to 818 billion cubic meters, according to the 2030 Water Resources Group. China – where Coke's sales have been in double-digit figures – is home to roughly 20% of the world's population, but only about 7% of the world's water. That means there are around 300 million people living in water-scarce areas. According to a 2007 World Bank report, water scarcity and pollution reduce China's gross domestic product by about 2.3%. Meanwhile, Coca-Cola sells 1.5 billion beverages a day in over 200 countries, using about 2.5 litres of water to produce just one litre of its products.

Coke realised that it needs to be seen as part of the solution, not part of the problem. As a result, it has put resources into water at an unprecedented scale. In 2007, the company announced it would spend $20 million over five years to help the WWF preserve seven of the world's major rivers. It also set up the $10 million Coca-Cola India Foundation, which began installing over 4,000 rainwater harvesting programmes and providing clean drinking water to 1,000 schools across the country. More significantly, in June of the same year, CEO Neville Isdell flew to Beijing and pledged that his company would become 'water neutral', saying, 'Water is the main ingredient in nearly every beverage that we make. Without access to safe water supply, our business simply cannot exist.'

Coke uses the term 'water neutral' to describe the ratio of ground water usage by any user as against the quantity put back into nature. It is a contentious topic and not everyone believes it is possible. But the scale of Coke's ambition – and indeed the progress it is making towards its targets – is going a long way to advancing the circularity agenda. Speaking in 2009, Coca Cola India's Director of Quality and Environment, Navneet Mehta, said: 'Our target is to neutralise all ground water usage by the company in India by the end of the current calendar year and become water neutral for all products and processes by 2012.' Mehta reported that the company had already achieved a replenishment level of 82% on its annual ground water usage in India and that their ground water usage ratio had improved over 42% between 1998 and 2008.

Having learned the lesson of circularity, CEO Neville Isdell makes it clear that this is not about charity: 'Water is the main ingredient in nearly every beverage that we make. Without access to safe water supply, our business simply cannot exist.' To which Seabright adds, 'We sell a brand. For us, having goodwill in the community is an important thing.'

Discussion 7.9: Coca Cola

1. In what way does Coca Cola's actions on water demonstrate a strategic approach to CSR?
2. Do you think 'water neutrality' is possible?
3. Coca Cola is also a major seller of bottled water. How sustainable is this?

7.10 Corporate Leaders Group on Climate Change

The Prince of Wales's Corporate Leaders Group on Climate Change (CLG) was set up in 2005 as part of The Prince's longstanding and pioneering Business and the Sustainability Programme that the University of Cambridge Programme for Sustainability Leadership has run on his behalf since 1994. As will become clear, CLG is an inspiring example of responsiveness by business, set against the backdrop of a world in which negative, obstructive lobbying by companies to avoid greater regulation by government has become the disappointing norm. In 2005, SustainAbility and WWF released a report entitled Influencing Power, which ranked the world's top 100 companies on the transparency of their lobbying activities and contrasted this with their public statements on CSR. Their conclusion was that that, even among those companies that ranked well in ethical terms on lobbying, 'their focus is generally on defending often controversial positions rather than on how corporate responsibility and related policy activities can support core business strategies.'

Given this reality then, how did a group of UK business leaders change lobbying from a dirty word and a defensive tactic into a force for genuinely progressive corporate sustainability responsibility? It all began in September 2004 when British Prime Minister Tony Blair, in a speech at the Prince of Wales's Business and the Environment Programme's 10th Anniversary event, issued a challenge to business to do more on climate change. In response, a group of CEOs and senior executives – initially representing 13 companies, ranging from HSBC and Sun Microsystems to Shell and Johnson Matthey – formed the CLG under the leadership and patronage of the Prince.

Having set themselves a bold mission 'to trigger the step-change in policy and action needed both to meet the scale of the threat posed by climate change, and to grasp the business opportunities created by moving to a low climate risk economy', the CLG's first action was to deliver a bold and surprising message to the Prime Minister, in the form of an open letter issued in May 2005. First, they stated that investing in a low-carbon future should be 'a strategic business objective for UK plc as a whole'. However, to do this, a debilitating impasse needed to be resolved. They explained that 'the private sector and governments are in a "Catch 22" situation with regard to tackling climate change, in which governments feel limited in their ability to introduce new climate change policy because they fear business resistance, while companies are unable to scale up investment in low carbon solutions because of the absence of long-term policies.'

Citing the International Energy Agency's calculations that $16 trillion dollars of energy infrastructure investment will be needed worldwide over the next 25 years to satisfy the world's growing energy needs, the CLG suggested that this can 'set the stage for enormous commercial opportunities for the UK if it is coupled with a shift to a low carbon economy.' However, to grasp these opportunities, it argued, business needs more, not less, regulation. In particular, the CLG asked Blair to work to extend targets for emissions trading policies to 2025 and thereby to increase market confidence and reduce the risk of investing in low carbon technology.

This savvy strategy of creating 'permission' for politicians to act boldly paid off. In an article in the International Chamber of Commerce International Energy Review, Cambridge University's Aled Jones and Margaret Adey state that 'by developing a high-level political strategy with well-positioned messages, the CLG has "emboldened" senior politicians to make decisions on climate policy that go further than they would have done otherwise. Indeed, UK Government insiders report that the CLG has had a direct impact on policy-making decisions relating to the UK's EU Emissions Trading Scheme National Allocation Plan Targets and the 2006 UK Energy Review.'

Encouraged by this success, the CLG continued to grow its corporate membership and issue ever more ambitious 'consensus statements', either in annual letters to the Prime Minister, or as communiqués at major international climate meetings. For example, in the 2006 Bali Communiqué, signed by the CEOs of 150 global companies, the CLG called for a comprehensive, legally binding United Nations framework to tackle climate change and concluded that 'as business leaders, it is our belief that the benefits of strong, early action on climate change outweigh the costs of not acting'.

Commenting further, Alain Grisay, CEO of F&C Asset Management said: 'Business and investors can only play their part in tackling climate change if governments take decisive action to make this possible. This problem will not get solved through market forces alone in the time that we have left to act, because climate change presents a textbook example of market failure. This means that voluntary targets won't do: business needs a level playing field in order to take on the financial risks that adequate action on climate change requires.'

In 2008, the CLG wrote to UK political party leaders and warned that while the 'global economic slowdown may cause some to question whether the UK can afford to act so boldly ... action cannot be delayed' and that 'decisive action will stimulate economic activity and job creation'. It went on to say that 'incremental change will not do', a message echoed in the Poznan Communiqué issued later that year. In particular, the CLG stated that 'we must deliver deep and rapid cuts in greenhouse gas emissions', adding that 'any credible comprehensive agreement must include mechanisms to reduce tropical deforestation'.

Meanwhile, the UK CLG had spun off an EU Group that was lobbying for bolder political leadership on climate change by Eurocrats. In the lead up to the UN climate negotiations in Copenhagen in 2009, the EU CLG sent an unequivocal message to sitting EU President José Manuel Barroso that a weak deal in Copenhagen would be 'bad for the climate and bad for the economy'. Furthermore, they expressed concern that the EU's 'leadership advantage' on the low carbon agenda was 'under threat' as other countries used their economic stimulus packages to promote investment in green technologies. The EU could 'see itself left behind in the clean technology race when China and other major emerging economies are already making large-scale investments in this area', it warned.

At the UN meeting itself, the CLG launched its Copenhagen Communiqué, endorsed by over 950 companies from more than 60 countries, calling on world leaders to agree 'an ambitious, robust and equitable global deal on climate change that responds credibly to the scale and urgency of the crisis facing the world today'. It went on to say that 'it is critical that we exit this recession in a way that lays the foundation for low-carbon growth and avoids locking us into a high carbon future.'

The Prince was also in attendance at the Copenhagen meeting, urging the world's political leaders to take their responsibility seriously, saying: 'We live in times of great consequence and, therefore, of great opportunity. ... Just as Mankind had the power to push the world to the brink so, too, do we have the power to bring it back into balance. You have been called to positions of responsibility at this critical time. The eyes of the world are upon you and it is no understatement to say that with your signatures, you can write our future.'

Given all of this momentum and business support, the failure to broker a deal in Copenhagen was a bitter disappointment to so many people at so many levels. But this hasn't blunted the CLG's resolve. In 2010, the group was still pressing the EU to go further, faster; in particular, to revise its 20% greenhouse gas reduction target for 2020 upwards 'towards a more ambitious target'. Garrett A.G. Forde, CEO of Philips Lighting said: 'Now is not the time for the EU to step on the brakes and give up its leadership position. ... At Philips we have set the ambitious target to improve the energy efficiency of our entire portfolio by 50% by 2015. We believe we can set even more ambitious targets for beyond 2015 if the EU provides a clear, ambitious and long term commitment towards a low carbon economy.'

The Prince has also not given up on setting a bold, responsive agenda. In a speech to the CLG in July 2010, he once again threw down the gauntlet: 'The challenge that I would like to lay before every single member of the Corporate Leaders Group on Climate Change is simple. Will you stand up and be counted? At every opportunity will you confront the sceptics and tell them they are wrong? Will you challenge your in house economists with the urgent need to define a new paradigm – in other words a macro economics for sustainability? Will you use the power of your brands and the power of your communications and, most of all, your marketing teams to support what the science tells us, and if necessary be prepared to take risks with your reputation to ensure you are on the right side of the debate? If you don't pick up this challenge and inspire many others, particularly those in your supply chains, then I fear the battle will be lost.'

Summing up, the Prince reminds us that responsiveness does not have to be all about doom and gloom or suffering and sacrifices. 'With issues of such magnitude,' he says, 'it is easy to focus solely on the challenges; the worst-case scenarios; the "what-if's" of failure. But take a moment to consider the opportunities if we succeed. Imagine a healthier, safer, and more sustainable, economically robust world. Because if we share in that vision, we can share the will to action that is now required.'

Discussion 7.10: Corporate Leaders Group on Climate Change (CLG)

1. Usually, corporate lobbying favours less government policy intervention, especially if associated regulation will result in expensive investments by business. How did the CLG achieve the opposite?
2. What was the 'catch-22' situation that the CLG was trying to break? Can you think of any other catch-22's between business and government, or between business and civil society, that are holding back progress towards sustainable development?
3. Despite the efforts of the CLG, the global negotiations on climate change have been unable to reach a strong, binding agreement on carbon reduction. Why is this?

7.11 Enron

Enron, formed in 1931, grew into one of the world's leading electricity, natural gas, pulp and paper, and communications companies. Enron was named "America's Most Innovative Company" by Fortune magazine for six consecutive years, from 1996 to 2001 and was on the Fortune's "100 Best Companies to Work for in America" list in 2000. It was also seen as a leader in Corporate Social Responsibility (CSR).

When financial irregularities were discovered in August 2001, the stock price plummeted and by December, Enron filed for bankruptcy.

Enron used an accounting technique called 'mark to market', which allowed it to mark future earnings at today's prices. In addition, they used 'related-party transactions' (i.e. businesses set up and controlled by Enron to whom they 'sold' services) to generate artificial revenues.

Arthur Andersen, Enron's accountants and at the time one of the top five accounting firms in the world, was implicated in the scandal, having shredded key documents, and collapsed in 2002.

Here are the facts: In 2000, Enron had revenues of $111 billion and employed over 20,000 staff. Enron's stock price dropped from $90 to cents in the space of 10 months in 2001. The average severance payment was $45,000, while executives received bonuses of $55 million in the company's last year. Employees lost $1.2 billion in pensions; retirees lost $2 billion, while executives cashed in $116 million in stocks. The dissolution of Andersen resulted in the loss of resulting 85,000 jobs around the world.

Jeffrey K. Skilling, the former chief executive of Enron, pleaded not guilty but was found guilty on 19 counts of fraud, conspiracy, insider trading and lying to auditors. He was sentenced to more than 24 years in prison and a fine of $45 million. Andrew S. Fastow, the former chief financial officer, was sentenced in September 2006 to six years in prison. Kenneth L. Lay, Enron's founder and chairman, was found guilty on 10 counts, but died of heart problems before sentencing was passed.

After a 6-year class action lawsuit by 1.5 million Enron shareholders who bought shares between 1997 and 2001, a settlement was reached whereby investors will receive $6.79 per share (despite many having paid up to $90 per share). The settlement will be paid for by a $7.2 billion compensation fund that was set up following class action lawsuits against the banks that did business with Enron, which shareholders allege were aiding and abetting fraud.

Some good sources of information on this case include: Smartest Guys in the Room (Mclean & Elkind, 2003); What Went Wrong at Enron (Fusaro & Miller, 2002); and Final Accounting (Toffler & Reingold, 2004).

Discussion 7.11: Enron
1. Enron was one of the most respected companies in America. What caused the company to implode and go bankrupt?
2. Apart from legal infringements (fraud, accounting irregularities, etc.), what was the role of leadership and corporate culture in Enron's demise?
3. In the light of the global financial crisis that began in 2008, what lessons did we fail to learn from Enron?

7.12 Freeplay

One innovation coming out of Africa started with music – or to be more precise – radios. It was whilst watching a BBC documentary in April 1994 that Chris Staines first realized the potential of an innovative idea from the British inventor, Trevor Baylis. 'The Clockwork Radio', as the device was first known, was proposed as a means of halting the spread of Aids in Africa through better education. Traditional radio, although widespread, relied on an electrical supply or the availability of disposable batteries – both of which were in short supply across the continent (in Sub-Saharan Africa only 29% of the population has access to electricity). By contrast, the wind-up radio was powered by a spring-charge mechanism that only required human power.

Staines and his business partner, Rory Stear, immediately realised the potential for self-sufficient electronics and so the Freeplay Energy Group (the company formed to develop the idea) was born. The growth of Freeplay, like so much innovation, was only possible through the support of many partners. Starting with a grant from the British government, subsequent investors have included, among others, the co-founders of the Body Shop, Gordon and Anita Roddick. On one of their community trade trips to South America, Gordon Roddick came across a Brazilian native who had obtained one of the Freeplay radios and was making a living selling people chances to listen to the radio in the jungle.

With a core purpose 'to make energy available to everybody all of the time', the company innovated to expand the product range to include a wind-up torches, lanterns, portable 'power-sticks' and mobile device chargers. Most recently, they have also ventured into primary healthcare. 'Freeplay itself is the first company in the world intended to make electronic products for deep-rural environments,' explained John Hutchinson, Chief Technology Officer of Freeplay Energy in Cape Town, South Africa. 'A number of people came to us and said, "Why don't you think of medical products because hospitals in Africa are littered with derelict Western-derived equipment. They require disposable or replaceable elements, and they're just not right for the job." Africa, you know, is a very harsh user environment. Things break in Africa.'

The opportunity came when Hutchinson met a doctor, John Wyatt, a professor of neonatology at University College of London Hospital. 'He works in a very up-tech environment', explained Hutchinson, 'and he had a bit of a crisis where he thought, "I spend so much money on saving one kid's life in this high-tech environment, whereas there are children dying elsewhere for lack of appropriate care".' Wyatt was painfully aware that 95% of infant-mortality happens in developing countris, but they only have 5% of the world's technology available to them. So Wyatt managed to get some seed money from the Halley Stewart Trust and worked with Hutchinson to look at three potential devices – a pulse oxymeter (which measures oxygen saturation in the blood of children), a syringe driver (which assists in giving newborns intravenous nourishment safely) and a jaundice pigment measurer (to determine degrees of jaundice in infants).

In the end, these turned out to be beyond the capacity of Freeplay, but they came up with an alternative product that they felt they could support: an off-grid foetal heart rate monitor. The Washington Post reports that half a million women die annually in childbirth, often from causes that could be prevented with basic care.

Getting an aid like this into the hands of midwives in the developing world could mean the difference between life and death, both for mothers and infants. Together with Philip Goodwin and Stefan Zwahlen, Hutchinson completed the design, which won a 'Design to Improve Life' Innovator's Award. Reflecting on why he continues to innovate for Freeplay, Hutchinson said: 'I've been with this company since the beginning in 1995, and it's still about providing the benefits of modern technology to people who otherwise would be completely excluded.'

Discussion 7.12: Freeplay

1.   What makes Freeplay such a good example of the process of social innovation?
2.   Freeplay has seen several product extensions beyond the initial wind-up radio. Can you think of further extensions they could make, using the same wind-up power principle?
3.   Freeplay is using creative design to address social and environmental needs in Africa. What product or solution would you design to address one of Africa's biggest social or environmental issues?

7.13 GlaxoSmithKline (GSK)

It is more than ten years since 39 of the largest pharmaceutical companies took the South African government to court for trying to offer cheap generic HIV/AIDS drugs (see Big Pharma case study) and the pharmaceutical industry is still trying to rebuild its reputation. As Mail & Guardian journalist Qudsiya Karrim reported for Inside Story in 2010, 'The past decade has been a public relations nightmare for big pharmaceutical companies – and deservedly so, their critics say. Activists and non-government organisations the world over have slated Big Pharma for putting profits ahead of people and vigorously enforcing their intellectual property rights, preventing many from gaining access to life-saving medication. It's an ugly story told repeatedly – in the media, over dinner, at AIDS conferences and during university seminars – and it has earned the pharmaceutical industry an unmatched notoriety.'

But have they learned their lesson? The latest and possibly most responsive action has been from GlaxoSmithKline (GSK). Early in 2009, CEO Andrew Witty announced a major reform in their corporate policy on drug affordability and accessibility. In particular, he said GSK will cut its prices for all drugs in the 50 least developed countries to no more than 25% of the levels in the UK and US – and less if possible – and make drugs more affordable in middle-income countries such as Brazil and India. In addition, GSK will reinvest 20% of any profits it makes in the least developed countries in hospitals, clinics and staff and invite scientists from other companies, NGOs or governments to join the hunt for tropical disease treatments at its dedicated institute at Tres Cantos, Spain.

Many NGOs remain sceptical. Michelle Childs, director of policy and advocacy for Médecins Sans Frontières says that in China, GSK charges over $3,000 for the antiretroviral Lamivudine in the absence of generic competition, while in Thailand, by comparison, another pharmaceutical company, Abbott, offers the Lopinavir/Ritonavir co-formulation for $500. And as for reinvesting profits, Catherine Tomlinson of the Treatment Action Campaign says, 'Wouldn't it simply be better to slash profits and allow for countries themselves to invest in improving health infrastructure? The GSK argument is circular: We charge so much money that we can give you some of your own money back!'

The most interesting and radical move, however, is that Witty committed GSK to put any chemicals or processes over which it has intellectual property rights that are relevant to finding drugs for neglected diseases into a 'patent pool', so they can be explored by other researchers. Explaining this move, Witty said, 'I think it's the first time anybody's really come out and said we're prepared to start talking to people about pooling our patents to try to facilitate innovation in areas where, so far, there hasn't been much progress.' He went on to say, 'Some people might be surprised it's coming from a pharma company. Obviously people see us as very defensive of intellectual property, quite rightly, and we will be, but in this area of neglected diseases we just think this is a place where we can carve out a space and see whether or not we can stimulate a different behaviour.'

On this score, some critics have been cautiously supportive. 'He is breaking the mould in validating the concept of patent pools,' said the head of Oxfam's medicines campaign, Rohit Malpani. 'That has been out there as an idea and no company has done anything about it. It is a big step forward. It is welcome that he is inviting other companies to take this on and have a race to the top instead of a race to the bottom.'

Discussion 7.13: GlaxoSmithKline (GSK)

1. How has GSK changed its business model to respond to society's needs? Is it sustainable?
2. GSK's patent pool is an example of 'wikinomics' and open-source thinking. Can you think of other business examples where this approach has been adopted?
3. What is the role of government in ensuring that pharmaceutical companies like GSK make life-saving drugs accessible, yet also remain profitable?

7.14 Google

Google is a good case because it tells us so much about the role of creativity in creating the Age of Responsibility. There was a time when we all believed that Google was a search-engine company. But that was before the 'Googlemorph' – that phenomenon that Google has perfected of not only changing its spots but almost magically shapeshifting before our very eyes into a completely different creature. Understanding how and why Google manages to do this leads us to some great insights.

It all begins with the leadership – or in this case two audacious Stanford PhD students who decided in 1996 that if they 'made a copy' of the internet and apply a complicated set of esoteric mathematical algorithms, they could make a search experience that was far superior to those offered by the highly respected, heavily funded and well entrenched Yahoo and Microsoft Explorer search engines. From this, we can gather that Google founders Larry Page and Sergey Brin are both highly ambitious and creative. But what happened next? They quickly became the most popular search engine, and once they figured out a clever pay-per-click-based advertising revenue model that worked (note that this came after figuring out the superior product), the money started pouring in. By the end of 2009, they were a $23 billion company.

That 13-year growth story is remarkable in and of itself, but far more interesting for us is how Google has used its success in search and its gargantuan wealth to pursue a much larger mission: to organise the world's information and make it universally accessible and useful. In practice, we see this manifesting in innovations that have changed and continue to shape all our lives: Google Maps, Google Earth, Google Finance, Google Docs, Google Books, Google Scholar, Google Images, Google Translate, Google Alerts – and so the list goes on and on. One of the latest is Google Health, which is in Beta testing and allows you to organise your health information all in one place, gathering medical records from doctors, hospitals, and pharmacies and then allowing you to share the information securely with a family member, doctors or caregivers.

To get an idea of the scale of Google's ambition and creativity, let's look briefly at two specific examples. In 2002, Google was grappling with the question: How long would it take to digitally scan every book in the world? No one knows. As part of this fact-finding mission, Page reached out to the University of Michigan, his alma mater and a pioneer in library digitization. When he learned that the estimate for scanning the university library's seven million volumes was 1,000 years, he told University president Mary Sue Coleman that Google could help make it happen in six. After experimenting with various scanning technologies, Google announced in 2004 that it's Print Library Project – in partnership with the New York Public Library and the Universities of Harvard, Michigan, Oxford and Stanford – would digitise 15 million volumes.

Then, in 2007, just when we'd got used to the idea that Google was not only about search, but also making the world's knowledge archive freely available, it Googlemorphed again. Through its Google.org fund, which it established with $1 billion in 2004, it announced a new strategic goal of RE<C, or renewable energy less than carbon. Translated, the goal is to produce one gigawatt of renewable energy capacity that is cheaper than coal (one gigawatt can power a city the size of San Francisco). 'We are optimistic this can be done in years, not decades,' said Page. 'If we meet this goal and large-scale renewable deployments are cheaper than coal, the world will have the option to meet a substantial portion of electricity needs from renewable sources and significantly reduce carbon emissions. We expect this would be a good business for us as well.' Google's proposal – 'Clean Energy 2030' – provides a potential path to weaning the U.S. off of coal and oil for electricity generation by 2030 (with some remaining use of natural gas as well as nuclear), and cutting oil use for cars by 44%.

What is particularly relevant for the CSR 2.0 Principle of Creativity is how Google has managed to sustain such a culture of innovation. One crucial element is that all engineering staff are allowed to spend one day a week (i.e. 20% of their work time) on their own pet projects. People are given the time and space to be creative. And when you foster such an enabling environment, innovation flows naturally and copiously. At Google, an ideas mailing list is open to anyone at the organisation who wants to post a proposal. Then Marissa Mayer has the task of making sure good ideas bubble to the surface and get the attention they need. What Mayer thinks will be essential for continued innovation is for Google to keep its sense of fearlessness. 'I like to launch [products] early and often. That has become my mantra,' she says. 'Nobody remembers Madonna's Sex Book or the Apple Newton. Consumers remember your average over time. That philosophy frees you from fear.'

So what's next? In 2009, Google Ventures was launched to invest in, among other areas, clean tech, biotech, and health care, all critical focus points for the Age of Responsibility. So watch this Googlemorphing space.

Discussion 7.14: Google

1. What enables Google to remain so creative and innovative?

2. Google has expanded its business to incorporate a variety of social and environmental issues. Do you think this will be a successful strategy?

3. How have the values of the founders of Google shaped the company's impact on issues of sustainability and responsibility?

7.15 Grameen Bank

In 1976, Professor Muhammad Yunus, Head of the Rural Economics Program at the University of Chittagong, launched an action research project, called the Grameen Bank Project, to examine the possibility of designing a credit delivery system to provide banking services targeted at the rural poor.

The project demonstrated its strength in Jobra and was extended to Tangail district in 1979 and several others thereafter, until in 1983, the Grameen Bank Project was transformed into an independent bank by government legislation.

Grameen Bank targets the poorest of the poor, providing small loans (usually less than $300) to those unable to obtain credit from traditional banks. Loans are administered to groups of five people, with only two receiving their money up front. As soon as these two make a few regular payments, loans are gradually extended to the rest of the group. In this way, the program builds a sense of community as well as individual self-reliance.

In 2006, the Nobel Peace Prize was awarded to Muhammad Yunus and the Grameen Bank "for their efforts to create economic and social development from below".

Today, the Grameen Bank concept has been extended to other businesses, including GrameenPhone, Grameen Check (loom woven cloths), Grameeen Fisheries Foundation, Grameen Cybernet and Grameen Shakti (Energy).

Here are the facts: Grameen means 'rural' or 'village' in the Bangla language. Most of the Grameen Bank's loans are to women, and since its inception, there has been an astonishing loan repayment rate of over 98%. Borrowers of the Bank own 90% of its shares, while the remaining 10% is owned by the government. The Grameen Bank is now a $2.5 billion banking enterprise in Bangladesh, with over 7 million active clients, affecting 35 million family members.

Microfinance advisory services by the International Finance Corporation (IFC) generated over $4.6 billion in new investment financing to over 2.3 million microentrepreneurs in 2006 (equivalent to 15% of the IFC's expenditure). According to the Microfinance Summit Campaign, by 2007 there were 3,316 microcredit institutions reaching over 133 million clients. 93 million (up from 7.6 million in 1997) were among the poorest when they took their first loan. Of these poorest clients, 85% per cent, or 79 million, are women. The microcredit model has spread to over 50 countries worldwide, from the U.S. to Papua New Guinea, Norway to Nepal.

Some good sources of information on this case include: *Banker To The Poor* (Yunus, 1999); *Creating a World without Poverty* (Yunus, 2008a); *Social Entrepreneurship* (Bornstein & Davis, 2010); *Money with a Mission* (Copestake et al., 2006); *Small Loans, Big Dreams* (Counts, 2008); and *A Billion Bootstraps* (Smith & Thurman, 2007).

Discussion 7.15: Grameen Bank

1. Grameen Bank uses the principle of 'social collateral' rather than 'financial collateral' to secure its loans. Can you explain the difference?
2. Why do you think microcredit has been so successful with women, rather than men?
3. Many big commercial banks have tried microcredit and failed. Why do you think Grameen Bank and others like it have succeeded?

7.16 Interface FLOR

'I stand convicted by me, myself alone, not by anyone else, as a plunderer of the earth, but not by our civilisation's definition. By our civilisation's definition, I'm a captain of industry. In the eyes of many, a kind of modern day hero.' This is how Ray Anderson – founder of Interface, one of the world's largest manufacturers of carpet tiles – usually starts his speeches these days. It is a far cry from where Anderson, now in his 70s, started out: an honours graduate of Georgia Institute of Technology who, after 14 years at various positions at Deering-Milliken and Callaway Mills, set about founding a company to produce the first free-lay carpet tiles in 1973.

The company was formed out of a joint venture, led by Anderson, between the British company Carpets International and a group of American investors. Modular carpet tiles grew in popularity and by 1978 Interface sales had reached $11 million. The company went public in 1983 and in 1987 changed its name to Interface, Inc. All of this growth and success – to sales of around $600 million by 1993 – took place pursuing a conventional industrial strategy. Green issues were simply not a big thing in the first 20 years of the company's history. But that was starting to change, especially with the 1992 Earth Summit in Rio shining a spotlight on sustainable development.

Interface, like many companies at the time, got caught up in the ferment. By the summer of 1994 Interface customers were starting to ask difficult questions, like:

What is your company doing for the environment? Anderson realised that 'the real answer was: not very much', so they set up a taskforce to assess the company's worldwide environment position. The group, naturally enough, asked Anderson to kick off their first meeting with an environmental vision. Anderson panicked. He didn't have an environmental clue, much less a vision.

Synchronistically, Paul Hawken's book The Ecology of Commerce had just landed on Anderson's desk. He devoured it and was shocked to find himself moved to tears. He still recalls the moment vividly – he had reached page 19, a chapter on the Death of Birth, which was E.O. Wilson's expression for species extinction. 'It was a point of a spear into my chest, and I read on, and the spear went deeper, and it became an epiphany experience, a total change of mindset for myself and a change of paradigm.' What was his great revelation? 'It dawned on me that the way I'd been running Interface is the way of the plunderer; plundering something that's not mine, something that belongs to every creature on earth. And I said to myself: "The day must come when this is illegal, when plundering is not allowed. It must come". So, I said to myself, "My goodness, some day people like me will end up in jail".'

In this moment of profound clarity, Anderson saw that carpet manufacturing 'is a pretty abusive industry'. The process uses lots of petroleum and petroleum derivatives, both as components of synthetic carpet and to power its production. Dyeing carpet is also water- and energy-intensive. And when people are finished with the carpet, it goes into landfills where it lasts probably 20,000 years. Anderson concluded that his company – and business more generally – is part of the problem, not the solution. Paraphrasing Hawken, he realised that 'there is not an industrial company on earth, not an institution of any kind, not mine, not yours, not anyone's, that is sustainable.'

And so Anderson had his vision: Interface would become the world's first truly sustainable company. In fact, not only sustainable, but restorative. They would put back more than they take, and actively do good, not just avoid doing harm. After the speech, Anderson recalls, 'I heard the whispers: Has he gone round the bend?' To which he replied at once that he had. 'That's my job, to see what's around the bend.' Today, Anderson confesses, 'I didn't know what the hell I was talking about', but it galvanised the task group, which after some preliminary research, concluded that they could meet his goal by 2000.

Filled with enthusiasm, Anderson's first move was to send a strong signal to the market. He held a Green the Supply Chain meeting, with a simple message: those who come with us will get the business, those who don't, won't. The following year,

1995, he pulled together an Eco-Dream Team, and introduced a system of EcoMetrics™, designed to quantify the 'metabolism' of Interface, i.e. the mass and energy flow through the company's operations. Simply put, EcoMetrics assesses how much Interface takes in, in terms of materials and energy, and what comes out, in the forms of products and waste. Later, Interface also implemented a system of SocioMetrics™, to measure impacts on their people – the associates and communities they serve.

Inspired by their new vision and metrics, in 1995 Interface started innovating their products, first by launching an Evergreen Lease, which they described as 'selling carpet without selling carpet'. This was based on the idea of selling a service, rather than a product. Hence, Interface produces, installs, cleans, maintains and replaces the carpet for customers. Customers lease the service of keeping a space carpeted, rather than buying carpet. They get the services of a carpet's warmth, beauty, colour, texture and acoustics. Interface saw it – rightly I believe – as 'a whole new sustainable business model'.

By 1996, Interface had learned enough to conceptualise what they were doing in a Model of a Sustainable Company. The next year, their definition of 'sustainable' received added scientific rigour when they became the first company to adopt the Natural Step principles, which are four 'system conditions', developed by Swedish cancer researcher, Karl-Henrik Robèrt. In 1998, Interface issued its first Sustainability Report and formed a Global Sustainability Council, while Anderson (1999) published his business biography of the journey so far, called Mid Course Correction. The company's product innovation also continued, with the introduction in 1999 of their Déjà vu™ collection, a carpet tile product using recycled nylon and 100% recycled vinyl secondary backing.

Despite all this great progress – which many described as revolutionary – as the millennium approached, it became blatantly obvious that their 'restorative company' goal was far more ambitious and difficult than Anderson or the environmental task team had ever imagined. It was time for a reality-check. The journey to a fully sustainable Interface would be like – as Anderson began to describe it – summiting 'a mountain higher than Everest' – difficult, yes, but with a careful and attentive plan, not impossible. So rather than change the goal, they changed the timeframe. The new deadline for 'Mission Sustainability' became 2020.

Carrying through the analogy, Interface identified Seven Fronts™ on Mount Sustainability through which they planned to ascend: 1) eliminating waste; 2) generating benign emissions; 3) using renewable energy; 4) closing the loop on production; 5) using resource-efficient transportation; 6) sensitising stakeholders;

and finally 7) redesigning commerce. Among the tools that have become central to the climb are life cycle assessment and biomimicry – Janine Benyus's idea of nature-inspired design.

These techniques have not only allowed Interface to choose the lowest impact options among existing processes, but also to innovate new products that are less resource- and energy-intensive and produce less waste. One of the first, in 2000, was called Entropy® - tiles that install non-directionally and have mergeable dye lots. This concept launched what became InterfaceFLOR's i2™ category, with the benefit that one person can install more than two and a half times as much i2 tile in one day as they could of broadloom carpet. Besides this, i2 floors result in as little as 1.5% waste, compared to broadloom with as much as 14%.

Other product innovations have included the Cool Carpet (offsetting greenhouse gas emissions) and carpets using fly ash waste and polylactic acid (PLA) fibres, derived from non-food grade corn. Perhaps most famously, in 2006, Interface invented the world's first totally glue-free, free-lay carpet tile (TacTile®), inspired by gecko-foot 'technology'. The result is less mess, less waste and greater savings, not to mention an environmental footprint that is over 90% lower than carpets using traditional glue adhesives.

In 2007, another technological breakthrough, dubbed ReEntry 2.0™, means that Interface can now recycle - or 'reinyarnate' – reclaimed and separated type 6 and 6,6 nylon, as well as separated GlasBac® and similar competitor backings into new non-virgin PVC carpet tile backing. This has been somewhat controversial, as there are those that argue that PVC should be phased out completely (including the authors of Cradle to Cradle). Anderson's response is that the world is awash with PVC and high performance natural alternatives are still in their developmental infancy. Hence, for now, it is essential to reclaim and reuse the PVC, rather than simply to burn or bury it.

Taking stock in 2010, Anderson's EcoMetrics™ tell him that they are about 60% of the way towards what Interface now calls its Mission Zero™ goal to have no negative environmental impacts by 2020. Translated into numbers, the results are impressive. Of the 400 million pounds of raw materials purchased in 2009, only 3.4 million pounds of waste went to landfills, 6.9 million pounds of raw material were recycled to be used again, and 9.6 million pounds of waste was sent to energy recovery as a use of last resort. Continued savings from Interface's QUEST program have netted $433 million in cumulative avoided costs since 1995. And ReEntry 2.0, Interface's reclamation and recycling initiative, diverted 25 million pounds of reclaimed carpet and post-industrial scrap from the landfill in 2009.

It has been a long and painful – but ultimately rewarding – journey. Anderson reflects on the transformational challenge that Interface faced, and we all still face, saying: 'The status quo is a very powerful opiate and when you have a system that seems to be working and producing profits by the conventional way of accounting for profits, it's very hard to make yourself change. But we all know that change is an inevitable part of business. Once you have ridden a wave just so far, you have to get another wave. We all know that. For us, becoming restorative has been that new wave and it's been incredibly good for business.'

Admittedly, Interface had a tough time through the financial crisis (who didn't), losing as much as 85% of its pre-crisis value in early March 2009, but has since rebounded strongly. In fact, Anderson regards their Zero Mission as one of the reasons they have survived and ultimately thrived through the recession. It's hard to bet against what has become a billion-dollar corporation, named by Fortune as one of the 'Most Admired Companies in America' and the '100 Best Companies to Work For', with sales in 110 countries and manufacturing facilities on four continents.

Anderson can't help but see the opportunities, saying: 'I believe there are new fortunes to be made as we define this, the next industrial revolution.' He is quick to add, however, that it's not all about the money. 'There's a lot of psychic income with people who feel they are associated with something bigger than themselves, something that's important'. But Anderson is also under no illusions about the scale of the challenge that we face. 'Part of what needs to change', he says, 'is our focus on short time horizons, i.e., the focus on the next quarter, for both companies and for their investors. Sustainability by its very nature requires a long view on the future, as we consider the impact of our decisions today on future generations.'

A long term view necessitates that we 'eventually cut the fossil fuel umbilical cord'. And this is where Anderson believes the government has a critical role to play in creating what he calls an 'honest bottom line'. By contrast, 'today that bottom line is vastly subsidized. If any one of us were paying the full cost of oil, our bottom lines would be very different. If you internalize the cost of oil, look at the cost of the war in the Middle East or the cost of global warming for future generations, if you internalize those external costs, that bottom line would look very different, whatever business you are in.' And it's not just about carbon. 'If we somehow put a value on species extinction and factor that into our costs, that bottom line would look very different. If we put any resource depletion into costs, our bottom line would change. So what we have is a dishonest market that does not take into account all the costs when it establishes its prices. We need an honest marketplace before we can let the market work for sustainability rather than against it as it works today.'

It is clear that sixteen years after creating his 'round-the-bend' vision of Interface becoming a truly sustainable and responsible company, Anderson is older and wiser. And despite all the success and accolades that Interface has enjoyed – both financial and in terms of its sustainability achievements – the piercing pain of the 'spear in the chest' has not dulled for Anderson. He remains profoundly concerned – disturbed even – at the growing state of crisis in the world's ecosystems. Asked in 2010 whether he was optimistic about the future and our chances of reaching sustainability, he said: 'I am optimistic that we [Interface] will get there. I am not optimistic that the industrial system will change quickly enough to avoid catastrophe.'

To me, Anderson's answer is both a celebration of what is possible, based on Interface's experience, and a warning of what is probable if we don't act more urgently and dramatically as a society and as business. A great source of further information is Anderson's (2009) biography Confessions of a Radical Industrialist.

Discussion 7.16: Interface FLOR

1. What characteristics does Ray Anderson embody that made him such a good sustainability leader?
2. Interface FLOR has demonstrated that financial profitability and environmental responsibility does not have to be a trade off. What has enabled them to achieve this?
3. Do you believe Misson Zero is achievable for Interface FLOR? What about for other companies?

7.17 Lehman Brothers[1]

Larry McDonald was a child of the 'greed is good' 80s. But, unlike me, he actually lived the dream – and is still haunted by the nightmare that ensued. Looking back, there are several obvious pieces to the puzzle; factors that explain McDonald's unrelenting drive to become a high stakes player on Wall Street. His father was obsessed with business, and plastics made him a stack of money, enough to start his own brokerage firm. That obsession took its toll on family life, and McDonald

---

[1] This vignette is a true story, précised and adapted from Larry McDonald's (2009) book *A Colossal Failure of Common Sense: The Incredible Inside Story of the Collapse of Lehman Brothers.*

soon found himself in a broken home, living with his mother and four siblings on a housing estate – at the wrong end of an 'urban version of Death Valley'.

Despite this, or more likely because of it, McDonald set his sights on escaping the mire of poverty. He now knew where he did not want to spend his life. And, thanks to his father's high-flying business career, he knew where wanted to get to. 'By the time I graduated from college in 1989,' McDonald recalled, 'I had learned enough about Wall Street to understand that was the place I wanted to be, right out there in New York with the big dogs, playing in the major leagues of finance. The trouble was, my chances of getting in were zilch'.

Wall Street became McDonald's personal holy grail. He was smart enough to realise that he was still light years away, but he set himself a secret five-year target to make it there. First, he tried to get into one of the brokerage houses in New England. Hundreds of rejection letters later, he changed his strategy – he became a self-confessed 'new specialist in low cunning, deviousness and subterfuge'. He began lying his way past office security guards and executive personal assistants, dressing up as a pizza delivery man, trying just about anything to get an audience with one of the branch managers.

One day, McDonald's chutzpah (if that's what you'd call it) paid off. But it wasn't the break he'd hoped for. 'Kid', the manager told him, 'I don't care what you sell for your first experience, but for Christ's sake get out there and sell 'em something, rather than wasting my time!' That was the clue, the key to breaking into the fortress of high finance. McDonald sprung into action and got a sales job, selling pork around the Cape and south-eastern Massachusetts. Midway through his second year, he was one of the top salesmen in the entire American Frozen Foods northeast region. Soon, there was an offer for a management job at their headquarters in Connecticut. He nearly accepted, but stopped himself just in time. Becoming the world's number one meat salesman was not his objective. Getting to Wall Street was. But how?

A friend from school convinced him that he needed to enrol at Philadelphia business school and sit for the Series 7 Exam, because without it 'a future bond trader would be like a butcher without a meat cleaver'. But he needed a sponsor and a 'sleazy bucket shop' – an underworld operation, selling stock in fake shells of corporations to raise cash – was the way in. The deal was that they would sponsor McDonald and when he passed his exam, he would work for them, joining their 'fat chain-smoking salesmen that would say anything to their victims'.

McDonald made the Faustian bargain and passed the exam, but managed to get a job with Merrill Lynch in Philadelphia instead, thereby avoiding the bucket shop, which he regarded distastefully as the 'totally unacceptable face of capitalism'. McDonald worked hard, began specialising in convertible bonds, made good money and plotted his next move. While he was still scheming, he ran into an acquaintance in a bar who worked for IBM and was about to start up one of the Cape's first Internet service providers. He convinced McDonald that, pretty soon, the dotcom boom would revolutionise everything – financial trading would go online.

Sensing a blockbuster opportunity, McDonald hatched a plot with an old friend to start up ConvertBond.com, which they launched in 1997. Pretty soon, The Wall Street Journal and CNBC television were featuring stories about them and the business took off. Despite running a seat-of-the-pants operation out of a small office above a strip mall, with 250,000 hits a day, their opinions on newly issued bonds started to hold considerable sway in the market. McDonald had caught the wave of the future, and it hadn't gone unnoticed by the 'big boys'. In the autumn of 1999, Morgan Stanley made an offer to take over ConvertBond.com. Suddenly, McDonald was a 33-year old millionaire and working in Morgan Stanley's Stamford office – another step closer to Wall Street.

The dotcom bubble burst soon afterward, so McDonald had got out just in time. And more drama was to come. In 2001, McDonald was in the thick of convertible bonds action, as first Pacific Gas and Electric filed for bankruptcy, then 9/11 happened, and finally the Enron debacle broke. He watched mesmerised as Enron, saddled with $65 billion in unpayable debt, spiralled to their death at the hands of the financial markets, with their share price plummeting from $90 to just a few cents. In the months that followed, a spate of bankruptcies rocked the world, all of which issued convertible bonds: Global Crossing, Qwest, NTL, Adelphia Communications and WorldCom. McDonald had a front-seat view of the whole financial operatic tragedy.

Alan Greenspan's response was to cut interest rates from 6% in December 2000 to 1% by July 2003. 'Thus began one of the greatest consumer borrowing bonanzas since the 1920s', reflected McDonald. 'This was the starting point of America living in a false economy, because all this free money was in defiance of the natural laws of the universe.' His father agreed: 'Here we go again' he warned. 'Straight back to the edge of the cliff.' But one person's poison is another's potion. Wall Street had just invented securitisation – turning mortgage debts into tangible, tradable entities. 'What a pure stroke of genius,' said McDonald. 'Hardly anyone noticed the minor flaws that would, in time, bankrupt half the world'.

As 2004 arrived, the flame of McDonald's ambitions burned strong as ever. 'I still wanted a seat at Wall Street's top table, right up there in the major leagues'.

Fortunately, he knew someone who worked for Lehman's, that pinnacle of his ambition that had survived and thrived for over 150 years. The friend encouraged McDonald to apply for a position and, after a series of gruelling interviews, he stepped into the lion's den. Admitted, it had taken 16 years, rather than the five he had hoped for, but here he was, 'into the hierarchy, alongside some of Wall Street's smartest guys'.

For the next few years, McDonald's dream became an intoxicating, head-spinning reality. He would wake at 4 am and be at his desk before 6, working in a chilled, oxygen-fed trading office, taking no lunch, and leaving more than 12 hours later. It was tiring, but he found it exhilarating. 'We were in the presence of gods, the new Masters of the Universe, a breed of financial daredevils who conjured Lehman's billion-dollar profits out of the one of the most complex markets ever to show its head above Wall Street's ramparts. This was the Age of the Derivative – the Wall Street neutron that provided atomic power to one of the most reckless housing booms in all of history'.

McDonald had his doubts about the sub-prime bonanza. But, he knew his limits: 'I didn't dare mention even a semblance of doubt, not to anyone. That would have been tantamount to high treason, as if the president of the United States had invited Osama Bin Laden to Camp David for the weekend'. Besides, McDonald was benefiting big time. Wall Street bonuses were 250% bigger than the average salary for all nonfinancial jobs in the city, and since 2003, thanks to derivatives, their total compensation had increased by nearly 50%. That was, in retrospect, 'on the high side', recalled McDonald. 'But that's what it was all about – record leverage, record bonuses'.

It later turned out that McDonald was not alone in his suspicions about the market's greed-fuelled behaviour. On 6 June 2006, all the staff in his unit in Lehman's were called into a meeting and addressed by one of the newly promoted managing directors. He said the U.S. real estate market was 'pumped up like an athlete on steroids, rippling with a set of muscles that did not naturally belong there'. It was based on 'money that was not real money, home prices that were not real prices, and mortgages that were not grounded in any definition of reality'. The presentation went down like a lead balloon among the traders. 'Have you missed the fact that this bull market is exploding?' retorted one.

The prevailing opinion of eternal sunshine was hardly surprising. True, U.S. consumer and corporate debt was stacking up –$1 trillion in 2000 and $2.7 trillion by 2005 – but Wall Street was still making shiploads of money, and everyone was bullish. Even Time magazine declared that 'the world economy is on track to enjoy another bumper year in 2006 as this twin American-Chinese engine continues to power ahead'. 'The outlook is basically for another Goldilocks kind of year', agreed Lara D. Tyson, then dean of London Business School. But some, including McDonald and a few bears2 at Lehman, had spotted the cracks in the shining edifice of global financial markets.

Despite these early warning signals, the tide of optimism and greed continued to sweep through Lehman's, America and the world, and McDonald was riding high, making more than a tidy golden nest egg in the process. By the time the spring tide had turned into an incontestable financial tsunami, it was too late – too late for Lehman's and too late for McDonald. When 158-year old Lehman Brothers filed for Chapter 11 bankruptcy on 15 September 2008, owing $660 billion, it took a good portion of Wall Street, Main Street and the world economy down with it.

McDonald still lives just a few city blocks from the old Lehman Brothers headquarters at 745 Seventh Avenue. Each time he walks past, he is overcome with mixed emotions – mainly nostalgia, edged by a lingering anger and still plagued by unanswerable questions. 'I stand and stare upward, sorrowful beyond reason', McDonald confesses, 'and trapped by the twin words of those possessed of flawless hindsight: if only'.

Discussion 7.17: Lehman Brothers
1. What do we learn from the Lehman Brothers case about the causes of the 2008 global financial crisis?
2. What was the role of Lehman Brothers' leaders in its downfall?
3. How could Lehman Brothers' corporate culture have been changed to support ethical and responsible behaviour?

7.18 McDonald's

In 1986, a UK environmental campaign group called The London Greenpeace Group published a six-page leaflet called "What's Wrong with McDonald's? Everything they don't want you to know".

The leaflet contained accusations of McDonald's complicity in starvation in the Third World, rainforest destruction, negative health impacts (including food poisoning, heart disease and cancer), exploitation of children through advertising, 'torture and murder' of animals, anti-union behaviour and poor employee working conditions.

---

2 Traders who bet on a falling prices for securities

In 1990, five members of the group were issued a writ by McDonald's for publishing and distributing the leaflet, of which two - Helen Steel and Dave Morris – went to trial in June 1994.

The resulting 313 day trial (popularly labelled 'McLibel') became the longest ever in British legal history and ended in June 1997, having heard 180 witnesses and reviewed 40,000 pages of documents and witness statements. The verdict was mixed – some of the allegations about McDonald's business practices were upheld, but Steel and Morris were found guilty of having libelled the company and were ordered to pay £60,000 in damages.

Steel and Morris refused to pay the damages (reduced on appeal to £40,000 in 1999), and in 2000, took their case to the European Court of Justice in Strasbourg, alleging that the original trial breached their human rights to a fair trial and freedom of expression. In February 2005, the Strasbourg judged in their favour and awarded compensation.

According to Gerry McCusker, author of Talespin: Public Relations Disasters, the trial cost McDonald's more than £10 million in legal fees.

Nearly 20 years later came Super Size Me, an Academy Award-nominated 2004 documentary film written, produced, directed by and starring Morgan Spurlock. Spurlock's film follows a 30-day time period (February 2003) during which he subsists entirely on food and items purchased exclusively from McDonald's.

He consumed an average of 5,000 kcal (the equivalent of 9.26 Big Macs) per day during the experiment. He gained 24.5 lb (11.1 kg), a 13% body mass increase, and his Body Mass Index rose from 23.2 (within the 'healthy' range of 19-25) to 27 ('overweight'). He also experienced mood swings, sexual dysfunction, and liver damage. It took Spurlock fourteen months to lose the weight he gained.

In 2005, McDonalds announced a Balanced Lifestyles initiative which involves offering healthier menu options, promoting physical activity and providing more nutritional information to customers about its products.

More information about this case study includes: Mclibel (Vidal, 1997); Fast Food Nation (Schlosser, 2005); and Talespin (McCusker, 2006).

Discussion 7.18: McDonald's

1. What have been the main criticisms that McDonald's (and other fast food chains) have faced relating to health, children, ethics, labour and environment?
2. How have McDonald's responded to these criticisms? Are you convinced? i.e. Do you regard McDonald's as a sustainable and responsible company?

3. Millions of customers *choose* to eat at McDonald's. Is ensuring healthy eating the responsibility of the company, or the customer, or the government? Is this any different for the health-related criticisms faced by the tobacco industry?

7.19 Nike

In November 1997, the Transnational Resource and Action Center (TRAC, now called CorpWatch), released a report called "Smoke from a Hired Gun: A Critique of Nike's Labor and Environmental Auditing in Vietnam as Performed by Ernst & Young."

The report exposed the findings of a confidential January 1997 report for Nike by Ernst & Young (leaked by a disgruntled employee) entitled ""Environmental and Labor Practice Audit of the Tae Kwang Vina Industrial Ltd. Co., Vietnam". The report's found various poor practices in areas of health and safety and working hours.

The *New York Times* picked up on the TRAC report and triggered a storm of negative publicity and pressure on Nike to address human rights in its supply chain.

Nike's initial response was to cite a report by Andrew Young of Good Works International (dated 27 June 1997), which evaluated their Code of Conduct and its application at the factory level, concluding that "Nike is doing a good job in the application of its Code Of Conduct. But Nike can and should do better." However, this just added to the controversy.

Among the more serious consequences was the Nike v Kasky case - a lawsuit filed in April 1998 in California against Nike for "unlawful and unfair business practices" that violate California's Business and Professions Code. The lawsuit claimed that Nike made the various misrepresentations about their standards of conduct.

Nike has since put a lot of effort and money into redressing its reputation, through a combination of public acknowledgements of past mistakes, stringent supply-chain policies, factory audits, transparent reporting and membership of partnerships such as the Global Alliance for Workers and Communities. The industry has also responded with the World Federation of Sporting Goods Industry Code of Conduct, launched in 1997.

Here are the facts: In 2006, Nike's three main product lines - footwear, apparel and equipment - used 800,000 workers in almost 700 contract factories in 52 countries. Today, Nike publishes a list of all contract factories currently approved to manufacture Nike-brand products, including those that are inactive. Between

2004 and 2006, Nike conducted 810 management audits in contract factories around the world, and in 2005, began collecting baseline environmental, health and safety data on more than 650 contract factories in 52 countries, conducting 65 audits and 15 in-depth root cause assessments. By 2011, Nike aims to eliminate excessive overtime and run include management training on workers' rights, women's rights, freedom of association and collective bargaining in contract factories.

There is also a positive story to the Nike case. Towards the end of the 1990s, the Nike Environmental Action Team (NEAT), led by Sarah Severn, then Nike's Director of Corporate Sustainable Development, began shaping what would become Nike's cradle to cradle approach. Working closely with Heidi McCloskey, Global Sustainability Director for Apparel, and Anne Peirson-Hills, Senior Manager of Environmental Affairs, Severn encouraged Nike's designers to go back to first principles, questioning basic design traditions in order to get to a new and better product outcome which addresses the environmental footprint required to source, manufacture, and recycle shoes.

Severn liked the innovative and ambitious approach of cradle to cradle: 'So much of the environmental debate had addressed end-of-pipe problems and end-of-pipe solutions,' she recalled. 'And here was a strategy that was turning that on its head. It was not about restriction or reaction. It created positive solutions at the front of the design process. That meshes very well with the culture in Nike. And it's an exciting message. If you talk about environmental management systems and eco-efficiency, people just roll their eyes. But if you talk about innovation and abundance, it's inspirational. People get very, very excited.'

The first manifestation of all that excitement was a new brand, 'Considered', which Nike launched with its Considered Boot in 2005: a single shoe lace woven between the leather parts of the upper, stitching that secured the upper to the sole, eliminating adhesives and allowing for easier disassembly. Design insights gained from this work helped inform future innovations such as the pinnacle Air Jordan XXIII, launched in January 2008, and the Nike Trash Talk, made from post-manufacturing waste.

Today, Considered design for shoes includes a number of modifications. Leather pieces are stitched in an overlapping fashion so as to produce smooth internal seams, obviating the need for comfort liners and reducing the shoes' material mass. The leather pieces are tanned using a vegetable-based process and metal eyelets aren't used. The two-piece outsole is designed to snap together, eliminating harmful adhesives and simplifying recyclability, and there is no use of PVC. Finally, where possible, materials are sourced locally to reduce transportation energy use. The result is that Considered shoes generate 63% less waste in manufacturing than a typical Nike design, the use of solvents has been cut by 80% and 37% less energy is required to create a pair of shoes.

It is also not just about shoes. In order to measure progress of all of its products and designs against its cradle to cradle principles, Nike developed a Considered Index, which is a tool for evaluating the predicted environmental footprint of a product prior to commercialisation. This system examines solvent use, waste, materials and innovation for footwear. Apparel products are evaluated on waste, materials, garment treatments and innovation. Nike claim that 'by continually raising that standard, we envision a future where the shoes you wear today become the shoes, shirts or equipment you use tomorrow. This closed loop manufacturing process, where nothing is wasted and everything is kept in play, is not just wishful thinking, it's the future.'

In order to create this future, Nike has committed to having all newly developed Nike footwear coming out of U.S. headquarters meet or exceed Considered Design baseline standards by 2011. This will be extended to apparel and European and Hong Kong offices by 2015, and sports equipment by 2020. One of the reasons Nike may very well succeed in meeting these targets is that Considered is bold and inspiring. As Ed Thomas, Director of Advanced Materials Research, put it, 'you've got to take the stake and you've got to plant it somewhere big and you've got to say that's what we're driving for. It's not just going more slowly. It's not just going to zero. It's actually turning around and picking a new direction.'

More sources of information about this case include: *Still Waiting For Nike To Do It* (Connor, 2001); and 'Beyond corporate codes of conduct: work organisation and labour standards at Nike's suppliers' (Locke, 2007).

Discussion 7.19: Nike

1. Companies like Nike are often criticised for the poor working conditions and low wages paid at the contract factories in their supply chain, as compared with the high price of their products and the large sums spent on advertising, promotion and celebrity endorsements. What is the best way to address these concerns?

2. How effective do you think Sportswear codes of conduct and initiatives like the Clean Clothes and Fair Play campaigns are in changing working conditions in the sporting goods supply chain?

3. Speaking about their Considered Design programme, one Nike representative said they would never sacrifice product performance for sustainability. What do you think of this statement in particular, and Considered Design in general?

7.20 Patagonia

'It was back in 1990 or so,' recalled Yvon Chouinard, founder and CEO of the $300 million Patagonia clothing company. 'We were growing the company by 40% to 50% a year and we were doing it by all the textbook business ways – adding more dealers, adding more products, building stores, growing it like the American dream, you know – grow, grow, grow. And one year we predicted 40% to 50% growth and there was a recession and all the sudden we only grew 20%. And at the same time, our bank was going belly-up and we had cash-flow problems and it went to absolute hell. And I realised that I was on the same track as society was – endless growth for the sake of growth.'

This was the turning point – the Damascus experience – on a journey that would lead Patagonia, founded in 1957 with Chouinard selling mountain-climbing pitons out of the boot of his car, to become one of the true business pioneers in sustainability and responsibility. Chouinard always had an affinity for nature and was a somewhat reluctant entrepreneur; he would rather have been out fishing or mountain climbing. So it was entirely natural that he would commit the company, since 1985, to giving at least 1% of its annual sales to environmental charities; or that, in 1988, he initiated a national environmental campaign to deurbanize the Yosemite Valley. But the real wake-up call, the U-bend in the pipe, was that 1990s recession.

Chouinard's first step was to kick the company's growth habit. He put the brakes on and reverted to what he called 'natural growth'. What that means is that 'only when our customers want something do we make more, but we don't prime the pump.' Taking this stance was a radical departure from 'business as usual' in an industry that runs on the steroids of aggressive advertising and celebrity endorsements. His competitors were dumbfounded, but Chouinard's mind was made up: 'I basically want to make clothing for people who need it rather than for people who want it.' The next step was to begin assessing the environmental impacts of Patagonia's products. This time, it was Chouinard's turn to be shocked.

The big surprise came from the results on industrially grown cotton. 'The "natural" fibre used in most of our sportswear proved to be by far the greatest environmental evildoer of the fibres studied. We learned that 25% of all the toxic pesticides used in agriculture was (and is) used in the cultivation of cotton, that the resulting pollution of soil and water was (and is) horrific, and that evidence of damage to the health of fieldworkers is strong, though difficult to prove. Cotton was the biggest villain – and it didn't have to be. Farmers had grown cotton organically, without pesticides, for thousands of years. Only after World War II did the chemicals originally developed as nerve gases become available for commercial use, to eliminate the need for weeding fields by hand.'

Chouinard has developed a philosophy over the years, namely that 'a company has a responsibility to not wait for the government to tell them what to do, or wait for the consumer to tell them what to do; that as soon as you find out you're doing something wrong, stop doing it.' And that's exactly what he did. In 1994, he gave Patagonia 18 months to wean itself off industrially grown cotton. And that was no mean feat. 'We had to revolutionize the industry,' Chouinard explains. 'We had to co-sign loans for farmers because if they went organic they couldn't get a loan from the bank because the bank's tied in with the chemical companies. We had to convince gins to clean their cotton gins and then process our stuff. We had to find the right mills. It was a really big process. But we've never made a single product using industrially grown cotton since then [1996] and it's working out fantastic. It put us on a whole other level from our competitors.'

By the early 2000s, the Age of Management was already in full swing and Chouinard started coming under pressure to produce a GRI-compliant sustainability report. In 2004, Patagonia audited itself against the GRI and produced a draft report, from which he concluded that it was 'absolute bullshit'. It was boring, it didn't challenge the company and, perhaps most importantly, he felt it was misleading. Chouinard wanted total transparency – warts and all – and he wanted it presented in an engaging way. 'We're very self critical and we're very idealistic,' Chouinard explains. 'I think only by being honest can we show the full extent of the problem. Right now there's a lot of green glossing going on, green marketing. There's a lot of misinformation out there, especially with all these companies claiming to be green. So we want to be absolutely dead honest with how difficult it is.'

As a result, and as part of Chouinard's commitment to 'lead an examined life', Patagonia launched its Footprint Chronicles® in 2007. The Chronicles are a remarkable experiment in transparency, tell the story of products from design through fibre creation to construction and shipment. To date, it has assessed the social and environmental impacts of over 150 of its products, the findings of which are available for all to see on its website. Let me take one recent addition – organic cotton jeans – to give you a flavour of how it works. The first thing I see when I click on a picture of the jeans is a map of the world, with pins in key locations and dotted lines joining them. As I hover my mouse over each pin, I get a quick snapshot of the supply chain: design in Ventura, California; fibre and fabric in Acola District, India; sewing in Tehuacan, Mexico; and distribution in Reno, Nevada. I can click on any one of these to get more information of that particular micro-process.

So let's look at what happens in India. I am taken to a slide-show with a colourful and insightful 19 page presentation on Patagonia's supplier, the Arvind Worldwide Inc.'s Fairtrade Organic Cotton Project. It describes how Arvind helped to organise struggling farmers into self-help groups consisting of 20 or so individuals who joined together to improve their yields and incomes, through the adoption of organic practices. Each step in the planting, growing, harvesting, packaging and shipping process is explained, with photographs that bring it all to life. And I can do the same for the other staging posts in manufacturing process. The result is that I am left with a much greater understanding of the supply chain and some sense of the people and processes involved. But what about the impacts?

Returning to the main Chronicles page for the organic cotton jeans, I notice five symbols on display, each of which reveals information when I hover my mouse over the icon. I find out that a single pair of jeans takes 187 megajoules (52 kWh) of energy, which I am helpfully told is equivalent to burning an 18 W energy saving bulb for 120 days, 24 hours a day. The jeans have travelled 14,300 miles (23,014 kms) to get to me, equivalent to a roundtrip from Annecy, France to Mar del Plata, Argentina. They have also produced 62 pounds (28 kgs) of CO_2 emissions and 82 oz (2.3 kgs) of waste, equivalent to 47 times and 4 times the weight of one pair of jeans respectively. Finally, 174 litres of water were used, enough to provide 58 people with drinking water for one day. I now have a much better handle on the impacts I am having by buying these jeans.

But there is more information: the Good, the Bad and What We Think. The Good states that 'we use organic cotton, working with contract farmers in India, teaching them about organic farming and fairtrade. The cotton is mainly rain-fed. During dry periods, it is irrigated with water previously captured in ponds. Fields are mulched to slow evaporation. We make them to last and when they wear out they can be recycled.' The Bad confesses that 'while the use of organically grown cotton is environmentally preferred to conventionally grown cotton, recycled cotton would be even better.' And What We Think provides some thought-provoking insights, saying 'many customers want jeans that look worn and faded. Distressing denim requires the use of chemicals, energy, water and manual labour, with some environmental downside. We continue to research new developments in demin processing, hoping to further reduce water use and employ even cleaner chemistry. Arvind makes demin with recycled content, but the cotton is not organic, so we do not use it. We hope to develop a recycled organic cotton blend.'

The Footprint Chronicles clearly have benefits for the customer, but what about for Patagonia? Elissa Loughman, Environmental Strategy Analyst, explains what they have learned from the process: 'Some of the earliest data that we found showed us that the transportation energy use is actually quite small in comparison to the total energy use to make a product. So this has allowed us to shift our focus from worrying about the distance that our products are travelling – as long as they are being shipped by boat, that's the most efficient way – to instead focusing on the energy use in the manufacturing process. Another thing we learned was that the treatment we were using on our wool to de-scale it, to make it shrink resistant and itch free, was using a lot of energy. It was a chlorine free process so it was good in terms of not using chlorine, but it was using more energy than we'd like. So we're currently looking for a less energy intensive solution that also avoids using toxins.'

The Chronicles have not only had environmental benefits. 'Changes have occurred with our partner suppliers as well,' says Loughman. 'One specific example is Everest, one of our fabric vendors. We had a group of Patagonia employees go to visit them and on their tour they noticed that there was a smell coming from the laminating area. They also noticed that the workers in that area weren't wearing masks, so they enquired about why the masks weren't being worn and they learned that the employees, during the monsoon season, found them unbearable to wear and refused to wear them. In an effort to resolve this issue and as part of their process to become Bluesign certified, Everest invested $1.3 million in a system to recover the solvent fumes on their coating line. The coolest thing about the Footprint Chronicles,' concludes Loughman, 'is that it has given us a venue to have an open and honest conversation with our customers and our [website] viewers, and it's allowed us to be transparent about our business and talk about the good things and the bad things. And the more we've learned about how we make our products, the more we want to know.'

Behind the Footprint Chronicles and many of Patagonia's other sustainability and responsibility initiatives is the key concept of cradle-to-cradle production and consumption. They have teamed up with some Japanese companies with the goal of making all of their clothing out of recycled and recyclable fibres. In particular, they are switching all their nylon to Nylon 6, which can be recycled infinitely. They're also recycling cotton and recycling wool. 'Of course, the best thing to do is make clothing so it never wears out, right?' says Chouinard. And failing that, he says, 'we're going to accept the responsibility. We're going to accept ownership for our products from birth 'til birth. So as much as we can, we're going to make all of our products so that if you buy a jacket, a shirt, a pair of pants or whatever, when you're done with it, you can give it back to us and we'll make more shirts and pants out of that, which is a different idea about consuming.'

Reflecting on the company's journey, Chouinard concludes that the key is curiosity. 'We had to ask a million questions. But then once you educate yourself, then you're left with choices. This company exists to ask the questions and make the choices and then to prove that it's good business to other companies so that they can do it.' As far as sustainability goes, Chouinard admits that he is 'trying to run this company as if it's going to be here 100 years from now', but believes that 'there's no such thing as sustainability. There are just levels of it. It's a process, not a real goal. All you can do is work toward it.' In the meantime, he admonishes that 'every business should say, "We're polluters, we're using nonrenewable resources, and therefore we should tax ourselves."' One way to do that is to join One Percent for the Planet, co-founded by Chouinard in 2001 as an alliance of mostly small companies that pledge to do the same. One Percent recently notched its 1,000th member; in total, its members have given $42 million to more than 1,700 groups.

Chouinard, despite his company being hailed as 'The Coolest Company on the Planet' by Fortune magazine, believes that we're a long way from having a sustainable society. To change that, he says we have to stop focusing on the symptoms and start focusing on the causes, which are growth, over-consumption and poorly designed manufacturing processes. 'I believe the accepted model of capitalism that demands endless growth deserves the blame for the destruction of nature, and it should be displaced. Failing that, I try to work with those companies and help them change the way they think about resources.' And the reward for that? 'Leading an examined life is a real pain the ass,' Chouinard says wryly. 'It adds an element of complexity to business that most businessmen just don't want to hear about.' So why has it done it? He sums it up in his business biography, Let My People Go Surfing (Chouinard, 2006): 'Not to do so would have been unconscionable'.

Discussion 7.20: Patagonia

1. Patagonia has publicly stated that, in order to be sustainable, growth is no longer one of their companies' objectives. Do you agree with this argument?
2. How are Patagonia's Footprint Chronicles different from traditional corporate sustainability reporting?

3. What role did Yves Chouinard play as a leader in Patagonia's journey to sustainability?

7.21 Seventh Generation

There are also smaller, more nimble companies, like Seventh Generation, that are able to go much further, much faster. Seventh Generation, an American household cleaning products business started more than twenty years ago by Jeffrey Hollender, took inspiration for its name and philosophy from the Iroquois Confederacy (a council of Native American Indian tribes), which included the admonition that 'in our every deliberation, we must consider the impact of our decisions on the next seven generations'.

From the beginning, this meant thinking in a circular way about the impact of their products. To begin with, this meant swimming upstream. 'When Seventh Generation told executives at the old Fort Howard Paper Company that we wanted to market bathroom tissue made from unbleached recycled fibre, they laughed,' recalls Hollender. Despite such early resistance, however, Seventh Generation has remained steadfast in its commitment to 'becoming the world's most trusted brand of authentic, safe, and environmentally-responsible products for a healthy home.' And indeed, it now has an impressive catalogue of cradle to cradle designed products, and has been doing extremely well, showing strong growth even through the recession.

However, ensuring that Seventh Generation lives up to their promise of authenticity is something that requires constant vigilance. For example, in March 2008, the company was 'exposed' by the Organic Consumers Association for having detectable levels of the contaminate 1,4-dioxane in their dish liquid. In fact, Seventh Generation's product was declared the safest of those available and they had been working with suppliers for more than 5 years to remove it, which they have since accomplished. But, as Hollender later declared, 'our effort was simply not good enough. Our real mistake was to exclude consumers and key stakeholders from our ongoing dialogue about dioxane. In short, we flunked the transparency test.'

Of course, the very foundation of transparency is information and the most basic kind is a full list of product ingredients, which, unbelievably, is not required by U.S. law for household products. Consequently, Seventh Generation launched a 'Show What's Inside' initiative, which included an educational website and an online Label Reading Guide, downloadable to shoppers' cell phones, which helped them interpret labels at the point of purchase, especially any associated risks. As Hollender and Breen (2010) report in their book, The Responsibility Revolution, not long after, SC Johnson launched a cloned version called 'What's Inside'. 'That's just what we had hoped for,' declared Hollender and Breen. 'When a $7.5 billion giant like SC Johnson puts its brawn behind ingredient disclosure, it's likely that the rest of the industry will follow, regardless of what the regulators do.'

Despite its green image, Seventh Generation also knows that it needs to create virtuous cycles in its social as well as its environmental impacts. As a result, in 2009, the company joined Women's Action to Gain Economic Security (WAGES) – an organisation committed to building worker-owned, cooperatively-structured, eco-friendly, residential cleaning businesses in San Francisco – to launch Home Green Home, WAGES' 4th worker-owned cooperative. This unique social enterprise, serves the city of San Francisco, and is creating healthy, dignified jobs for women in an industry known for long hours and low pay. The women who own and work in the business earn wages that average 50% more than their non-coop counterparts, and receive health care and paid vacation benefits. In future, Seventh Generation and WAGES hope to expand the innovative practice beyond San Francisco.

Discussion 7.21: Seventh Generation

1. Seventh Generation is an example of a mission-driven company. The Body Shop is another example. What are the strengths and weaknesses of this type of company?
2. What can we learn from how Seventh Generation responded to criticism on one of its products?
3. Jeffrey Hollender demonstrated what might be called 'radical' or 'revolutionary' leadership, yet he was eventually removed from his CEO position by the board. What does this say about the potential for transformative change through business?

7.22 Shell

In 1994, following extensive decommissioning studies, Shell decided to dispose of its Brent Spar oil platform through "deep sea disposal" (i.e. sinking it) in the North Sea.

In April 1995, Greenpeace occupied the platform to protest against the method of disposal, which it believed was environmentally harmful. Their campaign resulted in mounting international protests and boycotts, including from some European governments.

After three months, and despite the support of the British government, Shell announced that it would not sink Brent Spar, and after a broad engagement process called "The Way Forward", announced in September 1998 that they would use the platform as a Norwegian Ro/Ro ferry quay.

In July 1998, all the governments of the north east Atlantic region agreed to ban future dumping of steel-built oil installations. However, with Greenpeace having admitted to misrepresenting some of the facts about the volume of oil on board Brent Spar, the debate about the whether the best environmental interests were served in the Brent Spar case continue to be hotly debated.

Shell's experiences in Nigeria show that it isn't always exclusively environmental issues that catalyse a crisis, nor is it only when the company is directly involved in an incident.

In the 1990s tensions arose between the native Ogoni people of the Niger Delta and Shell. The concerns of the locals were that very little of the money earned from oil on their land was getting to the people who live there, and the environmental damages caused by Shell's practices.

In 1993 the Movement for the Survival of the Ogoni People (MOSOP) organised a large protest against Shell and the government. Shell withdrew its operations from the Ogoni areas but the Nigerian government raided their villages and arrested some of the protest leaders.

Some of these arrested protesters, Ken Saro-Wiwa being the most prominent, were tried for murder (which they denied) and were executed in November 1995, despite a plea by Shell for clemency and widespread opposition from the Commonwealth of Nations and international human rights and environmental activists.

Despite Shell's opposition to the executions, there were widespread perceptions of their complicity with the government, which resulted in sustained international protests and boycotts. In 2002, close relatives of Ken Saro-Wiwa also won the right to bring a case brought against Royal Dutch Shell in the US.

After 1995, Shell began implementing extensive policy reforms, including increased stakeholder engagement and community support and improved performance reporting on social and environmental issues, both in Nigeria and internationally.

More sources of information on this case include: Decommissioning the Brent Spar (Rice & Owen, 1999); The Principles and Practice of Crisis Management: The Case of Brent Spar (Ahmed, 2006); and Where Vultures Feast: Shell, Human Rights and Oil (Okonta et al., 2003).

Discussion 7.22: Shell

1. What, if anything, could Shell have done differently in the way it handled the Brent Spar and Nigeria crises in 1995 to prevent the reputational damage it suffered?
2. After 1995, Shell became a pioneer in triple-bottom line strategy and reporting, yet it is still regularly targeted as an irresponsible and unsustainable company, in Nigeria and around the world. Is the triple-bottom line approach an adequate strategy for creating sustainable businesses? If not, what strategy should companies use?
3. One approach Shell and other oil companies have adopted in Nigeria and elsewhere is to create 'global MOUs', also sometimes known as 'good neighbourly agreements', with the communities where they operate. How do these work, and have they been effective?

7.23 Tesco

An illustration of circularity is the trend towards carbon neutrality, which has been embraced by, among others, multinationals like Dell, HSBC and Tesco. Let's look at Tesco, the third largest retailer in the world and a member of the Prince of Wales's Corporate Leaders Group on Climate Change. CEO Sir Terry Leahy believes the company is uniquely positioned to 'make sustainability a significant, mainstream driver of consumption' because 17 million consumers visit its 1,900 stores every week. The challenge is significant, as Tesco emits 4 million tonnes of carbon a year, according to The Guardian.

One of Leahy's first steps was a pledge in 2007 to plough £500m (around $770m) over five years to turn the fringe green lobby into a mass consumer movement, starting with a donation of £5m ($7.7m) a year to help fund academic research into greener consumption. With this money, the Sustainable Consumption Institute was established, in partnership with Oxford University, to develop an accepted measure of the carbon footprint of every one of the roughly 70,000 products Tesco sells. Leahy thinks of this as establishing a 'carbon calories' system. Speaking to The Indendent, he said, 'there aren't many things that keep me awake at night but this is one.'

Next, in 2008, Tesco launched a plan to reduced the carbon emissions of each of its stores by 50% by 2050, using a 2006 baseline, and to be carbon neutral as a company by 2050. Explaining this ambitious target in an interview with MeetTheBossTV, Tesco's global technology and architect director Mike Yorwerth said: 'We see the role of our customers, consumers of the world, as playing a huge role in moving us towards a more sustainable economy and more sustainable consumption in a world where by, in 30 or 40 years' time, people will need to live on possibly a fifth of the carbon they use today.'

In 2009, Tesco extended the pressure to its suppliers, requiring that they achieve a 30% reduction in the carbon footprint of their products by 2030. By then, the company had already published the carbon footprints of 114 of the products it sells with special labels and was hoping to expand that to 500 products by the end of the year. This is not just about public relations. According to Leahy, 'a low-carbon strategy is vital if we are to minimize the risk to our business [which include] the physical threat of climate damage to our supply chains, the resulting economic damage, and the serious effects of rushed and inefficient regulation if we fail to act in time and governments are forced to take draconian action.'

Most recently, in 2010, Tesco launched its first carbon neutral store in Ramsey, Cambridgeshire in the UK. The sustainable design is timber-framed rather than steel, and uses skylights and sun pipes to cut lighting costs. It also has a combined heat and power plant powered by renewable bio-fuels, exporting extra electricity back to the national grid. In addition the refrigerators have doors to save energy and harmful HFC refrigerant gases have been replaced. The store cost 30% more to build, but it uses 50% less energy, which Leahy believes 'is a business case in itself'. To coincide with the store opening, Tesco also announced that it intended to spend more than £100m ($154m) with green technology companies. What's more, with sales up 10% in 2010, it does not appear that its bold carbon strategy is harming business. Ultimately, the Principle of Circularity is a path to profitability.

Discussion 7.23: Tesco

1. Terry Leahy talked about wanting to create a mass green consumer movement. Do you think this is a good approach, or is he simply passing on the responsibility to consumers?
2. Do you think carbon footprint labels on grocery products will change consumer behaviour? What would need to happen for this to succeed?
3. What does it mean to be 'carbon neutral'? Does this represent an effective strategy for tackling climate change, or is it simply 'greenwashing'?

7.24 Vodafone

In a Vodafone sponsored study of 92 countries over the period 1996 to 2003, it was concluded that a developing country with an average increase of 10% mobile penetration showed 0.59% higher growth in GDP than an otherwise identical country. This study was replicated by Deloitte in 2007 using more recent data, which found that a 10% increase in mobile penetration would produce an additional 1.2% increase in annual GDP growth rate.

Today, two thirds of the world's mobile phone subscriptions are in developing nations, with the highest growth rate in Africa. It took just six years – from 1994 to 2000 – for mobile phones to overtake fixed lines on the continent, with an average 1000% annual growth rate. And the rapid take-up continues: while just 1 in 50 Africans had a mobile in the year 2000, now 28% have a cellular subscription. There are many reasons for this phenomenal growth, including shorter payback periods on investment, the relatively low skill levels needed to operate a mobile phone (as compared, say, with a computer), low barriers to entry (especially in terms of infrastructure) and business model innovations (such as prepaid systems, Grameen-style micro-entrepreneurship and mobiles as public telephones or telecentres).

Beyond simply expanding traditional mobile services to Africa, however, companies like Vodafone have also used the continent as an incubator for innovation. In Kenya in 2005, for example, 80% of the population did not have a bank account. Also, more money was coming into the country through remittances from family members living abroad than through oversees development assistance. However, these transfers were expensive, with Western Union typically taking a big slice in commission. Hence, Vodafone developed and piloted a new service called M-PESA, whereby customers could use their mobile phones to perform basic financial services, including depositing, withdrawing and transferring money using SMS texts.

The project was jointly funded by the UK Department for International Development (DFID) Financial Deepening Challenge Fund and the pilot ran for over 6 months in Kenya from October 2005, in partnership with Faulu Kenya, a local Microfinance Institution. Since rolling out through its national partner, Safaricom, the service has been wildly successful. For many, the service has been life-changing, giving access to financial services from which they were excluded and allowing them to receive remittance payments from the UK directly. Besides employing and empowering thousands of M-PESA agents, the scheme has also cut out a lot of corruption, as all transactions are electronic.

When Vodafone extended the M-PESA service to Tanzania in April 2008, they signed up more than 3 million customers in less than a year. In 2009, Safaricom also launched the continent's first commercial solar powered mobile phone, the Coral-200. Building on their success in Kenya, Tanzania and Roshan in Afghanistan (branded M-Paisa), they announced in February 2010 that they would bring M-

PESA to South Africa as well, which is Africa's biggest economy. Given its efforts, it is not surprising that Vodafone was placed first as a sustainable business in the Tomorrow's Value Rating of the ICT and Telecoms sector. Building on the success of Vodafone and others, a 2010 study by Arthur D. Little estimates that global transaction volume in mobile financial services will reach approximately $280 billion by 2015.

Discussion 7.24: Vodafone

1. Why do you think Vodafone's MPESA innovation happened in Kenya, rather than, say, the UK or the USA?
2. What makes mobile phones such a potent enabler of social and economic empowerment? What has enabled mobile phones to scale so rapidly in developing countries?
3. What is the role of government in supporting social innovations such as MPESA? Why have we not seen more of these kind of technological breakthroughs?

7.25 Walmart

'Rapacious behemoth', 'aggressive', 'bully' and 'evil empire' are just some of the public epithets Walmart had acquired by the time Harold Lee Scott Junior took over as President and CEO in 2000. Fortune magazine said 'the firm had what could be charitably described as an "us-versus-them" mentality, in which "us" was Walmart and "them" was everybody else, from critics to the competition, the government, and yes, sometimes even its own employees. The company's public image as a rapacious behemoth reflected that.' Business Week reported a 'mounting socio-political backlash to Walmart's size and aggressive business practices' and urged Walmart to 'stop the bullying ... stop squeezing employees and suppliers, and charge customers a little more.'

The source of all these jibes and accusations can be traced to two killer facts. One, ever since founder Sam Walton opened the company's first store in Arkansas in 1962, Walmart has been all about discount operations – low cost and low price. And two, from its humble beginnings, Walmart mushroomed into the largest company in the world – a $405 billion giant with over 2 million employees, serving customers more than 200 million times each week at more than 8,400 retail units under 55 different banners in 15 countries around the world. There is nothing about Walmart that can be described as small, other than its prices.

'When it comes to price, it's hard to beat Walmart,' admits Business Week, 'but the "everyday low prices" come at a high cost to its employees.' The result has been dozens of lawsuits brought by employees claiming to be overworked and underpaid, including 'the mother of all sex discrimination class actions', which alleges the company discriminated against 1.6 million women. In fact, there are two union-funded activist organisations, Wakeup Walmart and Walmart Watch, that exist for the sole purpose of criticising Walmart. And that's just on labour issues.

When it comes to green issues, 'the name "Walmart" has always triggered a shudder', says Grist magazine. The company has been charged with 'exacerbating suburban sprawl, burning massive quantities of oil via its 10,000-mile supply chain, producing mountains of packaging waste, polluting waterways with runoff from its construction sites, and encouraging gratuitous consumption.' The litany of alleged sins doesn't end there either – putting small companies out of business, maltreating suppliers, offering inferior employee benefits, the list goes on and on.

The point is that when Scott took charge, and for at least the first five years of his reign, Walmart was under siege, with a siege mentality to fit. 'We would put up the sandbags and get out the machine guns,' Scott recalls. 'If somebody criticized us, my first thought was, "Why don't they like us?" Or, "What could we do to them?" versus now, when I think, "Could the criticism have some truth?" Fortune later concluded that 'Scott had apparently learned that the best way to respond to an attacker was not with an attack of one's own, but to embrace them'. And embrace them he did, to the extent that his journey to openness – alongside that of Walmart – is today one of the most remarkable leadership stories of our time. So what happened? And why, and how?

It seems some of the seminal credit must go to one of Sam Walton's sons and to the NGO Conservation International (CI). Rob Walton is a lover of the outdoors and found himself in February 2004 on a 10-day trip to Costa Rica, hosted by Peter Seligmann, co-founder and CEO of CI. After pointing out the destructive havoc that fleets of fishing boats were wreaking on the delicate Costa Rican marine habitat, legend has it that Seligmann looked the Walmart chairman in the eye as said: 'We need to change the way industry works. And you can have an influence.' Sam was moved and promised to introduce Seligmann to Scott.

The timing was serendipitous, as Scott had just concluded a review of Walmart's legal and public relations problems, and it wasn't a pretty picture. The discrimination lawsuit had been certified as a federal class action, new stores were blocked by activists in Los Angeles, San Francisco and Chicago, and the company had just forked out millions to regulators for air and water pollution infringements. The findings of two recent studies only made matters worse: one that showed that Walmart's average spending on health benefits for its employees was 30% less than the average of its retail peers, and another, by McKinsey, concluded that up to 8% of shoppers had stopped patronizing the store because of its reputation.

The watershed meeting took place without fanfare in June 2004, with Rob Walton, Scott, Seligmann, Glenn Prickett (also of CI) and Jib Ellison, a river-rafting guide turned management consultant. Whatever was said, it convinced Scott to dip Walmart's toes into green waters. No doubt it helped that CI's board included former Intel chairman Gordon Moore, BP chief executive John Browne, and former Starbucks CEO Orin Smith, and that CI were already advising Starbucks on fairtrade issues and McDonald's on sustainable agriculture and fishing. Whatever the reasons, Scott commissioned Ellison's management consulting firm, BluSkye, to measure Walmart's total environmental impact.

It was a bold move, but it quickly paid off. BluSkye found that, for example, by eliminating excessive packaging on it's Kid Connection private-label line of toys, Walmart could save $2.4 million a year in shipping costs, 3,800 trees and one million barrels of oil. And on its fleet of 7,200 trucks, rather than letting the truck engine idle during the drivers' mandatory ten-hour breaks, it could save $26 million a year in fuel costs by installing auxiliary power units to heat/cool the cabs. In short, Walmart had belatedly discovered the win-win world of eco-efficiency, which WBCSD had been promoting since 1992. 'As we headed down this first path in our sustainability journey and started to see these results, we really got excited', recalls Scott.

If the truth be told, these initiatives were neither radical nor especially high impact in the context of Walmart's global footprint. And Scott could easily have stopped there, having gained the PR-benefits and the easy-picking cost savings. Fortunately, however, fate intervened. On 29 August 2005, Hurricane Katrina hit the Louisiana coast and devastated New Orleans. 'Katrina was one of the worst disasters in the history of the United States,' reflected Scott (2007), 'but it also brought out the best in our company. ... We responded by doing what we do best: We empowered our people and leveraged our presence and logistics to deliver the supplies that hurricane victims so desperately needed. Hurricane Katrina changed Walmart forever. And it changed us for the better. We saw our full potential – with absolute clarity – to serve not just our customers, but our communities, our countries and even the world. We saw our opportunity and our responsibility. In the aftermath of the storm, we asked ourselves: How can we be that company – the Walmart we were during Katrina – all the time? Sustainability became a big part of the answer.'

And so began one of the most unexpected and remarkable stories of corporate transformation. Scott soon announced three radical goals: 1) to be supplied 100 per cent by renewable energy; 2) to create zero waste; and 3) to sell products that sustain people and the environment. Admittedly, they are described as 'aspirational' with no timelines are attached, but if they get anywhere close, or even half-way there, they will have been a major catalyst for the post-industrial revolution. Already, we see the Walmart Effect of scalability in action in three areas: fish, cotton and lightbulbs. Let's look at each in turn.

Walmart plans to purchase all of its wild-caught fresh and frozen fish for the U.S. market from Marine Stewardship Council (MSC) certified fisheries by 2011. They are also working work with Global Aquaculture Alliance (GAA) and Aquaculture Certification Council (ACC) to certify that all foreign shrimp suppliers adhere to Best Aquaculture Practices standards in the U.S. by 2011. By 2009, they were already halfway there. Speaking to the Wall Street Journal, George Chamberlain, president of the Aquaculture Alliance put the move in perspective: 'The endorsement drew attention; Walmart buys more shrimp than any other U.S. company, importing 20,000 tons annually – about 3.4% of U.S. shrimp imports. With Walmart's nod, we went from trying to convince individual facilities to become certified to having long waiting lines.'

Scott also made a commitment to phase out chemically-treated textile crops. By 2008, Walmart was the largest buyer of organic cotton, with more than 10 million pounds purchased annually. They are also the world's largest purchaser of conversion cotton – cotton grown without chemicals, but waiting to be certified as organic. Scott is under no illusions about the ripple effects: 'Cotton farmers can now invest in organic farming because they have the certainty and stability of a major buyer. Through leadership and purchasing power, all of us can create new markets for sustainable products and services. We can drive innovation. We can build acceptance. All we need is the will to step out and make the difference.'

Another product Scott targeted for greening was light-bulbs. A compact fluorescent light bulb (CFL) has clear advantages over the widely used incandescent light — it uses 75% less electricity, lasts 10 times longer, produces 450 pounds fewer greenhouse gases from power plants and saves consumers $30 over the life of each bulb. But it is eight times as expensive as a traditional bulb, gives off a harsher light and has a peculiar appearance. As a result, the CFL bulbs only ever achieved 6% penetration, B.W. (Before Walmart). To tip the scales in favour of CFLs, Walmart set the goal of selling 100 million energy-saving bulbs. Success would mean total sales of CFLs in the U.S. would double, saving Americans

$3 billion in electricity costs and avoiding the need to build additional power plants for the equivalent of 450,000 new homes.

To ram home the point about Walmart's mighty sway, according to the New York Times, when they proposed this audacious goal, light-bulb manufacturers, who sell millions of incandescent lights at Walmart, immediately expressed reservations. In a December 2005 meeting with executives from General Electric, Walmart's largest bulb supplier, 'the message from G.E. was, "Don't go too fast. We have all these plants that produce traditional bulbs". The response from the Walmart buyer was uncompromising: "We are going there. You decide if you are coming with us".' Unsurprisingly, G.E. decided to tool up and scale up to meet the demand.

Today, these and other initiatives are all part of Walmart's Sustainability 360° programme. Compounding the scalability effect is the fact that Walmart plans to take its more than 100,000 suppliers along with it on this sustainability journey. In 2009, it announced the creation of a 'worldwide sustainable product index'. Step 1 was providing each of its suppliers with a survey of 15 simple, but powerful, questions to evaluate their own company's sustainability in four areas: energy and climate; natural resources; material efficiency; and people and community. Step 2 is to develop a global database of information on the lifecycle of products, to be shared on a public platform. And step 3 will be to translate the findings into a simple, convenient, easy to understand rating, so customers can make choices and consume in a more sustainable way.

Walmart is not second-guessing what these assessment, measurement and information systems will look like. However, it has said that by 2012, all direct import suppliers will be required to source 95% of their production from factories that receive one of Walmart's two highest ratings in audits for environmental and social practices, including standards of product safety, quality and energy efficiency. In February 2010, it also committed to reducing 20 million metric tons of carbon pollution from its products' lifecycle and supply chain over the next five years. That's equivalent to the annual greenhouse gas emissions from 3.8 million cars by 2015.

To be sure, Walmart still has plenty of critics – of its Sustainability Index, its labour practices, its supply chain performance and its Goliath tactics. But – to borrow from the Marvel comic-adapted movie Transformers – it is getting harder and harder to cast Walmart as the evil Megatron (part of the Deceptacon race) and far more plausible to see it as Optimus Prime, an awesomely powerful yet ultimately well-intentioned Transformer. The moral of the Walmart story is that it is making sustainability and responsibility scalable. Scott's take on it is that 'more than anything else, we see sustainability as mainstream. ... We believe working families should not have to choose between a product they can afford and a sustainable product.' That is nothing short of the CSR holy grail, and the jury is still very much out – especially since Scott stepped down in 2009 – but if anyone can tip us into the Age of Responsibility, it's the new 'sustainability superpower' Walmart.

Discussion 7.25: Walmart

1. What caused Lee Scott to take Walmart down the sustainability path? Do you think he is a good example of a sustainability leader?
2. Explain the concept of 'choice editing', using examples, and how this can contribute to scalability of sustainable products and solutions.
3. How would you rate Walmart's performance today on social, environmental, labour and ethical issues?

CHAPTER 8: THE FUTURE OF CSR

8.1 The Age of Greed

To understand the future of CSR, we must understand the past. In Chapter 2, I reviewed the history of CSR. Here, I want to focus on the most recent past, namely the global financial crisis that began in 2007/8. Gordon Gekko's words, although spoken by a fictitious character of Oliver Stone's imagination in the movie Wall Street, captures the spirit of a very real age: the Age of Greed. Gekko said:

'The point is, ladies and gentleman, that greed, for lack of a better word, is good. Greed is right, greed works. Greed clarifies, cuts through, and captures the essence of the evolutionary spirit. Greed, in all of its forms; greed for life, for money, for love, for knowledge has marked the upward surge of mankind.'

The Age of Greed was an age that, in my view, began when the first financial derivatives were traded on the Chicago Mercantile Exchange in 1972 and ended (we hope) with Lehman's collapse in 2008. It was a time when 'greed is good' and 'bigger is better' were the dual-mottos that seemed to underpin the American Dream. The invisible hand of the market went unquestioned. Incentives – like Wall Street profits and traders' bonuses – were perverse, leading not only to unbelievable wealth in the hands of a few speculators, but ultimately to global financial catastrophe.

The story of Gordon Gekko (and his modern day real-life equivalents like Richard Fuld, the captain of the titanic Lehmans before it hit the iceberg) gets to the heart of the nature of greed. The word 'greed' – from the old English grædig – has etymological roots that relate to 'hunger' and 'eagerness'. This is similar to the older word, avarice, coming from Old French and Latin (avere), meaning 'crave or long for'. Those are characteristics that Gekko and Fuld had in spades. The Greek word for greed – philargyros, literally 'money-loving' – also has a familiar echo in their stories. The trouble is that capitalism in general, and the American Dream in particular, has tended to interpret greed as a healthy trait. Gekko and Fuld didn't believe they were being unethical, or doing anything wrong. Each was playing the capitalism game – extremely well – and being rewarded handsomely.

Perhaps we would do well to recall the German root of the word for greed (habsüchtig), which means 'to have a sickness or disease'. Greed acts like a cancer in society – whereby an essentially healthy cell in the body becomes selfish and ends up destroying its host. As important as the greedy cell is the environment which enables it to live and prospers. A certain measure of selfishness is natural, but it needs to be moderated by norms, rules and cultural taboos that keep its destructive tendencies in check.

The Age of Greed was not something 'out there'. It was not the preserve of a few rogue traders or evil moguls. We were all caught up in its web. It is in fact a multi-level phenomenon, incorporating executive greed, banking greed, financial market greed, corporate greed and ultimately the greed embedded in the capitalist system. These different facets of greed are each explored in turn below, before considering what the alternatives might be.

8.2 Executive Greed

The most convenient explanation for the financial crisis is to point a finger at the greed and irresponsibility of a few individual executives, like Enron's former CEO Jeffrey K. Skilling and Lehman's Fuld. It is an argument with significant weight.

In 2000, Enron was the 7th largest company in America, with revenues of $111 billion and over 20,000 staff. When the company collapsed in 2001, due to various fraudulent activities fuelled by a culture of greed, the average severance payment was $45,000, while executives received bonuses of $55 million in the company's last year. Employees lost $1.2 billion in pensions; retirees lost $2 billion, but executives cashed in $116 million in stocks.

At the end of 2007, when the GFC writing was already writ large on the wall, in large part due to the greed-hyped activities of Lehman and other financial institutions, CEO Fuld and president Joseph Gregory paid themselves stock bonuses of $35 million and $29 million respectively. Fuld lived in an enormous Greenwich mansion, over 9,000 square feet, valued at $10 million. He had four other homes and an art collection valued at $200 million. Hardly a picture of responsible restraint.

Taken on their own, these executive pay packages are outrageous enough. But the extent of creeping executive greed comes into even sharper focus when we look at trends in relative pay. In 1965, U.S. CEOs in major companies earned 24 times more than a typical worker, a ratio that grew to 35 in 1978 and to 71 in 1989. By 2000, it had hit 298, and despite falling to 143 in 2002 (after the post-Enron stock market slump), it bounced back again and has continued rising through the noughties (2000s).

According to Fair Economy, in 2007, despite the looming economic recession, CEOs of the largest 500 companies in America (S&P 500) averaged US$10.5 million, 344 times the pay of typical American workers and 866 times as much as minimum wage employees. The same year, the top 50 hedge and private equity fund managers earned an average of $588 million, according to Alpha magazine – more than 19,000 times as much as average worker pay. And in 2008, while the financial crisis was beginning to bite for ordinary citizens, average CEO pay went up to US$10.9 million, while CEO perks averaged US$365,000—or nearly 10 times the median salary of a full-time worker.

It is easy to go cross-eyed or brain-fried when confronted by a barrage of numbers like that. And yet, there was one particular number that shocked me so much at the time (in 1997) that it stuck in my conscience. I believe I read it in Anita Roddick's book, Body and Soul. She claimed that it would take one Haitian worker producing Disney clothes and dolls 166 years to earn as much as Disney's then president, Michael Eisner, earned in one day. Reflecting on this, I wrote in my book Beyond Reasonable Greed: 'rather than spreading around the wealth for the common good, it seems to us that Adam Smith's invisible hand has a compulsive habit of feeding itself'.

8.3 Banking Greed

As horrific as these trends in executive greed are – and they certainly represent a responsibility train-wreck – I do not believe that the GFC can be adequately explained by 'bad apples' (as the media liked to characterise these now-disgraced captains of industry). In addition to those leaders who were driven by personal greed, the sub-prime crisis was also a story of institutional greed, aided and abetted by deregulation of the financial sector since the 1980s.

Aside from this general trend of deregulation, we can point to a number of poor U.S. policy decisions that were to have disastrous consequences. The first was Bill Clinton's campaign promise to increase home ownership in poor and minority communities – a noble cause, to be sure, but one which put pressure on the banks to make riskier loans: two million of them between 1993 and 1999. The folly of this policy, while obvious in retrospect, didn't pose any immediate concerns, as the housing market was strong and prices continued to rise.

Over the same period, Clinton was coming under increasing pressure by the banking lobby to repeal the Glass-Steagall Act of 1933, a piece of post-Wall Street crash legislation that prevented commercial banks from merging with investment banks. The law was specifically put in place to prevent another global financial crisis and ensuing depression. At first, Clinton resisted. But the banks were relentless. In 1998, one of them, Citicorp, decided to flaunt the law, announcing a $70 billion merger with Travelers Insurance. Clinton tried to block it but failed in the Senate, despite the fact that the merger was technically illegal.

A year later, Clinton bowed to rising pressure and repealed the Glass-Steagall Act. This single action proved to be the 'butterfly effect' that would bring the world financial system to its knees. With the stroke of a pen, and bullied by the greed of the banks, Clinton had given permission for speculative financial traders to start gambling with the hard-earned deposits of ordinary Americans. Soon, all manner of financial instruments exploded onto the market – from CDOs (collaterized debt obligations) and CLOs (collaterized loan obligations) to CMBSs (commercial mortgage-backed securities) and CDSs (credit default swaps).

For a year or two, it seemed like the party may have ended before it had begun. Saddled with $65 billion in unpayable debt, Enron spiralled to their death at the hands of the financial markets, with their share price falling from US$90 to just a few cents. In the months that followed, a spate of bankruptcies rocked the world, all of companies which had issued convertible bonds: Global Crossing, Qwest, NTL, Adelphia Communications and WorldCom. The 9/11 tragedy and Dotcom crash happened around the same time, and some measure of caution returned to the markets, but not for long.

Alan Greenspan took an action that, like Clinton's repeal of Glass-Steagall, would cause another 'butterfly effect'. Between December 2000 and June 2003, he cut interest rates from 6 per cent to 1 per cent, and kept them there. Suddenly, not only was the housing market growing, but money was almost free. With the help of the newly invented financial voodoo instruments, the sub-prime party bonanza really got going.

Preposterous loans like the NINJA mortgage were invented – that stands for No Income, No Job, no Assets. It didn't matter that you were poor and had no collateral. Not only would you get a mortgage, the broker would pay you 10% more than you needed to buy the house. The initial interest rate (what the brokers called the 'teaser rate') would also be next to nothing, although it would increase five or ten fold in the years to come. The infallible logic behind this – if that isn't an inappropriate use of the term – was that house market prices would continue to rise steadily, and everyone would be a winner.

The result was that, according to the Mortgage Bankers' Association, the number of subprime loans offered to borrowers with below average credit increased nearly 15 times between 1998 and 2007, from 421,330 to 6.2 million. And the banks were in a feeding frenzy, leveraging themselves to the hilt, so that they could make obscene profits from the market boom. Historically, a leverage of 10 times EBITDA (Earnings before Interest, Taxes, Depreciation, and Amortization), i.e. where the company has debts of 10 times its actual value) was considered very high. But by the time it hit the iceberg, Lehman Brothers was well on the way to being leveraged to 44 times its value, owing more than $700 billion. The face of banking greed was unmasked.

8.4 Financial Market Greed

Many GFC analysts would stop there, satisfied that the combination of executive greed and banking greed provide sufficient explanation for the Crisis of Responsibility. And while they certainly represent the most obvious signal failures that caused the mother-of-all meltdowns, I still do not believe that these two factors tell the whole story. To understand banking greed, we need to look at the nature of the broader financial markets – how they are designed, how they operate and the behaviours that they incentivise.

In order to understand what 'greed is good' really means – in terms of hard numbers – we must wrap our heads around the concept of financial derivatives. Larry McDonald (2009), a Lehman's insider who called the collapse 'a colossal failure of common sense', refers to derivatives as 'the Wall Street neutron'. They are essentially speculative bets on changes in various market indicators (like currencies and interest rates) and they have been growing exponentially since their introduction in 1972. By the turn of the century, these wizz-kid invented, esoteric financial instruments were just hitting their stride, growing at around 25% per year over the last decade. Today, according to some accounts, the derivatives market is worth over US$1,000 trillion (that's 15 zeros!).

Why this is so significant is that most of this 'trade' is not happening in the 'real economy'; it is a casino economy. Take trade in currencies, for example. In 1998, around US$1.5 trillion (that's 12 zeros) in currency was traded daily on the global markets, up 46% from 1994. But only 2.5% was linked to 'real economy' transactions such as trade, tourism, loans or genuine investment on stock markets. The other 97.5% (up from 20% in the 1970s) was pure speculation – a casino economy in which financial traders were making eye-popping truckloads of money, without actually contributing anything tangible to the products and services that give us quality of life.

One of the more modern varieties of derivatives is the credit default swap (CDS). Larry McDonald reflects that 'in the merry month of May 2006, Wall Street took hold of this gambling concept and decided to transform itself into something between a Las Vegas casino and an off-track betting parlour'. Early in 2006, there were $26 trillion of CDS bets outstanding in the market. By the beginning of 2008, it was $70 trillion, with just 17 banks carrying that risk. And there was another $15 to $18 trillion in other derivatives and fancy instruments (an alphabet soup of CDOs, RMBSs, CMBSs, CLOs and ABSs).

This was all well and good when it was just a high-stakes game for rich kids to play. But as we have seen, with the repeal of the Glass-Steagall Act and the introduction of the Financial Services Modernization Act in 1999, the greed-infused, short-term obsessed gambling habits of Wall Street traders can have (and have had) very real and devastating effects on very real economies and very real people. And even today, in the aftermath of the GFC, very few of these financial market agents have taken responsibility, or been made accountable, nor have the financial market rules been significantly changed.

As it happens, that great post-Depression economist, John Maynard Keynes, had foreseen this and warned: 'Speculators may do no harm as bubbles on a steady stream of enterprise. But the position is serious when enterprise becomes the bubble on a whirlpool of speculation. When the capital development of a country becomes a by-product of the activities of a casino, the job is likely to be ill-done'. And ill-done it has been, woefully ill-done. No wonder billionaire investor Warren Buffet first described derivatives as 'weeds priced as flowers', and later as 'financial weapons of mass destruction'. If Kenyes were here today, standing with us on financial 'ground zero ', gazing at the post-apocalyptic debris of our once gleaming citadels of commerce, he might quite justifiably shake his head and mutter, 'I told you so!'

8.5 Corporate Greed

Even financial market greed may not be ultimate cause. Could it be that unbridled greed is, by design, the unavoidable consequence of the corporation? We often forget that when corporations were originally introduced in America in the mid-1800s, it was with the explicit purpose of serving the public good (enshrined in a charter), with liable shareholders. But the nature of the corporation changed when the US Supreme Court ruled that a corporation should have the same rights as individuals, thus making it a legal person. The problem, according to critics, is that the corporation is a 'person' with no moral conscience and an exclusive focus on the benefits of shareholders. This results in a pattern of social costs imposed by business in exchange for private gains for its executives and owners.

In his controversial, yet hugely influential book and documentary, The Corporation, Canadian legal academic Joel Bakan, suggests that corporations are, by their legal constitution, pathological in nature: 'The corporation has a legally defined mandate to relentlessly pursue—without exception—its own self-interest regardless of the often harmful consequences it might cause to others. Lying, stealing and killing are not rare aberrations but the duty of the corporation when it serves the interests of its shareholders to do so'. This, according to Bakan, means that corporations have all the characteristics of a psychopath, as defined by the World Health Organisation.

Not everyone – even among those concerned about business responsibility – would go this far in their diagnosis. But there is certainly little doubt about the in-built greed of the modern corporation. David Korten, author of When Corporations Rule the World, is among the many critics that remind us of the power of modern business, in which more than half of the top 100 'economies' in the world are in fact multinational corporations. With such power comes responsibility, but left their own devices, many corporations are cost externalisation machines – meaning that they will naturally try to avoid paying for any negative human, community or environmental costs that they impose on society.

In an interview I did with Korten (2008), he told me that the problem is even more fundamental than the corporations themselves: 'If I were to rewrite the book now, I would probably put the title When Corporations Rule the World with a slash through 'Corporations' and a little carrot pointing to 'Money'. It's actually When Money Rules the World. This has become so much more obvious, so much stronger and so much more disruptive as we've seen the rampant speculation in the financial markets. That very structure drives a predatory dynamic in the corporate system that you really can't do very much about at the level of the individual corporation. You can do a little tinkering around the edges, but those are pretty limited relative to the depth of the changes that we need to navigate'.

8.6 Capitalist Greed

So this begs the question: is capitalism itself fundamentally flawed? Will capitalism – with its short-term, cost-externalisation, shareholder-value focus – always tend towards greed, at the expense of people and the planet? Will the scenario of 'overshoot and collapse' that was computer modelled in the 1972 Limits to Growth report (and confirmed in revisions 20 and 30 years later) still come to pass? Has Karl Marx been vindicated in his critique (if not his solution) that by design, capitalism causes wealth and power to accumulate in fewer and fewer hands?

To answer these quintessential questions, we need to look at the facts. According to WWF, humanity's Ecological Footprint, driven by the spread of capitalism globally, has more than tripled since 1961. Since the late 1980s, we have been in overshoot – meaning that the world's Ecological Footprint has exceeded the

Earth's biocapacity. Between 1970 and 2003, WWF's Living Planet Index, which tracks over 6,000 populations of 1,313 species, fell by 29%. By their estimates, we would need three planets if everyone on earth were to adopt the energy intensive, consumptive lifestyle of the capitalist Western world.

The UN Millennium Ecosystem Assessment, issued in 2005, reaches similar conclusions: 60% of world ecosystem services have been degraded; of 24 evaluated ecosystems, 15 are being damaged; water withdrawals have doubled over the past 40 years; over a quarter of all fish stocks are overharvested; since 1980, about 35 per cent of mangroves have been lost; about 20% of corals were lost in just 20 years and 20% more have been degraded; and species extinction rates are now 100-1,000 times above the background rate. So, by all accounts, capitalism is failing spectacularly to control the environmental impacts of the economic activities that it is so successful at stimulating.

The social impacts of capitalism are more ambiguous. On the one hand, critics like Naomi Klein (author of No Logo and Disaster Capitalism) argue that 'Gucci capitalism' results in labour exploitation and a 'race to the bottom'. In other words, capital flows to wherever the social or environmental standards are lowest. Not only this, but capitalism is designed to create the instability that we have seen in the markets and those that suffer the most from this volatility are always the most vulnerable, namely the poor of the world.

On the other hand, largely thanks to its adoption of capitalism, China has enjoyed economic growth of more than 9% a year over the past 30 years and as a result, between 1981 and 2005, their poverty rate fell from 85% to 16%, or by over 600 million people. That represents real positive impacts on real people. But at what cost? Some estimate that environmental damage robs China of 5.8% of its GDP every year. What's more, the gaps between rich and poor in China are growing.

Perhaps the trillion-dollar question is not whether capitalism per se acts like a cancer gene of greed in society, but whether there are different types of capitalism, some of which are more benign than others? To date, the world has by and large been following the American model of shareholder-driven capitalism, and perhaps this is the version that is morally bankrupt and systemically flawed? Management guru, Charles Handy, seems to agree. In an interview I conducted with him, Handy (2008) confessed: 'I've always had my doubts about shareholder capitalism, because we keep talking about the shareholders as being owners of the business, but most of them haven't a clue what business they're in. They are basically punters with no particular interest in the horse that they're backing, as long as it wins'.

What then is the alternative version of capitalism? Can there be an economic system that is not fuelled by greed? The jury is still out on this, but at least we are starting to explore the idea. We hear Bill Gates talking about creative capitalism which combines the 'two great focuses of human nature - self-interest and caring for others'. Jonathon Porritt calls for 'capitalism as if the world matters' and Paul Hawkens, Amory Lovins and Hunter Lovins propose 'natural capitalism'.

Whichever version we ultimately go for, I am convinced it will have to be a more regulated capitalism. We sometimes forget that Adam Smith was a moral philosopher and always assumed that markets would take place within a rules-based system of norms and controls. Having witnessed the disaster of unregulated capitalism and deregulated financial markets, it is time for the pendulum to swing back to greater government involvement. History has taught us that, without a strong policy framework, we will not get responsible markets or sustainable products at the scale and with the urgency that we need them.

Discussion 8.1: The Age of Greed

1. Do you think the global financial crisis could have been prevented by better corporate responsibility alone?
2. Do you think it is possible to change the short-termism and narrow shareholder-focus of the financial markets? If so, how?
3. Some argue that capitalism needs to be reformed to achieve a sustainable and responsible economy? Do you agree, and if so, how?

8.7 The Ages and Stages of CSR

The impotence of CSR in the face of more systemic problems has been nowhere more evident than in the global financial crisis. As illustrated above, the global financial crisis represents a multi-level failure of responsibility – from the individual and corporate level to the finance sector and entire capitalist system. Underlying this failure of responsibility lies a cancer of greed that has corrupted our business systems, governance and ethics, particularly in our Western economies.

However, it would be unfair and inaccurate to characterise all business activity as motivated by greed. Rather, it is my contention that the evolution of business responsibility can be best understood in terms of five overlapping ages – the Ages of Greed, Philanthropy, Marketing, Management and Responsibility. I believe that each of these ages typically manifests a different stage of CSR, namely Defensive, Charitable, Promotional, Strategic and Transformative CSR respectively.

My contention is that companies tend to move through these ages and stages (although they may have activities in several ages and stages at once), and that we should be encouraging business to make the transition to Transformative CSR in the dawning Age of Responsibility. If companies remain stuck in any of the first four stages, I don't believe we will turn the tide on the environmental, social and ethical crises that we face. Simply put, CSR will continue to fail.

Defensive CSR

The Age of Greed is characterised by Defensive CSR in which all corporate sustainability and responsibility practices – which are typically limited – are undertaken only if and when it can be shown that shareholder value will be protected as a result. Hence, employee volunteer programmes (which show evidence of improved staff motivation, commitment and productivity) are not uncommon, nor are expenditures (for example in pollution controls) which are seen to fend off regulation or avoid fines and penalties.

Charitable CSR

Charitable CSR in the Age of Philanthropy is where a company supports various social and environmental causes through donations and sponsorships, typically administered through a Foundation, Trust or Chairman's Fund and aimed at empowering community groups or civil society organisations.

Promotional CSR

Promotional CSR in the Age of Marketing is what happens when corporate sustainability and responsibility is seen mainly as a public relations opportunity to enhance the brand, image and reputation of the company. Promotional CSR may draw on the practices of Charitable and Strategic CSR and turn them into PR spin, which is often characterised as 'greenwash'.

Strategic CSR

Strategic CSR, emerging from the Age of Management, means relating CSR activities to the company's core business (e.g. Coca-Cola and water management), often through adherence to CSR codes and implementation of social and environmental management systems, which typically involve cycles of CSR policy development, goal and target setting, programme implementation, auditing and reporting.

Transformative CSR

Transformative CSR in the Age of Responsibility focuses its activities on identifying and tackling the root causes of our present unsustainability and irresponsibility, typically through innovating business models, revolutionising their processes, products and services and lobbying for progressive national and international policies.

Hence, while Strategic CSR is focused at the micro level – supporting social or environmental issues that happen to align with its strategy (but without necessarily changing that strategy) – Transformative CSR focuses on understanding the interconnections of the macro level system – society and ecosystems – and changing its strategy to optimise the outcomes for this larger human and ecological system.

Ideally, therefore, businesses should make the journey to Systemic CSR in the emerging Age of Responsibility, building on each previous stage of maturity. If on the other hand companies remain stuck in any of the first four stages, our ability to turn the tide on the environmental, social and ethical crises that we face will be seriously compromised. Simply put, CSR will continue to fail.

Discussion 8.2: The Ages and Stages of CSR

1. What are the strengths and weaknesses of the Ages and Stages model of CSR?
2. Can you think of any examples of companies in each of the five ages and stages of CSR? What about companies that have evolved through one or more stages?
3. On the whole, what age and stage of CSR do you think your country and/or industry sector is mainly occupying? What might cause it to change?

8.8 The Age of Responsibility

Most companies are stuck in the Ages of Greed, Philanthropy, Marketing and Management, with approaches to CSR that are failing to solve the global challenges we face. What makes the Age of Responsibility – and showcase leaders like Ray Anderson and Interface – different from, say, BP (Age of Marketing) or Cadbury (Age of Management), is the depth of their admission and the scale of their ambition.

In Anderson's (2009) book, Confessions of a Radical Industrialist, he conceded not only that today's economic system is broken, but that he and his company were part of the problem. He was able to see himself as a plunderer – not through malicious intent, or even greed, but by failing to question the true impacts of business on society and the environment. As Alcoholics Anonymous will tell you, admission is the first step to recovery. Unfortunately, most companies stuck in the Ages of Greed, Philanthropy, Marketing and Management are all still in denial, thinking that either there is no problem, or it's not their problem, or that it's a problem to benefit from, or that it's only a minor problem.

The Age of Responsibility is not just about admission though; it's also about ambition. As far as I can tell, Interface was the first major company to set the BHAG (big hairy audacious goal) of zero negative impact, as well as going beyond 'no harm' to also become a restorative business – to genuinely make things better and leave this world with a net-positive balance. It is only such audacious goals that can lift the triple curses of incremental, peripheral and uneconomic CSR. As Robert Francis Kennedy reminds us: 'There are those who look at things the way they are, and ask why. I dream of things that never were, and ask why not?' We need more pragamatic dreamers, business leaders who practice what brain-mind researcher and author Marilyn Ferguson calls 'pragmagic'.

Anderson was not the first radical business leader, nor perhaps even the most radical. The late Anita Roddick, founder of the Body Shop International, had a missionary zeal that few will ever rival. Famous for her business-led activism, which began as an alliance with WWF in 1986 to save the whale, she went on to tackle issues as far ranging as animal rights, women's self-esteem, human rights, fair trade and indigenous people's rights. In her autobiography, Business As Unusual (Roddick, 2001), she distilled her philosophy as follows: 'Business is a renaissance concept, where the human spirit comes into play. It does not have to be drudgery; it does not have to be the science of making money. It can be something that people genuinely feel good about, but only if it remains a human enterprise.'

Ben Cohen and Jerry Greenfield who 'hated running but loved food' and therefore founded Ben & Jerry's ice cream, became flag bearers for a more radical kind of responsibility as well. Their mission 'to make the best possible ice cream in the nicest possible way' was not just sweet talk. They put it into action in various ways, from going free range and supporting fairtrade to setting up a Climate Change College and sponsoring research into eco-friendly refrigeration. Their biography, The Inside Scoop: How Two Real Guys Built a Business with a Social Conscience and a Sense of Humor (1994), tells the story. 'If you open up the mind,' they concluded, 'the opportunity to address both profits and social conditions are limitless. It's a process of innovation.'

Ricardo Semler (1989, 1993), CEO of the Brazilian manufacturing company Semco, is another self-confessed maverick who turned many assumptions about 'good management' on their head. For example, at Semco he allowed workers to set their own salaries and working hours; he taught everyone in the company, including shop floor workers, how to read a balance sheet; and he made everyone's salary public. 'If you're embarrassed about the size of your salary', he said, 'you're probably not earning it'. His radical philosophy was this: 'Most companies hire adults and then treat them like children. All that Semco does is give people the responsibility and trust that they deserve.'

8.9 Web 2.0: Seeds of a Revolution

Throughout my 20 year career in corporate sustainability and responsibility, these are the kinds of pioneers I have looked to for hope and inspiration. The frustration has been that these 'radical industrialists' have always remained the exception, rather than the rule. They are the outliers, which is fine if – in line with Everett Rogers' Diffusion of Innovation model – they are the innovators that make up 2.5% of the population. The problem is that most their ideas and practices haven't diffused to the early adopters and the early majority, let alone the late majority and laggards.

So what will it take to get the kind of transformation we need to move beyond innovation towards mass change? I find an analogy is always helpful and in early 2008, I discovered the perfect metaphor: Web 2.0. The term, of course, had been around for a while – coined in 1999 by IT consultant Darcy DiNucci in an article called 'Fragmented Future' and popularised in 2004 by the landmark O'Reilly Media Web 2.0 conference. Tim O'Reilly's 2005 article 'What is Web 2.0' had already become an Early Adopters' touchstone for a rapidly evolving new lexicon, and remains a classic piece. People like me, part of the technosphere's Early Majority, were a bit slower in waking up, and it took Dan Tapscott and Anthony Williams' book Wikinomics (2006) to switch me on to the revolution in progress.

Before coming to why Web 2.0 is a good metaphor for the transformation of CSR, let me try to bed down the concept. Today, Wikipedia defines Web 2.0 as 'web applications that facilitate interactive information sharing, inter-operability, user-centered design and collaboration.' Fair enough, but let's dig a little deeper, drawing on the term's evolution. In 1999, DiNucci was writing for programmers, challenging them to adapt to the increasing use of portable Web-ready devices. This was just a small part of what Web 2.0 would come to mean. In 2005, O'Reilly brainstormed a far more wide ranging list of examples and contrasts between Web 1.0 and Web 2.0. Examples included DoubleClick versus Google AdSense, Britannica Online versus Wikipedia, personal websites versus blogging, publishing versus participation, directories (taxonomy) versus tagging (folksonomy) and stickiness versus syndication, to mention but a few. His article concluded with seven core competencies of Web 2.0 companies:

1. Services, not packaged software, with cost-effective scalability;

2. Control over unique, hard-to-recreate data sources that get richer as more people use them;

3. Trusting users as co-developers;

4. Harnessing collective intelligence;

5. Leveraging the long tail through customer self-service;

6. Software above the level of a single device; and

7. Lightweight user interfaces, development models and business models.

Tapscott & Williams (2006) gave an applied view on Web 2.0 in the form of wikinomics, which they defined as 'the effects of extensive collaboration and user-participation on the marketplace and corporate world'. Wikinomics, they said, is based on four principles:

1. Openness, which includes not only open standards and content but also financial transparency and an open attitude towards external ideas and resources;

2. Peering, which replaces hierarchical models with a more collaborative forum, for which the Linux operating system is a quintessential example;

3. Sharing, which is a less proprietary approach to (among other things) products, intellectual property, bandwidth and scientific knowledge; and

4. Acting globally, which involves embracing globalisation and ignoring physical and geographical boundaries at both the corporate and individual level.

8.10 The Birth of CSR 2.0

By May 2008, it was clear to me that this evolutionary concept of Web 2.0 held many lessons for CSR. I published my initial thoughts in a short article online entitled CSR 2.0: The New Era of Corporate Sustainability and Responsibility (Visser, 2008b), in which I said:

The field of what is variously known as CSR, sustainability, corporate citizenship and business ethics is ushering in a new era in the relationship between business and society. Simply put, we are shifting from the old concept of CSR – the classic notion of 'Corporate Social Responsibility', which I call CSR 1.0 – to a new, integrated conception – CSR 2.0, which can be more accurately labelled 'Corporate Sustainability and Responsibility'. The allusion to Web 1.0 and Web 2.0 is no coincidence. The transformation of the internet through the emergence of social media networks, user-generated content and open source approaches is a fitting metaphor for the changes business is experiencing as it begins to redefine its role in society. Let's look at some of the similarities.

In Web 1.0, we had flat world just beginning to connect itself and finding a new medium to push out information and plug advertising. We saw the rise to prominence of innovators like Netscape, but these were quickly out-muscled by giants like Microsoft with its Internet Explorer. And the focus was largely on the standardised hardware and software of the PC as its delivery platform, rather than multi-level applications.

Similarly, CSR 1.0 was a vehicle for companies to establish relationships with communities, channel philanthropic contributions and manage their image. It included many start-up pioneers like Traidcraft, but has ultimately turned into a product for large multinationals like Walmart. And we travelled down the road of 'one size fits all' standardisation, through codes, standards and guidelines to shape its offering.

Web 2.0, on the other hand, is being defined by watchwords like 'collective intelligence', 'collaborative networks' and 'user participation'. Tools include social media, knowledge syndication and beta testing. Is as much a state of being as a technical advance - it is a new philosophy or way of seeing the world differently.

Similarly, CSR 2.0 is being defined by 'global commons', 'innovative partnerships' and 'stakeholder involvement'. Mechanisms include diverse stakeholder panels, real-time transparent reporting and new-wave social entrepreneurship. And we are recognising a shift in power from centralised to decentralised; a change in scale from few and big to many and small; and a change in application from single and exclusive to multiple and shared.

As our world becomes more connected and global challenges like climate change and poverty loom ever larger, businesses that still practice CSR 1.0 will (like their Web 1.0 counterparts) be rapidly left behind. Highly conscientised and networked stakeholders will expose them and gradually withdraw their social licence to operate. By contrast, companies that embrace the CSR 2.0 era will be those that collaboratively find innovative ways tackle our global challenges and be rewarded in the marketplace as a result.

Discussion 8.3: CSR 2.0 and the Age of Responsibility

1. Can you think of any examples (other than those in the text) of leaders or companies that demonstrate the levels of *admission* and *ambition* that are needed to create an Age of Responsibility?
2. Do you think CSR 2.0 is a useful metaphor for how CSR needs to evolve? What do you or don't you like about it?
3. What role could Web 2.0, including social media, play in bringing about CSR 2.0?

8.11 Principles of CSR 2.0

So much for the metaphor of CSR 1.0 and CSR 2.0. However, a metaphor can only take you so far. What was needed was a set of principles against which we could test CSR. These went through a few iterations, but I eventually settled on five, which form a kind of mnemonic for CSR 2.0: Creativity, Scalability, Responsiveness, Glocality and Circularity. These principles can be described briefly as follows:

Principle 1: Creativity

In order to succeed in the CSR revolution, we will need innovation and creativity. We know from Thomas Kuhn's (1996) work on The Structure of Scientific Revolutions that step-change only happens when we can re-perceive our world, when we can find a genuinely new paradigm, or pattern of thinking. This process of 'creative destruction' is today a well accepted theory of societal change, first introduced by German sociologist Werner Sombart and elaborated and popularised by Austrian economist Joseph Schumpeter (2008). We cannot, to a paraphrase Einstein, solve today's problems with yesterday's thinking.

Business is naturally creative and innovative. What is different about the Age of Responsibility is that business creativity needs to be directed to solving the world's social and environmental problems. Apple, for example, is highly creative, but their iPhone does little to tackle our most pressing societal needs. By contrast, Vodafone's M-PESA innovation by Safaricom in Kenya, which allows money to be transferred by text, has empowered a nation in which 80% of the population have no bank account and where more money flows into the country through international remittances than foreign aid. Or consider Freeplay's innovation, using battery-free wind-up technology for torches, radios and laptops in Africa, thereby giving millions of people access to products and services in areas that are off the electricity grid.

All of these are part of the exciting trend towards social enterprise or social business that is sweeping the globe, supported by the likes of American Swiss entrepreneur Stephen Schmidheiny, Ashoka's Bill Drayton, e-Bay's Jeff Skoll, the World Economic Forum's Klaus Schwabb, Grameen Bank's Muhammad Yunus and Volans Venture's John Elkington. It is not a panacea, but for some products and services, directing the creativity of business towards the most pressing needs of society is the most rapid, scalable way to usher in the Age of Responsibility.

Principle 2: Scalability

The CSR literature is liberally sprinkled with charming case studies of truly responsible and sustainable projects and a few pioneering companies. The problem is that so few of them ever go to scale. It is almost as if, once the sound-bites and PR-plaudits have been achieved, no further action is required. They become shining pilot projects and best practice examples, tarnished only by the fact that they are endlessly repeated on the CSR conference circuits of the world, without any vision for how they might transform the core business of their progenitors.

The sustainability problems we face, be they climate change or poverty, are at such a massive scale, and are so urgent, that any CSR solutions that cannot match that scale and urgency are red herrings at best and evil diversions at worst. How long have we been tinkering away with ethical consumerism (organic, fairtrade and the like), with hardly any impact on the world's major corporations or supply chains? And yet, when Walmart's former CEO, Lee Scott, had his post-Hurricane Katrina Damascus experience and decided that all cotton products in Walmart will be organic and all fish MSC-certified in future, then we started seeing CSR 2.0-type scalability.

Scalability not limited to the retail sector. In financial services, there have always been charitable loans for the world's poor and destitute. But when Muhammad Yunus (1999), in the aftermath of a devastating famine in Bangladesh, set up the Grameen Bank and it went from one $74 loan in 1974 to a $2.5 billion enterprise, spawning more than 3,000 similar microcredit institutions in 50 countries reaching over 133 million clients, that is a lesson in scalability. Or contrast Toyota's laudable but premium-priced hybrid Prius for the rich and eco-conscious with Tata's $2,500 Nano, a cheap and eco-friendly car for the masses. The one is an incremental solution with long term potential; the other is scalable solution with immediate impact.

Principle 3: Responsiveness

Business has a long track-record of responsiveness to community needs – witness generations of philanthropy and heart-warming generosity following disasters like 9/11 or the Sichuan Earthquake. But this is responsiveness on their own terms, responsiveness when giving is easy and cheque-writing does nothing to upset their commercial applecart. The severity of the global problems we face demands that companies go much further. CSR 2.0 requires uncomfortable, transformative responsiveness, which questions whether the industry or the business model itself is part of the solution or part of the problem.

When it became clear that climate change posed a serious challenge to the sustainability of the fossil fuel industry, all the major oil companies formed the Global Climate Coalition, a lobby group explicitly designed to discredit and deny the science of climate change and undermine the main international policy response, the Kyoto Protocol. In typical CSR 1.0 style, these same companies were simultaneously making hollow claims about their CSR credentials. By contrast, the Prince of Wales's Corporate Leaders Group on Climate Change has, since 2005, been lobbying for bolder UK, EU and international legislation on climate change, accepting that carbon emission reductions of between 50-85% will be needed by 2050.

CSR 2.0 responsiveness also means greater transparency, not only through reporting mechanisms like the Global Reporting Initiative and Carbon Disclosure Project, but also by sharing critical intellectual resources. The Eco-Patent Commons, set up by WBCSD to make technology patents available, without royalty, to help reduce waste, pollution, global warming and energy demands, is one such step in the right direction. Another is the donor exchange platforms that have begun to proliferate, allowing individual and corporate donors to connect directly with beneficiaries via the web, thereby tapping 'the long tail of CSR' (Visser, 2008d).

Principle 4: Glocality

The term glocalization comes from the Japanese word dochakuka, which simply means global localization. Originally referring to a way of adapting farming techniques to local conditions, dochakuka evolved into a marketing strategy when Japanese businessmen adopted it in the 1980s. It was subsequently introduced and popularised in the West in the 1990s by Manfred Lange, Roland Robertson, Keith Hampton, Barry Wellman and Zygmunt Bauman. In a CSR context, the idea of 'think global, act local' recognises that most CSR issues manifest as dilemmas, rather than easy choices. In a complex, interconnected CSR 2.0 world, companies (and their critics) will have to become far more sophisticated in understanding local contexts and finding the appropriate local solutions they demand, without forsaking universal principles.

For example, as cited in Chapter 3, BHP Billiton was vexed by their relatively poor performance on the (then) Business in the Environment (BiE) Index, run by UK charity Business in the Community. Further analysis showed that the company had been marked down for their high energy use and relative energy inefficiency. Fair enough. Or was it? Most of BHP Billiton's operations were, at that time, based in southern Africa, home to some of the world's cheapest electricity. No wonder this was not a high priority. What was a priority, however, was controlling malaria in the community, where they had made a huge positive impact. But the BiE Index didn't have any rating questions on malaria, so this was ignored. Instead, it demonstrated a typical, Western-driven, one-size-fits-all CSR 1.0 approach.

To give another example, in contrast to Carroll's (1991) CSR pyramid with its economic, legal, ethical and philanthropic layers, in a sugar farming co-operative in Guatemala, they have their own CSR pyramid – economic responsibility is still the platform, but rather than legal, ethical and philanthropic dimensions, their pyramid includes responsibility to the family (of employees), the community and policy engagement. Clearly, both Carroll's pyramid and the Guatemala pyramid are helpful in their own appropriate context. Hence, CSR 2.0 replaces 'either/or' with 'both/and' thinking. Both SA 8000 and the Chinese national labour standard have their role to play. Both premium branded and cheap generic drugs have a place in the solution to global health issues. CSR 2.0 is a search for the Chinese concept of a harmonious society, which implies a dynamic yet productive tension of opposites – a Tai Chi of CSR, balancing yin and yang.

Principle 5: Circularity

The reason CSR 1.0 has failed is not through lack of good intent, nor even through lack of effort. The old CSR has failed because our global economic system is based on a fundamentally flawed design. For all the miraculous energy unleashed by Adam Smith's 'invisible hand' of the free market, our modern capitalist system is faulty at its very core. Simply put, it is conceived as an abstract system without limits. As far back as the 1960s, pioneering economist, Kenneth Boulding, called this a 'cowboy economy', where endless frontiers imply no limits on resource consumption or waste disposal. By contrast, he argued, we need to design a 'spaceship economy', where there is no 'away'; everything is engineered to constantly recycle.

In the 1990s, in The Ecology of Commerce, Paul Hawken (1994) translated these ideas into three basic rules for sustainability: waste equals food; nature runs off current solar income; and nature depends on diversity. He also proposed replacing our product-sales economy with a service-lease model, famously using the example of Interface 'Evergreen' carpets that are leased and constantly replaced and recycled. McDonough & Braungart (2002) have extended this thinking in their Cradle to Cradle industrial model. Cradle to cradle is not only about closing the loop on production, but about designing for 'good', rather than the CSR 1.0 modus operandi of 'less bad'.

Hence, CSR 2.0 circularity would, according to cradle-to-cradle aspirations, create buildings that, like trees, produce more energy than they consume and purify their own waste water; or factories that produce drinking water as effluent; or products that decompose and become food and nutrients; or materials that can feed into industrial cycles as high quality raw materials for new products.

Circularity needn't only apply to the environment. Business should be constantly feeding and replenishing its social and human capital, not only through education and training, but also by nourishing community and employee wellbeing. CSR 2.0 raises the importance of meaning in work and life to equal status alongside ecological integrity and financial viability.

8.12 Shifting from CSR 1.0 to CSR 2.0

These principles are the acid test for future CSR practices. If they are applied, what kind of shifts will we see? In my view, the shifts will happen at two levels. At a meta-level, there will be a change in CSR's ontological assumptions or ways of seeing the world. At a micro-level, there will be a change in CSR's methodological practices or ways of being in the world.

The meta-level changes can be described as follows: Paternalistic relationships between companies and the community based on philanthropy will give way to more equal partnerships. Defensive, minimalist responses to social and environmental issues will be replaced by proactive strategies and investment in growing responsibility markets, such as clean technology. Reputation-conscious public-relations approaches to CSR will no longer be credible and so companies will be judged on actual social, environmental and ethical performance, i.e. are things getting better on the ground in absolute, cumulative terms?

Although CSR specialists still have a role to play, each dimension of CSR 2.0 performance will be embedded and integrated into the core operations of companies. Standardised approaches will remain useful as guides to consensus, but CSR will find diversified expression and implementation at very local levels. CSR solutions, including responsible products and services, will go from niche 'nice-to-haves' to mass-market 'must-haves'. And the whole concept of CSR will lose its Western conceptual and operational dominance, giving way to a more culturally diverse and internationally applied concept.

How might these shifting principles manifest as CSR practices? Supporting these meta-level changes, the anticipated micro-level changes can be described as follows: CSR will no longer manifest as luxury products and services (as with current green and fairtrade options), but as affordable solutions for those who most need quality of life improvements. Investment in self-sustaining social enterprises will be favoured over cheque-book charity. CSR indexes, which rank the same large companies over and over (often revealing contradictions between indexes) will make way for CSR rating systems, which turn social, environmental, ethical and economic performance into corporate scores (A+, B-, etc., not dissimilar to credit ratings) and which analysts and others can usefully employ in their decision making.

Reliance on CSR departments will disappear or disperse, as performance across responsibility and sustainability dimensions are increasingly built into corporate performance appraisal and market incentive systems. Self-selecting ethical consumers will become irrelevant, as CSR 2.0 companies begin to choice-edit, i.e. cease offering implicitly 'less ethical' product ranges, thus allowing guilt-free shopping. Post-use liability for products will become obsolete, as the service-lease and take-back economy goes mainstream. Annual CSR reporting will be replaced by online, real-time CSR performance data flows. Feeding into these live communications will be Web 2.0 connected social networks that allow 'crowdsourcing', instead of periodic meetings with rather cumbersome stakeholder panels. And typical CSR 1.0 management systems standards like ISO 14001 will be less credible than new performance standards, such as those emerging in climate change that set absolute limits and thresholds.

Discussion 8.4: Shifting from CSR 1.0 to CSR 2.0

1. Can you think of examples of companies that are demonstrating one or more of the five principles of CSR 2.0?
2. What are the incentives for companies to move to Transformative CSR in an Age of Responsibility? Are the incentives strong enough?
3. In order for CSR 2.0 to emerge successfully, what actions will non-business sectors (government, civil society, academia, etc.) need to take?

8.13 Drivers of the Future

Of course, CSR 2.0 is just one scenario of how the future of CSR might evolve. Scenarios, or stories of possible futures, are an incredible powerful tool. Far from simply being an exercise in light entertainment, they are a glimpse of the very real future landscape of business that will emerge over the coming decades. Underpinning the CSR trend is a number of conditions – what scenario planners call 'rules of game'. The rules of the game are the conditions that we are fairly certain will apply within the foreseeable future. They govern our behaviour and up to a point are beyond our control.

Unlike the rules of sport which are conveniently written down in a rulebook somewhere, the rules of business are normally unwritten. At times, they are subject to intense debate – particularly when they change as they are doing at the moment. However, there are certain rules that never change such as the moral rules of the game. Many lion companies either ignore or fail to understand that business is as subject to the moral rules as an individual is. Nor are they sensitive to those changes in the rules which are taking place as a result of alterations in the environment around them.

In my book Beyond Reasonable Greed (Visser & Sunter, 2002), we identified seven rules of the game that underpin the world that is emerging. Let's look at these briefly in turn.

Spaceship Earth

Recalling Kenneth Boulding's 1960s metaphor, we live within an insular planetary system. The only external input is the sun's radiation. To all intents and purposes, nothing comes in and nothing leaves. There is no backup store of resources to tap into once our planet is all used up. And there is no 'away' for the waste and pollution that we create. We can try to hide it by burying it or diluting it, but it doesn't disappear; it just accumulates. For even with our technological wizardry, we cannot replicate the planet's ingenious processes. Up till now, this rule hasn't been a problem. We've got away with ignoring it because for most of the Earth's history the population has been relatively small and only a small proportion of that population has consumed resources at a rate which might cause a problem.

Now, Spaceship Earth is what we would call a 'showstopper'. It is literally a 'killer concern' because, by ignoring this rule, we are in danger of killing ourselves off as a species on this planet. The planet will survive, by the way. This may sound overly melodramatic but it is pure, measurable science: we are slowly poisoning ourselves on the one hand, and threatening the delicate equilibrium of various ecosystems on which we depend on the other. More about this in the key uncertainties.

Demographic Multipliers

Population has a double whammy effect as a rule of the game. Obviously, a growing population puts more strain on limited resources, such as the environment, food and habitat. And, even with the most optimistic projections on declining fertility rates, the latent population growth that is already 'in the pipeline' will almost certainly result in a doubling of today's six billion people. That would be challenge enough for our Spaceship Earth, but it is only the first multiplier.

The second multiplier is tied up with the industrial lifestyle which developing countries are seeking to emulate, and which is highly resource intensive and extremely unhealthy, wasteful and polluting. What would happen if the one million pounds of annual waste generated by each American citizen were multiplied by seven billion as opposed to 300 million? Or if on the same basis we extrapolated the $100 billion that America spends to combat the harmful effects of air pollution, or the $50 billion in health costs associated with their fast-food diet? Quite simply, if every country adopts these lifestyles, the environmental and social impacts will be catastrophic. The crazy thing is that America has to rely on the rest of the world not catching up with it in order to continue with the wasteful lifestyle to which it has grown accustomed.

Pervasive poverty, Growing Resentment

Poverty is a crisis of global proportions. Three billion people still live on less than $2 a day, while more than one billion do not have access to proper food or clean water. According to the United Nations, worldwide poverty has got worse not better over the past 50 years. That's in absolute terms. Relatively speaking, the gap between the 'haves' and the 'have-nots' is also widening as we alluded to earlier. And being a complex issue, the problem is not going to go away at any time soon. For decades to come, poverty will remain the single biggest threat to social sustainability.

Poverty acts like a cancer in the human society: it eats away at the body from the inside out; there is no simple cure; and by the time it is usually recognised as a threat, it is already too late. Our current belief in 'trickle down' economics is like an ineffective, superstitious placebo. It may make us feel better for a while, but it hasn't rooted out the cause. It's as if we naively believe that if the privileged few keep eating ice-cream which happens to taste great, the good feeling will eventually spread to the less fortunate masses and just melt away the cancer. In practice, the reverse is happening. With the advent of mass media, the poor now know what they're missing out on and a sense of relative deprivation is spreading out like a shock-wave. Accompanying the resentment is something to which we refer later on: the access to weapons of mass destruction which the poor increasingly have. Combined with religious fervour, this whole mixture becomes pretty potent.

Declining Ecosystems

Some of the facts previously mentioned in the book bear repeating here: we have lost over thirty per cent of the species that were living a few hundred years ago; the Earth is losing an estimated three or more species per hour, a rate one hundred to one thousand times greater than the average over the preceding hundreds of millennia; and conservation biologists are predicting that half of the diversity of life will be lost in the next century if the present rates of habitat destruction and disturbance continue.

Need more facts? In the past 50 years, the world has lost a quarter of its topsoil and a third of its forest cover. At present rates of destruction, we will lose 70 per cent of the world's coral reefs in our lifetime, host to a quarter of marine life. In the past three decades, one-third of the planet's natural resources has been consumed. We are losing freshwater ecosystems at the rate of six per cent a year, marine ecosystems at four per cent a year. At the same time, we are starting to wreak havoc with our climate system. There is no longer any serious scientific dispute that things are getting worse, even in the twenty years since the Rio Earth Summit of 1992.

On the other hand, a very powerful driving force behind modern business was introduced unwittingly by Peter Drucker, the American guru, when he invented 'management by objectives' in the middle part of the last century. Nowadays, MBO as it is known is at the centre of all strategic, operational and budgetary processes. You set objectives and then you measure your performance against those objectives whether they are financial ones, production ones, marketing ones, etc. Because we naturally aspire to do better in the eyes of the people we fear and respect (for underlings read bosses, for bosses shareholders) our objectives tend to reflect this. We select targets which will lower costs, raise production and produce more profit. Nobody budgets lower profit unless it is due to factors beyond his or her control. Thus, while Drucker himself may be an open-minded and balanced individual, his product – MBO – has entrenched a culture of 'more' just when we need a culture of 'less' according to this rule of the game.

Worse still, MBO creates the impression that the future is certain and management is in control. The objectives must be attained whatever the future has in store. It's rather like the pilots of an airliner having a flight plan and no radar system to indicate that the flight plan should be changed in the event of bad weather ahead. The facts we have quoted under this heading show that some really bad weather is about to be encountered if we don't change course immediately.

Techno-scientific Boom

The pace of scientific discovery and technological innovation shows no signs of abating. Whether it is mapping the human genome, building artificial intelligence machines, or cloning animal life, each new revelation sparks a whole industry of possibilities. We just need to look at how many mainstream career options today did not exist 50 years ago: mobile phone design and engineering, computer science, biotechnology, corporate environmental management, microelectronics, website design, contamination remediation - the list could go on and on.

In our struggle to cope with the whirlwind of change that surrounds us, we should resist the temptation to react like the Luddites of old – those bands of English artisans bent on destroying machinery in the early nineteenth century in the belief that all new technology was evil. The information technology revolution has reshaped our world forever; and wave upon wave of scientific breakthroughs in the twenty-first century will continue to toss and tumble us about, until we learn to surf each new change. The hope is that technological advance can create environmentally-friendly substitutes in the fields of materials and energy, so vital for people to improve their standard of living within the constraints of inhabiting Spaceship Earth.

Networked Planet

Hand in hand with the spread of democracy around the globe, the planet has become a world wide web. The so-called information superhighway is a vast network of fibre optic cables, radio waves, micro-waves and satellite signals. Whether you are standing on the top of Mount Kilimanjaro or at the bottom of the Grand Canyon, a little black box called a cellphone can connect you with anyone else on earth. Or a web-cam can teleport someone live into your home for a chat, as if he or she were sitting across the coffee table from you.

This is the fishbowl reality of today's world – real-time, larger than life news about anything, anywhere; near-instantaneous duplication and dissemination of information; and cyber-societies of virtual relationships between like-minded people scattered around the globe. Commit any corporate sins against sustainability and there is nowhere to run, and nowhere to hide. On the other hand, if you are one person trying to make your voice heard, just plug into the Internet and go on a surfing safari. On the way, you will make lots of friends and learn all you need to know to make a difference collectively.

Renaissance in Values

The social and environmental movements that have gained momentum over the past five decades are more than just a collection of events, or a passing phase of human introspection. In the process, our global society has been changing at its very core. We have seen the bubbling up of age-old values – like honesty and selflessness and compassion – in a shift that may prove with hindsight to be as profound as the triumph of democratic principles over dictatorial monarchy, or civil freedom over human slavery.

In essence, what the sustainability trend is in the process of doing is renting the veil on the hypocrisy of today's political institutions, economic ideologies, and business organisations, all of which exist within societies that proclaim the virtues of one or more of the great religious or spiritual traditions of the world. As in the children's parable of Snow White, the shift in values now underway in society is acting like that 'mirror, mirror on the wall' which sees beyond superficial appearances (like political speeches, economic mumbo-jumbo, and corporate values statements), and judges character solely on the basis of the actions of the person or institution concerned. We have moved from 'tell me' to 'show me'.

8.14 Future Uncertainties

In addition to rules of the game, there are key uncertainties - variables that could go one way or the other. They are the pivotal points on which the future swivels. Let's look at some briefly.

Willingness to Share Power

One of the things that made South Africa's transition to democracy so remarkable was that F.W. de Klerk was prepared to surrender his position of supreme power as President in the interests of the country's future. He had the strategic insight to realise that holding onto power in a pariah state would, sooner or later, result in civil war and unnecessary bloodshed. The temporary power sharing arrangement negotiated between de Klerk and Nelson Mandela was the only sane solution, but it took great courage and vision to let go of control and begin to trust those formerly regarded as enemies.

Business faces the same dilemma. Either they continue to cling to their already awesome power and dominance in the world at the expense of future environmental and social sustainability; or they have the wisdom to start sharing that power – with Third World countries, with local communities, with environmental interest groups, and so on. The key uncertainty is the extent to which greed-minded businesses will realise that their current winner-takes-all course is a path towards self-destruction, and that power sharing is the only sustainable way forward. Equally, a key uncertainty overhangs the attitude of the West – particularly America – in promoting a more democratic system of world governance. Will the UN Security Council be modified with this in mind?

Direction of Innovation

The techno-scientific boom is a rule of the game. What remains uncertain, however, is the direction that this spring tide of innovation is going to take. In the same way that nuclear energy can power whole cities while nuclear weapons can destroy them in seconds, we are increasingly faced with ethical choices in our use of technology. Some types of biotechnology can help clean up pollution, while other kinds increase the dependence of already marginalized farmers on multinational chemical companies. On the one hand more powerful personal computers, combined with faster Internet access, has enabled small business to carve out global niches in a way that would have been impossible 30 years ago. On the other hand, software development in procurement programmes has allowed large companies to rationalise the number of their supplies, which has resulted in many small companies being struck off the list.

To some extent, technology is neutral; the direction in which we develop and apply it, however, is anything but neutral. Consider the current debate on the pros and cons of genetically modified food, or the cloning of human beings, for example. Guided by the principles of sustainability, some of these dilemmas become less ambiguous. Expand the use of carbon-based fuels by subsidisation, or invest in renewable energy? The former is environmentally unsustainable, so the answer is obvious. Install high tech manufacturing facilities in a country with high unemployment, or support labour intensive methods? The former is socially unsustainable, so the solution is self-evident. Or at least it should be in the future. The uncertainty lies in the extent to which governments and financial markets and ordinary consumers are going to support this trend towards sustainable technology.

Economic and Trade Policies

Will we see economic reforms that put a cost on environmental degradation through eco-taxes? Or that help to lift people out of the poverty trap through basic income grants? Will speculators be given free reign to wreak havoc with international markets and national economies, or will they be reigned in through 'Tobin taxes'? Will 'parallel currencies' be supported and promoted as a way of empowering local communities? How will we balance the interests of pension funds, life insurance companies and other institutional shareholders who need gains in the stock prices to run their businesses effectively against the need to create incentives for companies to become more elephant-like in their approach to all stakeholders? Will the monetary system be adapted to give greater access to capital to entrepreneurs and communities, or will excessively high interest rates and the overhang of foreign debt continue to thwart economic development in Third World countries?

Likewise, the way in which the rules of international trade evolve will either support greed-driven behaviour or be sensitive to society's needs. The World Trade Organisation smacks of an exclusive club – established by the already dominant players with only their own interests in mind. Will it pry open new markets no matter what the cost is to the vulnerable countries concerned? Or will it be counterbalanced by the fair trade movement which is more concerned with sharing the benefits of trade equitably and sustainably? On a different note, will sustainability-oriented certification and labelling schemes become part and parcel of the international trading system in order to allow trading partners to differentiate between irresponsible and responsible companies?

Political Maturity

If countries were children, we would not hesitate to tell some of them, in no uncertain terms, to stop their petty squabbles and temper tantrums, to cut out their selfish, brattish behaviour and to quit their senseless, destructive ranting. The disquieting flare-up of nationalistic, regional, cultural and religious rivalries is a key uncertainty that can destroy all the best intentions for a sustainable world. Whether it is Zimbabwe's troubles, the Middle Eastern conflict, or the West versus Islam, the threat to social and environmental sustainability is very real.

To create a sustainable future, politicians and countries will need to grow up. They have to be big enough to put their ideological differences aside, to allow wounds of the past to heal, and to realise that the only viable future is one in which everybody compromises to keep the peace and share the prosperity. This may sound like starry-eyed, wishful thinking, but that's exactly how the political miracle brokered between Mandela and de Klerk in South Africa sounded in the early 1990s. Then again, as any parent will attest, children are a notoriously unpredictable lot, and some never seem to grow up!

In the global kindergarten, the possibility of some regional conflict getting out of hand – for example India and Pakistan ending up in a nuclear exchange – is considerable. We don't have the two 'teachers' that we used to have in charge of the 'classroom'. When a regional dispute arose during the old 'Cold War' days, America took one side and the Soviet Union the other and somehow they contained the situation. Even when we came close to nuclear war over the Cuban missile crisis, sense prevailed in the end. Nowadays, America does not want to commit its young men to conflicts which have nothing to do with America's interests, Russia has troubles of its own and the United Nations is simply too weak and too stretched to cope. Against this backdrop nuclear proliferation continues unchecked, which means the boys in the classroom have some very dangerous toys.

Rate of Environmental Decline

The current decline of virtually every ecosystem on the planet is only in dispute by those who choose, usually for conveniently selfish reasons, to turn a blind eye to the overwhelming body of scientific evidence that is mounting up day by day. Facts and figures aside, it is common sense. Virtually every substance on earth is a potential poison – it is just a matter of concentration. In other words, there is a certain threshold beyond which almost all substances are toxic to life, including the human body. Since everything on earth disperses, but nothing disappears, our biggest problem is that persistent substances (like many chemicals and heavy metals) are steadily building up in our environment. It is only a matter of time before they become 'toxic'.

We are reminded of the African tale of the Earth Mother placing a fig tree into the care of a troupe of monkeys. However, the monkeys not only ate the fruit, they stripped the bark and broke off the branches as well. In other words, they went beyond reasonable greed. When the Earth Mother returned, the fig tree had withered and died and the skeletons of the monkeys lay scattered on the ground.

What is uncertain is the rate of environmental decline, and exactly when we will start to feel the system biting back – when crops yields will plummet; or fishing stocks pass the point of no return; or wild swings in weather patterns become the norm; or chemicals in the environment start manifesting as health defects in humans. The Natural Step calls these feedback loops "hitting the walls of the funnel". Another uncertainty is whether it will be too late to take corrective action by the time the problem becomes obvious. For instance, even if the whole world stopped emitting greenhouse gases tomorrow, we would still feel the effects of the damage already done for centuries to come. Will we be like the many species who perished in the last ice age? By the time they noticed the temperature change, they could not adapt quickly enough.

Social Unrest

The past 100 years of industrial development have been building up to a situation of intolerable social inequity. The widening gap between the 'haves' and 'have-nots', now exacerbated by the digital divide, is a breeding ground for social discontent. We should be heeding the lessons of history. After all, how many popular revolts have been directed against unjust rule and too great a concentration of wealth and power? And yet, this is exactly the kind of situation we find in our world today: between the First and Third Worlds, between billionaire tycoons and slave-wage workers, between the Wabenzi (Mercedes-driving politicians) and their starving, unemployed constituents.

Are the anti-globalisation protests of Seattle and the terror attacks of September 11 merely a hint of what is to come? How much longer will the billions of poor people in Third World countries put their faith in the hollow promises of the 'trickle down' economics of globalisation? Can the materialistic goals of American free market capitalism ever be reconciled with the cultural traditions of the Islamic Middle East? We are at a critical stage in the world's history, somewhere just below boiling point, when a few degrees one way or the other could make all the difference – the difference between social unrest boiling over or simmering down.

However, there is something that moves social unrest straight up the uncertainty charts to a prime position: the change in the mathematics of destruction. It is now quite possible for some shadowy cult of extremely evil people to gain access to weapons of mass destruction – nuclear, biological or chemical. $E = mc^2$ is a genie which will never be put back in the bottle. Extremist cults and terrorist organisations will exploit social unrest as a launchpad for their evil deeds. Thus, a requirement for a peaceful world is a level of social stability which allows nations to cooperate in establishing an effective global intelligence network against such criminals.

Lifestyle Choices

The simple illusion of business-friendly capitalism that has kept most of the world under a spell for the past 50 years is that 'we can have our cake and eat it'. Even sustainable development is twisted by politicians to mean that more economic growth will solve our social and environmental problems. However, when US President George W. Bush pulled out of the Kyoto Protocol agreement on climate change because (he argued) it would hurt the American economy, we were left in no doubt as to the illusion that we are asked to accept. A switch to a sustainable economy will require short term sacrifices and investments that will only pay off down the line.

The key uncertainty is whether individuals and companies and countries will follow a path leading to sustainable lifestyles, or whether we will shun the short-term sacrifices necessary for long term environmental integrity and social well-being. How many of us will pay extra cash to have a catalytic converter fitted onto our car's exhaust? How many of us can afford it? Will our companies combat HIV/AIDS by making the required investment in educational programmes leading to behavioural change and the infrastructure required to deliver antiretroviral drugs to the community? Will our politicians eliminate perverse subsidies relating to unsustainable lifestyles and direct these towards social banking and renewable energy? There are a multitude of lifestyle choices that will shape our future.

8.15 Future Scenarios

Given the rules of the game and key uncertainties just described, we have chosen two contrasting scenarios to illustrate how the future landscape of business and the world could turn out. As mentioned already, the actual outcome will partly depend on the options we choose over the coming decade. The two scenarios are: (1) Oases in the Desert; and (2) Plains of the Serengeti. Remember scenarios are stories of what can happen in the future – they are not forecasts of what is going to happen. Their purpose is to educate rather than prescribe. To liven things up, we return to the metaphor of lions and elephants as irresponsible/unsustainable and responsible/sustainable companies respectively.

Oases in the Desert

Oases in the Desert is where we end up if the lions continue on their path of ascendancy towards global domination. The scenario's oasis image points to pockets of plenty existing in the midst of a desert of deprivation. It is almost as if the excesses of water and lush greenery in the oasis have been sucked out of the rest of the landscape and accumulated at just a few spots. Some golf courses give one that impression! Generally, the scenario is the net result of the present lions' tendency to accumulate power and concentrate wealth in fewer and fewer hands (or should that be paws?). Additional consequences are that the majority of the world's population is pushed into a marginal existence and the natural environment is systematically degraded. Only the cats get fatter. Like black holes in astronomy, wealth becomes so condensed that it creates its own 'singularity of greed'. All the money that flows into the lions never escapes.

Those that are familiar with Frank Herbert's bestselling science fiction series, Dune, will have no difficulty imagining the scene. The story is set on the desert planet of Arakas, the sole source of spice, which is a mineral on which the galactic population is dependent. The mercenary tycoons that control the spice control the universe, and they're not about to share their accrued benefits of power, wealth and water with anybody else.

At first, the lion kings – individuals, businesses and politicians that have exploited the current global situation relentlessly for their own selfish gain – may revel in their opulence without concern. They will think that they are simply collecting their just reward for being superior players of the modern game of material gain. Most likely, their mesmerised fans will worship them as heroes. They will form exclusive clubs where only royalty is welcome, so that they can show off their treasures to one another, strategise about how they can shape the destiny of the world and reassure one another that they deserve everything they've got. Occasionally, they will fall out with one another and have trade wars, but they never allow these differences to jeopardise their overall control.

Their self-indulgent lives will lack only one thing – peace of mind. Because, as everyone knows, water is a priceless commodity in the desert. And if you own and control the water supply, all those billions that are dying of thirst in the desert will do desperate things to gain access to the fountain, or just to vent their stored up hatred – they may even commit murder! Therefore, security will become a primary and constant concern for lions. High walls, alarm systems, bodyguards, hidden vaults, police investigators, secret escape tunnels, private armies, you name it: they will install and employ them. But they will never feel completely safe. Lingering in the background will always be the fear of the next crazed suicide bomber or undetected anthrax delivery.

Of course, the lion kings will own what is left of the living environment – all the most pristine ecological reserves will be their exclusive playground. Their homes, their offices and their vehicles will be fitted with all the latest technological wizardry to insulate them from the pervasive pollution and saturation of toxins that incessantly plague the masses. And yet there will still be some things that they just can't buy or own or control. The unpredictable weather patterns will continue to be an expensive source of irritation, as will the seemingly random collapse of shares in their portfolio when the company or the industry in which they are invested is implicated in the latest health scare, fatal accident or environmental disaster.

The era of the lion kings will not last forever and it will probably end with bang or a squelch. As the vast majority of the world's population sees the gap ever widening between their own poverty-ridden and environmentally-degraded existence and the insular wealth of rich executives, large multinationals and First World countries, a global mass protest movement gathers momentum and becomes increasingly volatile and violent, eventually making the kingdom of the lion king ungovernable. This popular discontent is exacerbated as ecosystems continue to topple like dominoes, and the most vulnerable populations begin to suffer the ravages of pollution-induced disease. Terror strikes against lion countries as well as lion companies become more common, fuelled by cultural and religious tensions. Ultimately, such developments lead to a chain reaction that descends into full-scale nuclear and bio-chemical warfare. A selection of oases meet their doomsdays ahead of schedule. You may recall our reference to butterfly wings causing the perfect storm if conditions are right – a tiny little thing triggering off a huge response.

Maybe the few hundred vote difference in Florida in the last US presidential election will be responsible for the Third World War. Who knows?

Plains of the Serengeti

Plains of the Serengeti is where we head for if the lions realise that their game of domination has a no-win conclusion and voluntarily or begrudgingly begin shapeshifting into elephants. The scenario conjures up breathtaking images of the fertile plains of East Africa and the Great Rift Valley teeming with wildlife, all living in a state of dynamic harmony with each other and the natural environment. A rich heritage of biological diversity exists, with even the predators finding their rightful place within the larger community of animals. Hence, although competition still takes place in the society, it is tempered by the more pervasive co-operative tendency in Nature which ensures that a healthy balance is maintained. The smaller, more entrepreneurial animals flourish in this setting.

The trail leading to the Serengeti requires that at various levels of society, from the individual through to the community, from business through to the economy, from politics through to global governance, a consensus emerges regarding new rules of the game that are in everyone's collective interest, including criteria for ecological sustainability and minimum equity requirements for social sustainability. As a consequence of these new governance principles, the sixth mass species extinction and the poisoning of the environment are halted and reversed, and the formerly marginalized and disempowered sections of the world's population are given a fair stake in global society and the economy.

Much of the success of the transition to a sustainable world has to do with the restructuring of the economy. The incentive mechanisms are redesigned in such a way that excessive accumulation of wealth and concentration of power are strongly discouraged, negative environmental impacts are prohibitively expensive and meeting social needs is a primary condition for operating at any level in the economy. Money still exists, but shapeshifts into a multi-tiered commodity with community currencies being created as and when required as a means of facilitating local exchange of goods. Modifications to the interest and discount rate mechanisms are devised, and speculation is heavily taxed. The main difference from the lion trail is that the economy is made to serve people and the environment and not the other way round.

Business still plays a critical role in the world, meeting people's needs with its products and services; but the power and influence that it previously had over global affairs is now subject to numerous social, environmental and ethical checks and balances. While an important purpose of companies remains the making of profit and the provision of a return to shareholders, their overall objective is widened to that of making a permanent contribution in the communities in which they operate. Work itself is seen as a means to an end, a 'space' in which people can develop their potential, express their talents and make a positive contribution to society. Survival is no longer dependent on having a formal job. Most places of work and living are digitally connected, with an emphasis on decentralising as much authority as possible to employees and providing them with congenial surroundings.

Among the fundamental principles that are embedded in society in this scenario are creative diversity, freedom with accountability and the philosophy of holism. Although the technological revolution has continued apace and has greatly assisted with meeting human needs and ensuring ecological sustainability, this has to be matched by a revolution in the outlook of humans towards their planet. The new wave of discovery will be focused on understanding the physiology and psychology of healthy living systems (including all levels of human interaction) and developing the personal and social skills to build these systems effectively. However, given the fact that the actual Serengeti is home to both elephants and lions, it would be wrong to typecast a scenario named after it as an elephant heaven devoid of all lions. You will still have highly competitive companies operating in the lion mode – but the rules of the park won't favour them anymore.

8.16 Future Options

Having depicted the possible paths that the future can take in two mainline scenarios, we must now consider the options within the control of the principal actors which will increase or reduce the probabilities of either scenario materialising. While we will concentrate on the options facing companies, multi-level shapeshifting makes it essential to bring countries and individuals into the picture. Continuing on with our lion/elephant metaphor, at the business level, we have nominated the three options: (1) Catwalk; (2) Leophancy; and (3) The Charge of the Heavy Brigade.

Catwalk

The first option for companies is to continue down the Catwalk. In other words, it's business as usual with the lions on the prowl. Sustained pressure from shareholders and the sanctity of the profit motive will continue the drive towards greater efficiencies, the expansion into new markets and the accumulation of capital. Repeated mergers and acquisitions will be necessary to secure survival, until eventually global industries are dominated by just a handful of multinational corporations. In order to facilitate the unrestricted operation of global companies and their access to potential markets, initiatives like the World Trade Organisation and the Multilateral Agreement on Investments will be strongly supported. Any criticism of these global 'rules of trade' will be called foul-play and an attempt to resist the levelling of the playing fields (which are anything but level).

The concept of stakeholders will be acknowledged, but a strict hierarchy of priority will be applied. Directors, shareholders and financial institutions will continue to take precedence over any other group. Employees and customers get the attention they need to ensure the successful sale of the companies' products and services. Other groups, like government, communities, media and environmental or social activists will be treated as necessary evils, to be negotiated with or influenced as and when required. A minimum level of charitable work and social and environmental contributions will be maintained to project the public image of a responsible corporate citizen. However, should any business decision require a trade-off between economic returns and social impacts or environmental degradation, the colour of money will always win the day.

Corporate executives will rise to the status of kings in a changing landscape of growing disparity. For most business directors and line managers, their actions will remain within the boundaries of the law as they steadily accumulate great fortunes of wealth. Given the rules of the free market game, they will simply be regarded as extremely talented players who are collecting their hard-earned and well-deserved prize of gold. The plight of the world's poor and the steady decline in global environmental conditions will be seen as problems for government or the United Nations to take care of (after all, that's what taxes are for!). Despite the waves of layoffs as industries consolidate, technologies improve and efficiencies go up, Catwalk managers will continue to argue that their contribution steadily trickles down to benefit everyone. Whatever happens, they consider this argument unassailable.

To illustrate the Catwalk option further, corporate responses to the climate change debate have been truly revealing. The biggest animals in the pride – including BP Amoco, Chevron, Daimler Chrysler, Exxon Mobil, Ford Motor Company, General Motors, Royal Dutch Shell and Texaco – initially gathered together under the umbrella of the Global Climate Coalition. The express objective of this grouping was to dispute and discredit the scientific basis of climate change and the global agreement being formulated to regulate greenhouse gas emissions (the Kyoto Protocol). It comes as no surprise that these companies are massive emitters of greenhouse gases, and that any regulation of this source of pollution would be extremely costly for them to implement. Interestingly, some of these lions have since shown signs of trimming their whiskers, which is a fitting introduction to the next option.

Leophancy

Like sycophants, leophants want to be all things to all people – sucking up to the shareholders when it suits them and rolling over for the 'greenies' when circumstances demand. They have recognised that some of their lion traits are going to get them into trouble sooner or later and that elephants are beginning to gain favour in the world. As a result, they are just starting to test the water – introducing an environmental policy here, adopting a corporate governance code there, adding a few non-financial performance measures, setting up community forums. They are not yet bold enough to whip off their lion suits and dive right into the refreshing pool of sustainability. After all, there may be sharp objects lurking beneath the surface; besides, other lions might laugh if they discover that their roar is bigger than their ... well, you know!

Leophants feel a little schizophrenic, as a result of being caught between two worlds. Their sensitive radar systems are picking up large grey blobs in the distance, but the growl of lions much closer by resonates in their ears. On the one hand, they hear the muffled cries of angry special interest groups; on the other the ticking of the share price is difficult to ignore. They can feel their ears starting to flap, their nose beginning to droop and their incisors about to protrude from their mouth, but they are a little embarrassed or scared to come out of the closet. Although they are aware of a few lone elephants in the desert, they have seen prides of lion take down some of these brave pioneers. Better just to hide out in the shadows, hedge the bets and play it safe.

Becoming a leophant is not necessarily the easiest option. Like an adolescent tripping into puberty, leophant companies risk looking awkward and ungainly. Their management and staff feel that every decision is now riddled with paradox and uncertainty. Apart from this, if the economy, political scene and the financial markets are not shapeshifting at the same rate, there is always the danger of being heavily criticised by the Greek chorus of fund managers in the background. Hence, leophants often begin with small elephant-friendly actions, but cover them up by still growling loudly like one of the old macho pride. They feel an incessant compulsion to justify their every move towards sustainability by saying that there is a business case for it, or that their actions are nothing more than good risk management.

Picking up on our climate change example, it has been fascinating to watch how some of the founding members of the Global Climate Coalition – such as BP Amoco, Ford, Shell and Texaco – have since defected. Following this change of heart, first BP and then Shell committed themselves publicly to reducing greenhouse gases, pioneered internal emissions trading systems and upped their investments in renewable energy. Likewise, under its new chairman Bill Ford, the family's motor manufacturing giant has suddenly become very vocal about its preparations for leadership in a post-fossil-fuel-based economy. Leophancy is catching on! Much of the inspiration for it comes from those that are less cautious in their approach to sustainability issues, and that brings us to our final option.

Charge of the Heavy Brigade

The final option for companies is to blaze a trail for the sustainable future by wholeheartedly and unashamedly joining The Charge of the Heavy Brigade. Strength lies in numbers and the greater the number of companies that make the switch from lions to elephants, the less they will be dismissed as mavericks. One lonely elephant trumpeting in the bush is not enough! Moreover, the public will find it refreshing to have a growing constituency of corporate leaders driven by a sense of values, purpose and destiny. Their zealous mission will be to show that it is not only possible, but essential, to transform businesses into an elephant-friendly force in society – an agent of change for good. It is not uncommon for CEOs pursuing the elephant option to have had some kind of 'revelation' about how unsustainable the traditional business model really is. They suddenly 'get it'; and they realise that life is not so much about making money as making a difference. Then instead of shouting about their conversion from the roof-tops, they quietly go ahead and change their lifestyle accordingly.

One of the first actions of the elephant pioneer is to shut up and start listening. They quickly establish various mechanisms for comprehensively surveying and understanding the complex needs of their numerous stakeholders. They also put in place a series of indicators to track their corporate performance in terms of these needs. However, as they begin to tune their senses to the incoming infrasonic messages, they realise that good communication is often not about the 'letter' but the 'spirit' of what is being said in return. They also realise that dealing effectively with stakeholders only works if power is balanced and shared. It cannot work if shareholders' selfish demands always take precedence over community or environmental concerns. Nor should customers' willingness to consume a harmful product or service necessarily imply that it should be produced and sold. Elephants will find that they are constantly required to revise their preconceived notions about the way that businesses should be run, and the valuable role that different stakeholder groups can play.

At the moment, the herd of fellow elephant-oriented companies is still relatively small. They therefore find themselves often mingling with NGOs and activists. This network of passionate comrades are their source of inspiration and 'insider' information. They give the company clues as to what issues are ticking time bombs and what products are hot prospects for a sustainable future. They act like a weather barometer, signalling how the mood of the sustainability debate is subtly shifting and what direction to head in to find sunshine and avoid the thunderstorms. Sometimes, these activist groups sit on corporate advisory boards or performance review panels. Elephant companies soon discover that their advice, more often than not, has its roots in a deep caring for people and the planet.

Returning to our climate change example, companies on the elephant trail actively support the phasing out of greenhouse gases and a shift to a hydrogen and solar economy. Not overnight, but over time. A case in point is OK Petroleum, Sweden's largest refiner and retailer of gasoline, who joined with twenty-four other companies to lobby the government to increase carbon taxes. This was partially due to the fact that OK had already shapeshifted far enough to design a low-carbon gasoline. But it was also because OK no longer sees itself as being in the petroleum business – it is a clean energy company of the future. Inevitably, the real elephant companies find themselves shifting their investments out of socially sensitive, environmentally-damaging businesses into more sustainable sectors and technologies.

8.17 Decisions

We don't know which option you will choose or what decisions you will make as a result of reading this book. But we can certainly offer you some tips. If you're a CEO, the best thing you can probably do is go through the line of reasoning that we've followed in this chapter at your company's next strategic planning session. This time, however, you get some unusual stakeholders to join you who might offer different perspectives on the future rules of the environmental and social game. Not just the generic ones that apply to business in general, but the specific ones that apply to your industry. You don't stifle the debate or try to steer it in the direction of your own vision. You just let it run where it will.

An alternative approach is to split your top management team into two or three small groups and ask each group to come up with their rules. It's amazing how different the results can be, leaving the CEO scratching his or her head that these people are in the same team supposedly playing the same game. Add in one or two outsiders to each group and the results can be even more surprising when they are compared in the plenary session. The prime purpose, of course, of putting the executive team through this hoop is to get across to its leo-leaning members that there are rules beyond their control. They will get shocked by an electric fence if they go too far. Even the supreme CEO, Jack Welch, singed his whiskers late in life when General Electric's bid to acquire Honeywell was blocked by the European Commission. There are always limits; and business can be unusual at the best and worst of times.

As far as the key uncertainties are concerned, it is vital to emphasise that this is a 'blue sky' discussion and no uncertainty can be too wild to consider. Back in 1986, HIV/AIDS was classified by a South African scenario team as a 'wild card' that might affect the country's future. It quickly became a primary rule of the game. In other words, a faint dot on the radar screen may emerge as the biggest threat.

Scenarios function as a bridging mechanism between the external world you don't control and the internal one that you do. Their purpose is to synthesise all the information contained in the rules of the game and the key uncertainties into two or three simple stories that the mind can grasp when making a decision. Scenarios are the narrow part of the hour-glass. Using this principle, one of the two authors presented South Africans with a stark but easily understandable choice back in the mid-1980s: The High Road of negotiation leading to a political settlement or The Low Road of confrontation leading to a civil war and a wasteland. As CEO, you want to present to your colleagues a set of clear-cut scenarios that differentiate between lion and elephant behaviour and the consequences for the company.

The discussion of options available to a company is where the bottom of the hour-glass widens out again. It should be as 'blue sky' as the conversation about uncertainties. If anybody says that such-and-such an option is far too wild, you can perfectly reasonably retort that it's just an option with no commitment. Remember that options are not a wish list. Each one is a decision you can take and implement right now if you decide to select that option. Again, outsiders are a valuable resource in broadening the terms of the debate.

Lastly, you make decisions which we hope after all the arguments we have presented in this book will point you down the elephant trail. And just as you start down a hiking trail with that first step, don't be too ambitious to start with. The initial step taken by a company should be to establish a process which means that each subsequent step is chosen with the new philosophy in mind: that of being a 'sustainable business'. Like elephants in the mist, you will never know in advance where the trail ultimately leads. Sometimes you will take wrong steps and you will have to reverse direction to get back on the path again. On other occasions, a single step will take you around a corner where a breath-taking view awaits you. And when you look back over your shoulder, you will wonder how you managed to come so far. But if you take no steps at all, the future has a nasty habit of catching up with you.

Discussion 8.5: Future Scenarios

1. Choose a country, sector or sustainability issue. What 'rules of the game' are shaping the future over the next 40 years?
2. What are the 'key uncertainties' that are influencing the future of this country, sector or sustainability issue?
3. What are your scenarios for the future of your chosen country, sector or sustainability issue?

8.18 A Test for Future-Fitness

Are you fit for the future? Will a product, organisation, community, city or country survive and thrive in 10, 20, 50 or even 100 years?

We live in a world that is changing faster and challenging us more than ever before. Great progress has been made in lifting people out of poverty, advancing scientific frontiers, connecting the globe with technology and making knowledge more accessible. At the same time, there are disturbing trends of increasing inequality, catastrophic destruction of ecosystems and loss of species, pervasive corruption, increasingly volatile and dangerous climate change, waves of forced migration and floods of refugees, a rise of religious extremism and the omnipresent threat of terrorism.

The question is: how can we – as individuals, businesses, communities and policy-makers – prepare for the future? How can we maximize our chances of success, not only by being ready, but also by helping to shape the future that we desire? I think it helps to view future-fitness in two ways: in terms of *alignment* – i.e. fitting, like a jigsaw piece, into the bigger picture of an emerging world; and in terms of *agility* – i.e. building up the kind of fitness that allows quick reflexes and strong performance in response to future conditions.

The biggest trends in society and our most enduring ideals suggest that there are five key criteria for future-fitness: our products, organisations, communities, cities or countries must be safe, smart, shared, sustainable and satisfying? These 5-Ss of Future-Fitness are summarised in the table below and then briefly defined in the subsequent sections.

Figure 8.1: The Kaleidoscope 5-S Future-Fitness Framework

Criteria	Test question	Keywords	Example indicators
Safe	Does X* protect and care for us?	Healthy, secure, resilient	OH&S, toxicity, risk & emergency preparedness
Smart	Does X connect and empower us?	Educated, connected, responsive	Connectivity, access to knowledge, R&D investment
Shared	Does X include and value us?	Fair, diverse, inclusive	Value distribution, stakeholder participation, diversity
Sustainable	Does X protect and restore our environment?	Renewable, enduring, evolutionary	Externality pricing, footprint analysis, renewability
Satisfying	Does X fulfil and inspire us?	Beneficial, beautiful, meaningful	Quality standards, levels of satisfaction, happiness

* 'X' could be a product, organisation, community, city or country

Safe

A safe future is one in which our products, organisations, communities, cities and countries do not damage our health and wellbeing; rather, they minimize our exposure to toxins, sickness, disease and danger, allowing us to feel physically and psychologically secure. Examples include the Zero Toxics campaign in the textiles industry, G.E.'s Healthymagination programme, Freeplay's off-grid fetal heart-rate monitor and HP's Global Social Innovation in Health programme.

Smart

A smart future is one in which our products, organisations, communities, cities and countries use technology to better connect us to each other and allow us to share what we value most. They also facilitate more democratic governance by allowing us (as customers or citizens) to give direct, immediate feedback. Examples include IBM's Smarter Planet initiative, Karmayog's online corruption reporting system, Wikirate, A Little World and the World Wide Web Foundation's Web Index.

Shared

A shared future is one in which our products, organisations, communities, cities and countries address issues of equity and access by being transparent about the distribution of value in society and working to ensure that benefits are fairly shared and diversity is respected. Examples include GSK's patent pool, the GreenXchange,

Kickstarter's crowdfunding site, the Fairtrade Foundation, the e-Choupal's farmer empowerment digital scheme and the Occupy movement.

Sustainable

A sustainable future is one in which our products, organisations, communities, cities and countries begin to operate within the limits of the planet by radically changing resource consumption patterns and ecosystem impacts. This includes a shift to renewable energy and resources, closing the loop on production and moving to a low carbon society. Examples include Interface's Mission Zero, Unilever's Sustainable Living Plan, energy-surplus houses and cradle-to-cradle certified companies.

Satisfying

A satisfying future is one in which our products, organisations, communities, cities and countries produce high quality services that satisfy our human needs, as well as enabling a lifestyle and culture that values quality of life, happiness and other indicators of wellbeing. Examples include Six Sigma quality systems, B-corporations (for benefit), GoodGuide's product rating system, NEF's Happy Planet Index, and the Slow Food and Downshifting movements.

Conclusion

The way to apply future-fitness thinking is to test the anticipated stocks and flows in society against these five criteria. For example, do the projected stocks of nature, infrastructure, institutions, people and capital suggest that our product, organisation, community, city or country will be more (or less) safe, smart, shared, sustainable and satisfying? Likewise, do the expected flows of materials, energy, knowledge, money and products suggest a future that is more (or less) healthy, inclusive, connected, renewable and fulfilling?

In the final analysis, our hope for the future is based on creating a better world tomorrow than we have today; a society that gives more freedom and fulfilment to our children and grandchildren than we have enjoyed. The Kaleidoscope 5-S Future-Fitness Framework is just one way to crystallize what a better future could look like – and to galvanise our efforts in shaping the products, organisations, communities, cities and countries that could turn such a bright vision into reality.

Discussion 8.6: Future-Fitness

1. How would you rate your country against each criteria of the 5-S framework?
2. What measurable indicators of progress would you use for each of the 5-Ss, if applied to your city?

3. What actions can companies take to improve performance on each of the 5-Ss?

8.19 Predictions for the Next 10 Years

I have argued that what is needed – and what is just starting to emerge – is a new approach to CSR, which I call Transformative CSR, or CSR 2.0. This is a purpose-driven, principle-based approach, in which business seeks to identify and tackle the root causes of our present unsustainability and irresponsibility, typically through innovating business models, revolutionizing their processes, products and services and lobbying for progressive national and international policies. This leads to my first forecast.

Forecast 1

Over the next 10 years, we will see most large, international companies having moved through the first four types or stages of CSR (defensive, charitable, promotional and strategic) and practicing, to varying degrees, Transformative CSR, or CSR 2.0.

But what will CSR 2.0 look like? How will we know it when we see it? The first test is Creativity. The problem with the current obsession with CSR codes and standards (including the new ISO 26000 standard) is that it encourages a tick-box approach to CSR. But our social and environmental problems are complex and intractable. They need creative solutions, like Freeplay's battery-free off-grid wind-up technologies (torches, radios, computers, etc.) or Vodafone's M-Pesa scheme, which allows the unbanked to perform basic financial transactions (depositing, withdrawing, transferring) using mobile phones.

Forecast 2

Over the next 10 years, reliance on CSR codes, standards and guidelines like the UN Global Compact, ISO 14001, SA 8000, etc., will be seen as a necessary but insufficient way to practice CSR. Instead, companies will be judged on how innovative they are in using their products and processes to tackle social and environmental problems.

Another shift which is only just beginning is taking CSR solutions to scale. There is no shortage of case studies of laudably responsible and sustainable projects. The problem is that so few of them ever go to scale. We need more examples like Walmart's 'choice editing': by voluntarily limiting the company to the use of organic cotton, Walmart forces its customers to do the same. Other examples are BYD making small electric cars in China or the Grameen Bank microcredit movement.

Forecast 3

Over the next 10 years, self-selecting 'ethical consumers' will become less relevant as a force for change. Companies – strongly encouraged by government policies and incentives – will scale up their choice-editing, i.e. ceasing to offer 'less ethical' product ranges, thus allowing guilt-free shopping.

A trend that is already underway and will continue to strengthen is the use of cross-sector partnerships. This is in recognition of the fact that the problems we face today are too global, complex and multifaceted for a single institution to solve. One good example is the Corporate Leaders Group on Climate Change, which has systematically and collectively urged UK and EU governments to set bolder climate policies.

Forecast 4

Over the next 10 years, cross-sector partnerships will be at the heart of all CSR approaches. These will increasingly be defined by business bringing its core competencies and skills (rather than just its financial resources) to the party, as Walmart did with its logistics capability in helping to distribute aid during Hurricane Katrina.

The idea of 'think global, act local' has been in circulation for some decades now, and indeed was given prominence at the original Rio Summit in 1992. However, companies are still learning to practice this balancing act, combining international norms with local contexts, finding local solutions that are culturally appropriate, without forsaking universal principles.

Forecast 5

Over the next 10 years, companies practicing CSR 2.0 will be expected to comply with global best practice principles, such as those in the UN Global Compact or the Ruggie Human Rights Framework, but simultaneously demonstrate sensitivity to local issues and priorities. An example is mining and metals giant BHP Billiton, which have strong climate change policies globally, as well as malaria prevention programmes in Southern Africa.

A clear failing of our current economic and commercial system is based on a fundamentally flawed design, which acts as if there are no limits on resource consumption or waste disposal. Instead, we need a cradle-to-cradle approach, closing all resource loops and ensuring that products and processes are inherently 'good', rather than 'less bad', as Shaw Carpets does when taking back its carpets at the end of their useful life and Nike is starting to do with its Considered Design principles.

Forecast 6

Over the next 10 years, progressive companies will be required to demonstrate full life cycle management of their products, from cradle-to-cradle. We will see most large companies committing to the goal of zero-waste, carbon-neutral and water-neutral production, with mandated take-back schemes for most products.

The way that we measure and report on social, environmental and ethical performance is changing. As the Global Reporting Initiative, the Carbon Disclosure Project and other standards are strengthened, a consensus on useful metrics is emerging. What is still missing, however, is an agreed set of mandatory metrics, publicly accessible in a database, which makes comparison possible. Current CSR indexes rank the same large companies over and over, often with differing conclusions.

Forecast 7

Over the next 10 years, much like the Generally Accepted Accounting Practices (GAAP), some form of Generally Accepted Sustainability Practices (GASP) will be agreed, including consensus principles, methods, approaches and rules for measuring and disclosing CSR. Furthermore, a set of credible CSR rating agencies will have emerged.

Still, the role of government in the next 40 years will be crucial. Many of the issues that CSR is currently trying to tackle on a voluntary basis will be mandatory in the future, especially with regards to emission reductions (toxics and greenhouse gases), waste practices and transparency. There will also be a gradual harmonisation of country-level legislation on social, environmental and ethical issues.

Forecast 8

Over the next 10 years, many of today's CSR practices will be mandatory requirements. However, CSR will remain a voluntary practice – an innovation and differentiation frontier – for those companies that are either willing and able, or pushed and prodded through non-governmental means, to go ahead of the legislation to improve quality of life around the world.

The form and media for transparency are rapidly evolving. We can expect annual CSR reporting to be increasingly replaced by online, real-time CSR performance data flows. Feeding into these live communications will be Web 2.0 connected social networks (such as those on Justmeans, where companies can stream their data and updates) and Wiki-style forums for crowdsourcing (such as

OpenEyeWorld, where companies can electronically interact with hundreds of sustainability experts and gauge the 'wisdom of the crowds').

Forecast 9

Over the next 10 years, corporate transparency will take form of publicly available sets of mandatory disclosed social, environmental and governance data – available down to a product life cycle impact level – as well as Web 2.0 collaborative CSR feedback platforms, WikiLeaks type whistleblowing sites and product rating applications (like the GoodGuide iPhone app).

The way that companies manage CSR will also change. CSR departments will most likely shrink, disappear or disperse, as the role for a CSR generalist is confined to small policy functions. By contrast, more specialists in various aspects of CSR will be required and performance across responsibility and sustainability dimensions will increasingly be built into corporate performance appraisal systems (salaries, bonuses, promotion opportunities, etc.), as is already the case in companies like Arcor, the confectionary company in Argentina.

Forecast 10

Over the next 10 years, CSR will have diversified back into its specialist disciplines and functions, leaving little or no CSR departments behind, yet having more specialists in particular areas (climate, biodiversity, human rights, community involvement, etc.), and more employees with knowledge of how to integrate CSR issues into their functional areas (HR, marketing, finance, etc.).

Collectively, these forecasts reflect a scenario of widespread adoption of CSR 2.0 over the next 10 years, a future in which companies become a significant part of the solution to our sustainability crisis, rather than complicit contributors to the problem, as they are today. Given the current global crises and mounting system pressures, and knowing business's ability to adapt and rapidly change, I regard this as a highly likely prediction sketched out by a concerned pragmatist, rather than the wish-list of a CSR 'true believer'.

Discussion 8.7: Ten-Year Predictions
1. Do you agree or disagree with the 10 forecasts?
2. What are some of your CSR/sustainability related forecasts for the next 10 years?
3. What would need to happen – in business and society – in order for your forecasts to come true?

CONCLUDING THOUGHTS

In my book, The Age of Responsibility (Visser, 2011), I conveyed the message that CSR has failed and we need a new approach (which I called CSR 2.0 or transformative CSR) that is better equipped to tackle the economic, social and environmental crises the world still faces.

However, as I travelled around the world sharing its ideas and collecting best practices – which, incidentally, is the subject of my new book, *The Quest for Sustainable Business* (Visser, 2012) – I discovered that many CSR students, teachers and professionals still lacked a basic grounding in CSR theory and practice, which is vital to understand first, in order to make the intellectual and practical leap to next generation CSR thinking.

This book, therefore, is my attempt to capture in once place the essence of what we have learned about CSR in recent decades – its evolution, impacts, failures and successes. I hope that CSR enthusiasts of all shapes and sizes, all colours and creeds, will not only have been informed by what has gone before, but also inspired by what is to come.

If I have learned anything in my journey through CSR over the past 20 years, it is that corporate sustainability and responsibility is a malleable beast; it is constantly changing. And more than that, I have seen that we are the CCEs – the Chief Change Agents – in the process of creating a better world for ourselves, for each other and for our children.

I fully expect that some of you who have read this book will become the next generation of social and environmental innovators that will not only change the CSR game, but also change the rules of the game – the way in which our economies, our communities and our companies operate in future.

I wish you all the very best in your quest. You are welcome to share your progress with me, or give feedback about this book, by emailing:

wayne@waynevisser.com.

Good luck and good business!

REFERENCES

Accenture & UN Global Compact, 2010. A new era in sustainability [CEO survey].

Acutt, N., Medina-Ross, V. & O'Riordan, T., 2004. 'Perspectives on Corporate Social Responsibility in the Chemical Sector: A Comparative Analysis of the Mexican and South African Cases'. *Natural Resources Forum* 28(4): 302–16.

Adair, J., 1984. *Action Centred Leadership*. London: McGrawHill.

Ahmed, M., 2006. *The Principles and Practice of Crisis Management: The Case of Brent Spar*. Palgrave Macmillan.

Amaeshi, K. M., Adi, B. C., Ogbechie, C., & Olufemi, O. A., 2006. 'Corporate Social Responsibility in Nigeria: Western Mimicry or Indigenous Influences?' *Journal of Corporate Citizenship*, 24, Winter: 83–99.

Ancona, D., 2010. 'Distributed leadership at work.' *Washington Post*, 22 September.

Anderson, R.C., 1999. *Mid-Course Correction: Toward a Sustainable Enterprise: The Interface Model*. Peregrinzilla Press.

Anderson, R.C., 2009. *Confessions of a Radical Industrialist*. Random House Business Books.

Araya, M. 2006. 'Exploring Terra Incognita: Non-financial Reporting in Latin America'. *Journal of Corporate Citizenship* 21, Spring: 25–38.

Arora, B. & Metz Cummings, A., 2010. A Little World: Safe and Efficient M-Banking in Rural India. UNDP Growing Inclusive Markets publication.

Autry, J.A., 1992. *Love and Profit: The Art of Caring Leadership*. William Morrow Paperbacks.

Bakan, J., 2004. *The Corporation: The Pathological Pursuit of Profit and Power*. Free Press.

Bakan, J., 2008. Interview with Joel Bakan, conducted by Wayne Visser as part of the University of Cambridge Top 50 Sustainability Books project, 5 August 2008.

Balasubramanian, N. K., Kimber, D., Pussayapibul, N., & Davids, P. 2005. 'Emerging Opportunities or Traditions Reinforced? An Analysis of the Attitudes Towards CSR, and Trends of Thinking about CSR, in India'. *Journal of Corporate Citizenship*, 17, spring: 79–92.

Barnard, C., 1938. *The Functions of the Executive*. Cambridge, MA: Harvard University Press.

Baskin, J. 2006. 'Corporate Responsibility in Emerging Markets'. *Journal of Corporate Citizenship*, 24, Winter: 29–47.

Bass, B.M., 1990. From transactional to transformational leadership: Learning to share the vision. *Organizational Dynamics*, Winter: 19-31.

Birch, D. & Moon, J. 2004. 'Introduction: Corporate Social Responsibiity in Asia'. *Journal of Corporate Citizenship*, 13, Spring: 18–23.

Blake, R.R. & Mouton, J.S., 1968. *The Managerial Grid; Key Orientations for Achieving Production through People.* Houston: Gulf Publishing Company.

Blowfield, M., 2003. 'Ethical Supply Chains in the Cocoa, Coffee and Tea Industries'. *Greener Management International*, 43, Autumn: 15–24.

Blowfield, M., 2004. 'Implementation Deficits of Ethical Trade Systems: Lessons from the Indonesian Cocoa and Timber Industries'. *Journal of Corporate Citizenship*, 13, spring: 77–90.

Blowfield, M., Visser, W. & Livesey, F., 2007. Sustainability Innovation: Mapping the Territory, *University Cambridge Programme for Sustainability Leadership Research Paper Series*, No. 2.

Bornstein, D., 2007. *How to Change the World: Social Entrepreneurs and the Power of New Ideas.* Oxford: Oxford University Press.

Bornstein, D. and Davis, S., 2010. *Social Entrepreneurship: What Everyone Needs to Know.* Oxford University Press.

Boulding, K.E., 1966. The economics of the coming Spaceship Earth. Paper presented at the Sixth Resources for the Future Forum on Environmental Quality in a Growing Economy, Washington, D.C., 8 March.

Bowen, H., 1953. *Social Responsibilities of Business.* New York, Harper.

Brandenburger, A.M. & Nalebuff, B.J., 1997. *Co-opetition: A Revolution Mindset That Combines Competition and Cooperation: The Game Theory Strategy That's Changing the Game of Business.* Currency Doubleday

Burns, J.M., 1978. *Leadership.* New York: Harper & Row.

Campbell, J. & Moyer, B., 1991. The Power of Myth. Anchor.

Carroll, A.B., 1979. A three-dimensional model of corporate performance. *Academy of Management Review* 4(4): 497-505.

Carroll, A.B., 1991. The Pyramid of Corporate Social Responsibility: Toward the Moral Management of Organizational Stakeholders. *Business Horizons*, July-August.

Carroll, A.B., 2009. A History of Corporate Social Responsibility: Concepts and Practices. In Crane, A. et al., *The Oxford Handbook of Corporate Social Responsibility.* Oxford: Oxford University Press.

Carroll, A. B. & Shabana, K. M., 2010. The Business Case for Corporate Social Responsibility: A Review of Concepts, Research and Practice. *International Journal of Management Reviews*, 12: 85–105.

Carson, N., 2010. Interview with Neil Carson, CEO of Johnson Matthey, conducted by Polly Courtice, 15 June 2010.

Carson, R., 1962. *Silent Spring*. Houghton Mifflin.

Center for Excellence in Leadership, London South Bank University & Forum for the Future, 2007. Leadership for sustainability: Making sustainable development a reality for leaders. Center for Excellence in Leadership (CEL).

Chapple, W. & Moon, J. 2005. 'Corporate Social Responsibility in Asia: A Seven-Country Study of CSR Web Site Reporting'. *Business & Society*, 44(4): 415–41.

Cheshire, I., 2010. Interview with Ian Cheshire, CEO of Kingfisher, conducted by Polly Courtice.

Chouinard, Y., 2006. *The Education of a Reluctant Businessman*. Penguin.

Christian Aid, 2004. Behind the Mask: The Real Face of CSR. London: Christian Aid.

Clark, J.M., 1939. *Social Control of Business*. 2nd ed. Chicago: University of Chicago Press.

Clay, J., 2005. Exploring the links between international business and poverty reduction: A case study of Unilever. Oxfam GB, Novib, Unilever and Unilever Indonesia.

Coch, L. & French, J.R.P., 1948. Overcoming resistance to change. *Human Relations* 1: 512-532.

Collins, J., 2001. *Good to Great: Why Some Companies Make the Leap ... and Others Don't*. HarperBusiness.

Connor, T., 2001. *Still Waiting For Nike To Do It*. Global Exchange.

Copestake, J., Greely, M., Johnson, S., Kabeer, N. & Simanowitz, A., 2006. *Money with a Mission, Volume 1: Microfinance and Poverty Reduction*. Practical Action.

Correa, M. E., Flynn, S. & Amit, A., 2004. 'Responsibilidan Social Corporative en América Latina: Una visión empresarial'. Série CEPAL Medio Ambiente y Desarrollo, 85. Santiago de chile: CEPAL.

Counts, A., 2008. *Small Loans, Big Dreams: How Nobel Prize Winner Muhammad Yunus and Microfinance are Changing the World*. London: John Wiley & Sons.

CPSL, 2011. A Journey of a Thousand Miles: The State of Sustainability Leadership 2011. Cambridge Programme for Sustainability Leadership.

Crane, A. & Matten, D. 2005. 'Can Corporations be Citizens? Corporate Citizenship as a Metaphor for Business Participation in Society'. *Business Ethics Quarterly*, 15(3): 427–51.

Crane, A. & Matten, D., 2010. *Business Ethics: Managing Corporate Citizenship and Sustainability in the Age of Globalization*. 2nd ed. Oxford: Oxford University Press.

Crane, A., McWilliams, A., Matten, D., Moon, J. & Siegel, D.S. (eds.), 2009. *The Oxford Handbook of Corporate Social Responsibility*. Oxford: Oxford University Press.

De Vries, M.K., 2001. *The Leadership Mystique: Leading Behavior in the Human Enterprise*. Financial Times/ Prentice Hall.

De Oliveira, J. A. P., 2006. 'Corporate Citizenship in Latin America: New Challenges to Business'. *Journal of Corporate Citizenship*, 21 Spring: 17–20.

Dolan, C. S. & Opondo, M., 2005. 'Seeking Common Ground: Multi-stakeholder Processes in Kenya's Cut Flower Industry'. *Journal of Corporate Citizenship*, 18, Summer: 87–98.

Doppelt, B., 2010. *Leading Change Toward Sustainability: A Change-Management Guide for Business, Government and Civil Society*, 2nd Edition. Sheffield: Greenleaf.

Drayton, B., 2010. Tipping the world: the power of collaborative entrepreneurship. McKinsey What Matters website, 8 April.

Drucker, P., 1993. *The Practice of Management*. Collins.

Egels, N., 2005. 'CSR in Electrification of Rural Africa: The Case of ABB in Tanzania'. *Journal of Corporate Citizenship*, 18 Summer: 75–85.

EIRIS, 2007. The state of responsible business: Global corporate response to environmental, social and governance (ESG) challenge. Ethical Investment Research Services.

Elkington J., 1994. Towards the sustainable corporation: win–win–win business strategies for sustainable development. *California Management Review* 36(2): 90–100.

Elkington, J., 1997. *Cannibals With Forks: The Triple Bottom Line of 21st Century Business*. London: Capstone.

Elkington, J., 2008. Interview with John Elkington, conducted by Wayne Visser as part of the University of Cambridge Top 50 Sustainability Books project, 23 May 2008.

Eurosif, 2010. European SRI Study 2010. European Social Investment Forum.

Fiedler, F.E., 1971. *Leadership*. General Learning Press.

Flowers, B.S., 2008. Interview with Betty Sue Flowers, conducted by Wayne Visser as part of the University of Cambridge Top 50 Sustainability Books project, 20 August 2008.

Frankl, V.E., 2006. *Man's Search for Meaning*. Beacon Press. [Originally published in 1968].

Freeman, R.E., 1984. *Strategic Management: A Stakeholder Approach*. Boston, MA: Pitman.

Friedman, T.L., 2008. *Hot, Flat, and Crowded: Why We Need a Green Revolution – and How It Can Renew America*. New York: Farrar, Straus and Giroux.

Fulham, R., 1988. *Everything I Ever Needed To Know, I Learned In Kindergarten*. Press of Ward Schori.

Fuller, R.B., 1969. *Operating Manual for Spaceship Earth*. New York: Simon and Schuster.

Fusaro, P.C. & Miller, R.M., 2002. What Went Wrong at Enron: Everyone's Guide to the Largest Bankruptcy in U.S. History. New York: John Wiley & Sons.

GlobeScan, 2005. The GlobeScan Survey of Sustainability Experts 2004-2.

GlobeScan, 2007. The GlobeScan Survey of Sustainability Experts 2006-2.

Globescan, 2011. Sustainability Survey 2011: Survey of Sustainability Leaders. April.

Goffee, R. & Jones, G., 2009. Authentic leadership. Leadership Excellence, May.

Greenleaf, R.K., 2002. *Servant Leadership: A Journey into the Nature of Legitimate Power and Greatness*. Paulist Press.

Griffin, J.J. & Mahon, J.F., 1997. The corporate social performance and corporate financial performance debate. *Business & Society*, 36, p.5.

Hamann, R., Kapelns, P., Sonnenberg, D., Mackenzie, A. & Hollesen, P., 2005. 'Local Governance as a Complex System: Lessons from Mining in South Africa, Mali and Zambia'. *Journal of Corporate Citizenship*, 18, Summer: 61–73.

Hammond, A.L., 2007. *The Next 4 Billion: Market Size and Business Strategy at the Base of the Pyramid*. WRI/IFC.

Handy, C., 1998. *The Hungry Spirit: Beyond Capitalism – A Quest for Purpose in the Modern World*. Arrow Books.

Handy, C., 2008. Interview with Charles Handy, conducted by Wayne Visser as part of the University of Cambridge Top 50 Sustainability Books project, 3 September 2008.

Hart, S.L., 2005. *Capitalism at the Crossroads: The Unlimited Business Opportunities in Solving the World's Most Difficult Problems*. Wharton School Publishing.

Hart, S.L., 2008. Interview with Stuart Hart, conducted by Wayne Visser as part of the University of Cambridge Top 50 Sustainability Books project, 13 August 2008.

Haslam, P. A., 2007. 'The Corporate Social Responsibility System in Latin America and the Caribbean', in Crane & Matten (eds.), 2007b. *Corporate Social Responsibility*, 3 vols. London: Sage.

Hawken, P., 1994. *The Ecology of Commerce: A Declaration of Sustainability*. New York: HarperBusiness.

Hawken, P., Lovins, A. & Lovins, L.H., 1999. *Natural Capitalism: Creating the Next Industrial Revolution.* London: Earthscan.

Henderson, H., 1988. *The Politics of the Solar Age: Alternatives to Economics.* Doubleday.

Hersey, P. & Blanchard, K. H., 1999. *Leadership and the One Minute Manager.* William Morrow.

Hollender, J. & Breen, B., 2010. *The Responsibility Revolution: How the Next Generation of Businesses Will Win.* Jossey-Bass.

IBM, 2009. Leading a sustainable enterprise - Leveraging insight and information to act. IBM Institute for Business Value.

Immelt, J., 2007. GE's Jeff Immelt on the 10 keys to great leadership. *Fast Company,* 19 December.

Immelt, J., 2010. Interview with Jeffrey Immelt, CEO of General Electric, conducted by Polly Courtice in February 2010.

ISO, 2010. The ISO Survey of Certifications: 2010. International Organization for Standardization.

Isos MORI, 2010. Skills for a Sustainable Economy: The Business Perspective, Report for Business in the Community/EDF Energy.

Ite, U. E., 2004. 'Multinationals and Corporate Social Responsibility in Developing Countries: A Case Study of Nigeria'. *Corporate Social Responsibility and Environmental Management,* 11(1): 1–11.

Juhasz, A., 2008. *The Tyranny of Oil: The World's Most Powerful Industry – and What We Must Do to Stop It.* William Morrow.

Kapelus, P., 2002. 'Mining, Corporate Social Responsibility and the Case of Rio Tinto, Richards Bay Minerals and the Mbonambi'. *Journal of Business Ethics,* 39: 275–96.

Kapstein, E., 2008. 'Measuring Unilever's Economic Footprint: The Case of South Africa'. INSEAD and Unilever and Unilever South Africa.

Karnani, A., 2007. Misfortune at the Bottom of the Pyramid. *Greener Management International,* 51, June.

Karnani, A., 2010. 'The case against corporate social responsibility'. *Wall Street Journal,* 23 August.

Kaufman, A., Tiantubtim, E., Pussayapibul, N. & Davids, P., 2004. 'Implementing Voluntary Labour Standards and Codes of Conduct in the Thai Garment Industry'. *Journal of Corporate Citizenship,* 13, Spring: 91–9.

Khoza, R.J., 2012. *Attuned Leadership: African Humanism As Compass.* Penguin Books.

King, M.E., 2010. Interview with Mervyn King, conducted by Wayne Visser as part of a University of Cambridge research project on non-executive directors, 13 January 2010.

Klein, N., 2000. *No Logo: No Space, No Choice, No Jobs*. Picador.

Koopman, A., 1994. *Transcultural Management*. Wiley-Blackwell.

Korten, D., 2008. Interview with David Korten, conducted by Wayne Visser as part of the University of Cambridge Top 50 Sustainability Books project, 3 September 2008.

Kotter, J. & Heskett, J., 1992. *Corporate Culture and Performance*. Free Press.

Kouzes, J.M. & Posner, B.Z., 2007. *The Leadership Challenge*, 4th Edition. Jossey-Boss.

KPMG, GRI & UNEP, 2010. 'Carrots and Sticks: An update on trends in voluntary and mandatory approaches to sustainability reporting'. KPMG Unit for Corporate Governance in Africa.

Krep, T., 1940. *Measurement of the Social Performance of Business*. Washington, DC: US Government Printing Office.

Kuhn, T.S., 1996. *The Structure of Scientific Revolutions*, 3rd edition. Chicago: University Of Chicago Press.

Laffer, A.B., Coors, A. & Winegarden, W., 2004. *Does Corporate Social Responsibility Enhance Business Profitability?* Laffer Associates.

Leopold, A., 1949. *A Sand County Almanac*. New York: Oxford University Press.

Lewin, K., Llippit, R. & White, R.K., 1939. Patterns of aggressive behavior in experimentally created social climates. *Journal of Social Psychology* 10: 271-301.

Locke, R., 2007. Beyond corporate codes of conduct: work organisation and labour standards at Nike's suppliers, *International Labour Review,* 146 (1-2): 21-40.

Lockett, A., Moon, J., & Visser, W. 2006. Corporate social responsibility In management research: Focus, nature, salience, and sources of influence. *Journal of Management Studies*, 43(1).

Lomborg, B., 2001. Ske*ptical Environmentalist: Measuring the Real State of the World*. Cambridge, UK: Cambridge University Press.

London, T., 2009. Making better investments at the Base of the Pyramid. *Harvard Business Review*, May.

Lopez, J., 2010. Interview with José Lopez, Executive Vice President Operations and GLOBE of Nestle, conducted by Polly Courtice, 17 June 2010.

Lovelock, J., 1979. *Gaia: A New Look At Life On Earth*. Oxford: Oxford University Press.

Lovelock, J., 2008. Interview with James Lovelock, conducted by Wayne Visser as part of the University of Cambridge Top 50 Sustainability Books project, 16 September 2008.

Luken, R. & Stares, R., 2005. 'Small Business Responsibility in Developing Countries: A Threat or an Opportunity?' *Business Strategy and the Environment*, 14: 38–53.

Lund-Thomsen, P., 2004. 'Towards a Critical Framework on Corporate Social and Environmental Responsibility in the South: The Case of Pakistan'. *Development*, 47(3): 106–113.

Lydenberg, S., 2005. *Corporations and the Public Interest: Guiding the Invisible Hand.* San Francisco, CA: Berrett-Koehler.

Margolis, J.D. & Walsh, J.P., 2001. *People and Profits? The Search for a Link between a Company's Social and Financial Performance.* Mahwah, N.J.: Lawrence Erlbaum Associates.

Mandela, N., 1994. *Long Walk to Freedom: The Autobiography of Nelson Mandela.* Little, Brown.

Maso, P., 2010. Interview with Philippe Maso, CEO of AXA, conducted by Polly Courtice.

Mbigi, L., 1997. *Ubuntu: The African Dream in Management.* Randburg: Knowledge Resources.

McCall, M.W. Jr. & Lombardo, M.M., 1983. Off the track: Why and how successful executives get derailed. Greenboro, NC: Centre for Creative Leadership.

McCusker, G., 2006. *Public Relations Disasters: Talespin – Inside Stories and Lessons Learnt.* Kogan Page.

McDonald, L., 2009, *A Colossal Failure Of Common Sense: The Inside Story Of the Collapse of Lehman Brothers.* Random House.

Mclean, B. & Elkind, P., 2003. *Smartest Guys in the Room: The Amazing Rise and Scandalous Fall of Enron.* Portfolio Trade.

Meadows, D.H., Meadows, D. & Randers, J., 1972. *The Limits to Growth: A Report to the Club of Rome's Project on the Predicament of Mankind.* Universe Books.

Mintzberg, H., 1976. Planning on the Left Side and Managing on the Right. *Harvard Business Review*, July.

Mitchell, R. Agle, B. & Wood, D., 1997. Towards a theory of stakeholder identification: defining the principle of who and what really counts. *Academy of Management Review*, 22(4).

Environics International, 2000. The Millennium Poll on Corporate Social Responsibility.

Morrison, A.J., 2000. Developing a global leadership model. *Human Resource Management*, 39(2&3): 117–131.

Muehlfeit, J., 2010. Interview with Jan Muehlfeit, Chairman of Microsoft Europe, conducted by Polly Courtice.

Musser, S.J., 1987. *The determination of positive and negative charismatic leadership.* Grantham: PA: Messiah College.

Nader, R., 1965. *Unsafe at Any Speed: The Designed-In Dangers of the American Automobile.* Grossman Publishers.

Nelson, J., 2003. 'Economic multipliers: Revisiting the core responsibility and contribution of business to development', IBLF Policy Paper 2003, Number 4.

Newell, P. & Muro, A., 2006. 'Corporate Social and Environmental Responsibiity in Argentina: The Evolution of an Agenda'. *Journal of Corporate Citizenship*, 24, Winter: 49–68.

Nielsen, M. E., 2005. 'The Politics of Corporate Responsibility and Child Labour in the Bangladeshi Garment Industry'. *International Affairs*, 81(3): 559–80.

Ogg, S., 2010. Interview with Sandy Ogg, Chief Human Resources Officer for Unilever, conducted by Polly Courtice.

Okonta, I., Douglas, O. & Monbiot, G., 2003. *Where Vultures Feast: Shell, Human Rights and Oil.* Verso.

Orlitzky, M., Schmidt, F. L., & Rynes, S. L., 2003. Corporate social and financial performance: A meta-analysis. *Organization Studies*, 24(3), 403-441.

Peindado-Vara, E., 2006. 'Corporate Social Responsibility in Latin America'. *Journal of Corporate Citizenship*, 21, Spring.

Peters, T., 1989. *Thriving on Chaos: Handbook for a Management Revolution.* HarperBusiness.

Peters, T. & Waterman, R.H., 2004. *In Search Of Excellence: Lessons from America's Best-Run Companies.* 2nd edition. Profile Books.

Polman, P., 2009. McKinsey conversations with global leaders: Paul Polman of Unilever. *McKinsey Quarterly*, October.

Porritt, J., 2005. *Capitalism as if the World Matters.* London: Earthscan.

Porter, M.E. & Kramer, M.R., 2006. Strategy and society: the link between competitive advantage and corporate social responsibility. *Harvard Business Review*, December.

Porter, M.E. & Kramer, M.R., 2011. Creating shared value. *Harvard Business Review*, January.

Prahalad, C.K., 2004. *The Fortune at the Bottom of the Pyramid: Eradicating Poverty Through Profits.* Wharton School Publishing.

Prahalad, C.K. & Hart, S.L., 2002. The Fortune at the Bottom of the Pyramid. *Strategy+Business*, 26: 54-67.

Prasad, B. C., 2004. 'Globalisation, Free Trade and Corporate Citizenship in Pacific Forum Island Countries'. *Journal of Corporate Citizenship*, 13, Spring: 65–76.

Prieto-Carron, M., 2004. 'Is there Anyone Listening? Women Workers in Factories in Central America, and Corporate Codes of Conduct'. *Development*, 47(3): 101– 5.

Prieto-Carron, M., 2006. 'Corporate Social Responsibility in Latin America: Chiquita, Women Banana Workers and Structural Inequalities'. *Journal of Corporate Citizenship*, 21, Spring: 85– 94.

Randers, J., 2008. Interview with Jorgen Randers, conducted by Wayne Visser as part of the University of Cambridge Top 50 Sustainability Books project, 8 July 2008.

Rice, T. & Owen, P., 1999. *Decommissioning the Brent Spar*. Spon Press.

Robeco & Booz & Co., 2009. Responsible investing: A paradigm shift.

Roddick, A., 2001. *Business As Unusual*. Thorstens.

Scharmer, O., 2007. *Theory U: Leading from the Future as It Emerges*. Berrett-Koehler Publishers.

Scharmer, O., 2008. Interview with Otto Scharmer, conducted by Wayne Visser as part of the University of Cambridge Top 50 Sustainability Books project, 26 August 2008.

Schlosser, E., 2005. *Fast Food Nation: The Dark Side of the All-American Meal*. Harper Perennial.

Schmidheiny, S., 2006. 'A View of Corporate Citizenship in Latin America'. *Journal of Corporate Citizenship*, 21, Spring: 21–4.

Schmidheiny & WBCSD, 1992. *Changing Course: A Global Business Perspective on Development and the Environment*. MIT Press.

Schrage, E. J. & Ewing, A., P. 2005. 'The Cocoa Industry and Child Labour'. *Journal of Corporate Citizenship*, 18, Summer: 99–112.

Schumacher, E.F., 1973. *Small is Beautiful: Economics as if People Mattered*. Harper & Row.

Schumpeter, J., 2008. *Capitalism, Socialism and Democracy*. Original edition 1942. Harper Perennial Modern Classics.

Scott, H.L., 2007. London Lecture of HRH Prince of Wales's Business and the Environment Programme. See www.cpsl.cam.ac.uk.

Semler, R., 1993. *Maverick: The Success Story Behind the World's Most Unusual Workplace*. Century.

Senge, P.M., 2003. *The Fifth Discipline: The Art and Practice of the Learning Organization.* 2nd edition. Random House.

Senge, P.M., Scharmer, O.M., Jaworski, J. & Flowers, B.S., 2005. *Presence: An Exploration of Profound Change in People, Organizations, and Society.* Crown Business.

Senge, P.M., Laur, J., Schley, S. & Smith, B., 2006. *Learning for Sustainability.* SoL, the Society for Organizational Learning.

Smith, J., 2010. Interview with James Smith, Chairman of Shell UK, conducted by Polly Courtice, June 2010.

Smith, P. & Thurman, E., 2007. *A Billion Bootstraps: Microcredit, Barefoot Banking, and The Business Solution for Ending Poverty.* McGraw-Hill.

Sustainability Leadership Institute, 2011. Website www.sustainabilityleadershipinstitute.org [Accessed 15 July 2011]

SustainAbility & UNEP, 2001. Buried Treasure: Uncovering the Business Case for Corporate Sustainability.

SustainAbility, IRC & Ethos Institut, 2002. Developing Value: The Business Case for Sustainability in Emerging Markets.

SustainAbility & Skoll Foundation, 2007. Growing Opportunity: Entrepreneurial Solutions to Insoluble Problems. London: SustainAbility.

SustainAbility & Skoll Foundation, 2008. The Social Intrapreneur: A Field Guide for Corporate Changemakers. London: SustainAbility.

Tannenbaum, R. & Schmidt, W.H., 1973. How To Choose a Leadership Pattern. *Harvard Business Review*, May-June.

Tapscott, D. & Williams, A.D., 2006. *Wikinomics: How Mass Collaboration Changes Everything.* Portfolio.

Tate, T. 2010. Interview with Truett Tate (2010), Group Executive Director, Wholesale, for Lloyds Banking Group, conducted by Polly Courtice.

Toffler, B.L. & Reingold, J., 2004. *Final Accounting: Ambition, Greed and the Fall of Arthur Andersen.* Crown Business.

Van Lawick van Pabst, J.A. & Visser, W., 2012. Theory U and CSR 2.0: Alignment of Two Conceptual Approaches to Create Profound Innovation and Transformative Change in Corporate Sustainability and Responsibility (February 22, 2012). Available at SSRN: http://ssrn.com/abstract=2009341

Vidal, J., 1997. *Mclibel: Burger Culture on Trial.* The New Press.

Visser, W., 2003. Corporate responsibility in a developing country context. *Ethical Corporation*, 20 August, pp.32-34.

Visser, W., 2005. 'Corporate Citizenship in South Africa: A Review of Progress Since Democracy'. *Journal of Corporate Citizenship*, 18, Summer: 29–38.

Visser, W., 2006a. 'Research on Corporate Citizenship in Africa: A Ten-Year Review (1995–2005). In Visser et al., 2006. *Corporate Citizenship in Africa: Lessons from the Past; Paths to the Future.* Sheffield: Greenleaf.

Visser, W., 2006b. Revisiting Carroll's CSR Pyramid: an African perspective. In Pedersen, E.R. & Huniche, M., *Corporate Citizenship in Developing Countries: New Partnership Perspectives.* Copenhagen: Copenhagen Business School Press, pp. 29–56.

Visser, W., 2008a. Corporate Social Responsibility in Developing Countries. In Crane, A., McWilliams, A., Matten, D., Moon, J. & Siegel, D. (eds.), *The Oxford Handbook of Corporate Social Responsibility.* Oxford: Oxford University Press, pp.473-479.

Visser, W., 2008b. CSR 2.0: The New Era of Corporate Sustainability and Responsibility. *CSR International Inspiration Series*, No. 1.

Visser, W., 2008c. *Making A Difference: Purpose-Inspired Leadership for Corporate Sustainability and Responsibility (CSR).* Saarbrücken: VDM.

Visser, W., 2008d. The Long Tail of CSR: Achieving Scalability in Corporate Sustainability and Responsibility, *CSR International Inspiration Series*, No. 5.

Visser, W., 2011. *The Age of Responsibility: CSR 2.0 and the New DNA of Business.* London: John Wiley & Sons.

Visser, W., 2012. *The Quest for Sustainable Business: An Epic Journey in Search of Corporate Responsibility.* Sheffield: Greenleaf.

Visser, W. & Courtice, P., 2011. Sustainability Leadership: Linking Theory and Practice. Available at SSRN: http://ssrn.com/abstract=1947221.

Visser, W., Matten, D., Pohl, M. & Tolhurst, N., 2010. *The A to Z of Corporate Social Responsibility: The Complete Reference of Concepts, Codes and Organisations.* 2nd ed. London: John Wiley & Sons.

Visser, W. & McIntosh, A., 1998. An evaluation of the historical condemnation of usury. *Accounting, Business & Financial History*, 8(2), July.

Visser, W., McIntosh, M. & Middleton, C. (eds.), 2006. *Corporate Citizenship in Africa: Lessons from the Past; Paths to the Future.* Sheffield: Greenleaf Publishing.

Visser, W., Middleton, C., & McIntosh, M. (eds.), 2005. 'Introduction to the Journal of Corporate Citizenship Special Issue on Corporate Citizenship in Africa'. *Journal of Corporate Citizenship*, 18, Spring: 18–20.

Visser, W. & Sunter, C., 2002. *Beyond Reasonable Greed: Why Sustainable Business is a Much Better Idea!* Cape Town: Tafelberg Human and Rousseau.

Visser, W. & Tolhurst, N., 2010. *The World Guide to CSR: A Country-by-Country Analysis of Corporate Sustainability and Responsibility*. London: John Wiley & Sons.

Vivarta, V. & Canela, G., 2006. 'Corporate Social Responsibility in Brazil: The Role of the Press as Watchdog'. *Journal of Corporate Citizenship*, 21, Spring: 95–106.

Vives, A., 2006. 'Social and Environmental Responsibility in Small and Medium Enterprises in Latin America'. *Journal of Corporate Citizenship*, 21, Spring: 39–50.

Vogel, D., 2005. *The Market for Virtue: The Potential and Limits of Corporate Social Responsibility*. Brookings Institution Press.

Volans Ventures, 2009. The Phoenix Economy: 50 Pioneers in the Business of Social Innovation. London: Volans Ventures.

Von Weizsäcker, E., Lovins, A.B. & Lovins, L.H., 1995. *Factor Four: Doubling Wealth, Halving Resource Use - The New Report to the Club of Rome*. Earthscan.

Vroom, V.H. & Yetton, P.W., 1973. *Leadership and Decision-making*. Pittsburg: University of Pittsburg Press.

Ward, B., 1966. *Spaceship Earth*. New York: Columbia University Press.

WBCSD, 2000. Corporate Social Responsibility: Making Good Business Sense. Geneva: World Business Council for Sustainable Development.

WCED, 1987. *Our Common Future: the Brundtland Report for the World Commission on Environment and Development*. Oxford Paperbacks.

Welford, R., 2005. 'Corporate Social Responsibility in Europe, North America and Asia'. *Journal of Corporate Citizenship*, 17, Spring: 33–52.

Weyzig, F., 2006. 'Local and Global Dimensions of Corporate Social Responsibility in Mexico'. *Journal of Corporate Citizenship*, 24, Winter: 69–81.

Wheeler, D. & Sillanpää, M., 1997. *The Stakeholder Corporation: The Body Shop Blueprint for Maximizing Stakeholder Value*. Financial Times/Prentice Hall.

Wood, D.J., 1991. Corporate Social Performance Revisited. *Academy of Management Review*, 16(4), October, pp. 691-718.

Yunus, M., 1999. *Banker To The Poor: Micro-Lending and the Battle Against World Poverty*. PublicAffairs.

Yunus, M., 2008a. *Creating a World Without Poverty: Social Business and the Future of Capitalism*. PublicAffairs.

Yunus, M., 2008b. Interview with Muhammad Yunus, conducted by Wayne Visser as part of the University of Cambridge Top 50 Sustainability Books project, 29 August 2008.

Zadek, S., 2008. Interview with Simon Zadek, conducted by Wayne Visser as part of the University of Cambridge Top 50 Sustainability Books project, 28 August 2008.

Zhuang, C. & Wheale, P. 2004. 'Creating Sustainable Corporate Value: A Case Study of Stakeholder Relationship Management in China'. *Business and Society Review*, 109(4): 507–47.

Zulkifli, N. & Amran, A., 2006. 'Realising Corporate Social Responsibility in Malaysia: A View from the Accounting Profession'. *Journal of Corporate Citizenship*, 24, winter: 101–14.

ABOUT THE AUTHOR

Dr Wayne Visser is Founder and Director of the think tanks Kaleidoscope Futures and CSR International. In addition, Wayne is Senior Associate at the University of Cambridge Programme for Sustainability Leadership and Visiting Professor of Corporate Responsibility at Warwick Business School in the UK.

Wayne is the author of seventeen books, including *The Quest for Sustainable Business* (2012), *The Age of Responsibility* (2011), *The World Guide to CSR* (2010) and *The A to Z of Corporate Social Responsibility* (2010). He has also published over 180 other works (chapters, articles, etc.) and has delivered more than 170 professional speeches all around the world, with his work taking him to more than 60 countries in the last 20 years.

Wayne was listed in the Top 100 Global Sustain Ability Leaders (2011 & 2012, rankings by ABC Carbon), the Top 100 Thought Leaders in Europe & the Middle East (2011, ranking by Centre for Sustainability & Excellence and Trust Across America), Top 100 CSR Leaders and Top 20 Sustainability Leaders (2009 & 2012, rankings by CSR International). He was also winner of the Outstanding Author Contribution Award at the Emerald Literati Network Awards for Excellence 2011 and recipient of the Outstanding Teacher Award of The Warwick MBA 2010/11 and 2011/12.

Before getting his PhD in Corporate Social Responsibility (Nottingham University, UK), Wayne was Director of Sustainability Services for KPMG and Strategy Analyst for Cap Gemini in South Africa. His other qualifications include an MSc in Human Ecology (Edinburgh University, UK) and a Bachelor of Business Science with Honours in Marketing (Cape Town University, South Africa).

Wayne lives in London, UK, and enjoys art, nature, writing poetry and learning about new countries and cultures.

A full biography and much of his writing and art is on www.waynevisser.com

OTHER BOOKS BY WAYNE VISSER

Non-fiction

The Quest for Sustainable Business: An Epic Journey in Search of Corporate Responsibility, Greenleaf Publishing, 2012.

The Age of Responsibility: CSR 2.0 and the New DNA of Business, John Wiley & Sons, 2011.

The World Guide to CSR: A Country-by-Country Analysis of Corporate Sustainability and Responsibility (with Nick Tolhurst), John Wiley & Sons, 2010.

The Top 50 Sustainability Books (with CPSL), Greenleaf Publishing, 2009.

Landmarks for Sustainability: Events and Initiatives that have Changed Our World (with CPSL), Greenleaf Publishing, 2009.

Making A Difference: Purpose-Inspired Leadership for Corporate Sustainability and Responsibility (CSR), VDM, 2008.

The A to Z of Corporate Social Responsibility (with Dirk Matten, Manfred Pohl & Nick Tolhurst), John Wiley & Sons, 2007.

Corporate Citizenship in Africa (with Malcolm McIntosh & Charlotte Middleton), Greenleaf Publishing, 2006.

Business Frontiers: Social Responsibility, Sustainable Development and Economic Justice, ICFAI Books, 2005.

South Africa: Reasons to Believe (with Guy Lundy), Aardvark Press, 2003.

Beyond Reasonable Greed: Why Sustainable Business is a Much Better Idea! (with Clem Sunter), Tafelberg Human and Rousseau, 2002.

Fiction

African Dream: Inspiring Words & Images from the Luminous Continent, Kaleidoscope Futures, 2012.

String, Donuts, Bubbles and Me: Favourite Philosophical Poems, Wayne Visser/Lulu, 2012.

Seize the Day: Favourite Inspirational Poems, 2nd ed., Wayne Visser/Lulu, 2012.

Wishing Leaves: Favourite Nature Poems, 2nd ed., Wayne Visser/Lulu, 2012.

I Am An African: Favourite Africa Poems, 3rd ed., Wayne Visser/Lulu, 2012.